Nepali

Phrasebook & Dictionary

Acknowledgments
Production Editors Kate Kiely, Bruce Evans
Book Designers Wibowo Rusli, Fabrice Robin
Language Writers Mary-Jo O'Rourke, Bimal Man Shrestha, Krishna Pradhan
Cover Image Researcher Naomi Parker

Thanks
James Hardy, Liz Heynes, Catherine Naghten, Sunny Or, John Taufa, Angela Tinson, Juan Winata

Published by Lonely Planet Global Limited
CRN 554153

7th Edition – July 2023
ISBN 978 1 78657 089 5

Cover Image Woman circling a prayer wheel, Boudhanath stupa, Kathmandu. Matteo Colombo/AWL Images ©

Printed in Malaysia 10 9 8 7 6 5 4 3 2 1

Contact lonelyplanet.com/contact

acknowledgments

about the authors

This edition was written by Mary-Jo O'Rourke, the primary author, and Bimal Man Shrestha, the consulting author. Krishna Pradhan provided the Sustainable Travel section of this book. Mary-Jo is a linguist, writer and editor with a special interest in Nepal and its people, in particular its languages and food. She has travelled, lived and worked in Nepal a number of times since the 1980s, and has completed a Master of Arts in Newari Linguistics at La Trobe University in Melbourne. Bimal is a Newar from Kathmandu, who now lives in Melbourne. He's bilingual in Newari and Nepali and speaks several other languages including English and Japanese. Among many other jobs, he has worked as a tour guide and as an interpreter in various languages.

from the authors

The authors wish to thank family and friends around the world for their support. Many have contributed to lively discussions of particular words and usages. Our young daughter Bellana has also been cooperative and helpful in her own special way. Particular acknowledgement goes to Dr Rita Tuladhar for her expert help with the Health chapter, especially Women's Health. *Dhan*·ya·bahd Rita. Thanks also to Yukiyoshi Kamimura for his care with the wonderful illustrations.

make the most of this phrasebook ...

Anyone can speak another language! It's all about confidence. Don't worry if you can't remember your school language lessons or if you've never learnt a language before. Even if you learn the very basics (on the inside covers of this book), your travel experience will be the better for it. You have nothing to lose and everything to gain when the locals hear you making an effort.

finding things in this book

For easy navigation, this book is in sections. The Basics chapters are the ones you'll thumb through time and again. The Practical section covers basic travel situations like catching transport and finding a bed. The Social section gives you conversational phrases, pick-up lines, the ability to express opinions – so you can get to know people. Food has a section all of its own: gourmets and vegetarians are covered and local dishes feature. Safe Travel equips you with health and police phrases, just in case. Remember the colours of each section and you'll find everything easily; or use the comprehensive Index. Otherwise, check the two-way traveller's Dictionary for the word you need.

being understood

Throughout this book you'll see coloured phrases on each page. They're phonetic guides to help you pronounce the language. You don't even need to look at the language itself, but you'll get used to the way we've represented particular sounds. The pronunciation chapter in Basics will explain more, but you can feel confident that if you read the coloured phrase slowly, you'll be understood.

communication tips

Body language, ways of doing things, sense of humour – all have a role to play in every culture. 'Local talk' boxes show you common ways of saying things, or everyday language to drop into conversation. 'Listen for ...' boxes supply the phrases you may hear. They start with the phonetic guide (because you'll hear it before you know what's being said) and then lead in to the language and the English translation.

about nepali 8

basics...35

practical 55

CONTENTS

nepali

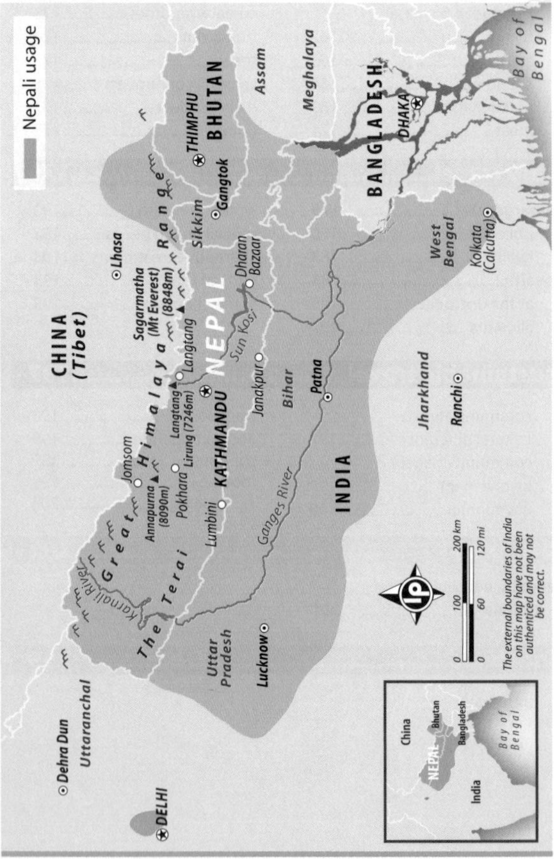
Nepali usage
CHINA
(Tibet)
Lhasa
Sagarmatha
(Mt Everest)
(8848m)
Great Himalaya Range
Jomsom
Annapurna
(8090m)
Langtang
Lirung (7246m)
Langtang
Pokhara
The Terai
Karnali River
Lumbini
KATHMANDU
NEPAL
Sun Kosi
Janakpur
Dharan
Bazaar
Sikkim
Gangtok
THIMPHU
BHUTAN
Assam
Meghalaya
BANGLADESH
DHAKA
Bay of Bengal
West Bengal
Kolkata
(Calcutta)
Jharkhand
Ranchi
Bihar
Patna
INDIA
Ganges River
Uttar Pradesh
Lucknow
Uttaranchal
Dehra Dun
DELHI
0
100
200 km
0
60
120 mi
The external boundaries of India on this map have not been authenticed and may not be correct.
China
Bhutan
NEPAL
Bangladesh
India
Bay of Bengal

ABOUT NEPALI

Nepali belongs to the Indo-European language family, and so is closely related to Hindi, and distantly related to various European languages, including English and French. It's been spoken (in older forms at least) since around 300 AD, when Hindu Indo-Aryans invaded the area from the south, displacing the Buddhist Kirantis.

When Nepal became a nation state in the 1760s, numerous small kingdoms were unified under one capital. There are still many ethnic groups throughout the country, each with its own culture and language. Some of these are the Kiranti, Newars, Tamang, Tharu and Tibetans (including the Sherpa), as well as the Nepali-speaking majority group. With over 100 indigenous languages, Nepali, the national language, acts as a unifying force in this heterogeneous nation of 23 million. It's also widely spoken in Sikkim, Darjeeling and other parts of India, as well as Tibet and Bhutan. In total, Nepali is spoken by some 35 million people and is a second language for about 50 per cent of the Nepalese population. Foreign-aid volunteers, researchers and other long-term foreign residents of Nepal are among the many non-native speakers.

Nepali has a number of dialects. This phrasebook uses the standard form, which is understood throughout most of the language area. It's written in the Devanagari script, a writing form also used for Hindi and the parent of both languages, Sanskrit. The Nepali alphabet has 67 characters and, unlike English, most of them have only one pronunciation. Likewise, most Nepali sounds have only one spelling. This almost one-to-one correspondence between sounds and letters means that spelling in Nepali is much more straightforward than in English.

This phrasebook includes the Devanagari script for every word, sentence and phrase (except in the Grammar chapter, where you've got enough to think about). The phonetic version is also provided in Roman script – we refer to it as the 'pronunciation guide' (you'll see it in colour next to the script). If you're having any difficulty with pronunciation, try pointing out the script to a local.

There are some significant differences between everyday spoken Nepali and the more formal written language. However, the information in this book is presented in the informal spoken style, which is all you'll need. Nepali has a smaller vocabulary than English, which means that a word can be more general in meaning and may have several translations. For instance, *rahm*·ro (राम्रो) means 'good' but can also mean 'nice' or 'beautiful', depending on the context.

Since Nepal opened its doors to foreigners and tourism in 1951, it has become very popular with travellers from all over the world. Most Nepalese in urban and popular tourist areas speak some English, as it's a compulsory school subject. However, as you move away from the main tourist centres, it does get harder to find local people who speak more than rudimentary English, as many hill villages continue to lack even the most basic educational facilities. Besides, as a traveller you'll find that life in Nepal is easier and a lot more interesting if you try to learn a little of the language. Even if you're not fluent, being able to communicate on a basic level will help to narrow the cultural gap and thus deepen your experience.

All you need to make learning enjoyable are a few Nepalese companions to practise with – impossible to avoid in friendly Nepal. Simply gather a few phrases from this book and prepare yourself for some fascinating encounters. Good luck in your travels and na·ma·*ste* (नमस्ते), 'best wishes'!

abbreviations used in this book

adj	adjective	m	masculine
ani	animate	pl	plural
f	feminine	pol	polite
inani	inanimate	poss	possessive
inf	informal	sg	singular
lit	literal translation		

Pronunciation

Nepali is fairly easy to pronounce because many of the vowel and consonant sounds of English are also found in Nepali.

In this book we provide both the Nepali script and the way you pronounce it – phonetic guides are in colour next to the phrases. We break up the Nepali words into syllables and where these are italicised, you should stress that part of the word as you say it.

vowels

Nepali has six vowels and two diphthongs (vowel combinations) – all but one of these (o) also occur as nasal vowels, making 15 vowels in total. The nasals are pronounced with the airstream coming out of the nose. Speakers of English can approximate this by putting a weak 'n' at the end of such a syllable. Nasals are indicated in the text by a tilde (~) over the vowel.

sound	description
a/ã	as the 'u' in 'cup'
ah/ãh	as the 'a' in 'father'
i/ĩ	as the 'ee' in 'see', but shorter
u/ũ	as the 'u' in 'put'
e/ẽ	as the 'e' in 'bet'
o	as the 'o' in 'hot'

diphthongs (vowel combinations)

Diphthongs consist of two vowels pronounced together as a single syllable, such as the 'ou' in 'out'. As with single vowels, diphthongs may also be nasalised in Nepali.

sound	description
ai/aĩ	as the 'ai' in 'aisle'
au/aũ	as the 'ow' in 'vow', but shorter

consonants

Most Nepali consonants are pronounced the same as you would expect in English, but for easy reference all are listed below in English alphabetical order:

sound	description
b	as the 'b' in 'bat'
c	as the 'ch' in 'chew'
d	as the 'd' in 'dog'
g	as the 'g' in 'get', always hard
h	more forcefully than in English, except in the middle of a word, where hardly pronounced at all
j	as the 'j' in 'jaw' (you may also hear it pronounced as the 'ds' in 'bands' or the 'z' in 'zebra')
k	as the 'k' in 'skin'
l	as the 'l' in 'last', always clear
m	as the 'm' in 'mother'
n	as the 'n' in 'now'
ng	as the 'ng' in 'finger'
ny	as the 'ny' in 'canyon'
p	as the 'p' in 'spot'
r	trilled slightly and clearer than the English 'r'
s	as the 's' in 'sit'
sh	as the 'sh' in 'ship' (you may also hear it pronounced as the English 's')
t	as the 't' in 'stop'
w	as the 'w' in 'word'
y	as the 'y' in 'yellow'

Occasionally, you'll come across doubled consonants in words. A doubled consonant means the sound is pronounced twice – this is important for the correct meaning to be conveyed:

ka·mal	lotus	*kam*·mal	blanket
chah·nu	sloping roof	*chahn*·nu	to choose

aspirated consonants

Aspirated consonants are pronounced much more forcefully than their unaspirated counterparts (listed above) and with a puff of air, like the 'th' in 'hothouse'.

Aspiration is indicated in the text by an h following the consonant, so th represents an aspirated t. Don't confuse this with the English sound 'th' (as in 'think' or 'then'), which doesn't occur at all in Nepali. There's one exception: sh is not an aspirated s but is pronounced as the 'sh' in 'ship'.

The aspirated consonants are listed below in English alphabetical order:

sound	description
bh	as the 'b' in 'bus', pronounced with a puff of air
ch	as the 'ch' and following 'h' in 'punch hard'
dh	as the 'd' in 'duck', pronounced with a puff of air
gh	as the 'g' in 'go', pronounced with a puff of air
jh	as the 'j' in 'jump', pronounced with a puff of air
kh	as the 'k' in 'kill'
ph	as the 'p' in 'pit' (you may also hear it pronounced like an 'f' made with both lips)
th	as the 't' in 'time'

Aspiration is used to differentiate between the meaning of words in Nepali, so the difference in pronunciation is important:

retroflex consonants

Retroflex sounds are made by curling your tongue up and back towards the roof of your mouth. In Nepali d and t – both unaspirated and aspirated – and n occur as retroflex sounds. These are the sounds that make the Nepali (and Indian) pronunciation so distinctive from English! They're not too difficult to get the hang of with a bit of practice – try saying the sound several times, moving your tongue a bit further back along the roof of your mouth each time.

Retroflex d and dh are sometimes also pronounced as a retroflex r which is a quick flap of the tongue against the roof of the mouth, like the 'd' sound in 'ladder' when said quickly. Retroflex consonants are indicated throughout the text by a dot beneath the letter.

As the following examples show, the pronunciation of retroflex consonants is important for the correct meaning to be conveyed:

top	cannon	ṭop	helmet
dho·kah	fraud	*ḍho*·kah	door/gate

stress

The position of the stressed syllable in Nepali words depends on whether the vowels are short or long, and whether the syllables end in vowels or consonants. As a rough guide, in two-syllable words the last syllable is normally the stressed one, while in words of three or more syllables it's normally the second-last syllable. The pronunciation guides show you the word stress: the emphasis in each word is indicated in italics.

ka·*lah*	art	din·*car*·yah	diary

the nepalese alphabet

Nepali is written in the Devanagari script. Each character contains part of (or is on) a horizontal line, and characters are joined together into words by this line. The vowel a is inherent in the basic form of all consonants, so k would be pronounced ka instead. Different symbols are written before, after or below the consonant to indicate different vowel sounds (see

ABOUT NEPALI

page 16). The complete Nepali alphabet is listed below (in Nepali alphabetical order). Note that there's no differentiation between upper and lower case; also, some sounds have two written forms but are said the same way.

the nepalese alphabet

Vowels

अ	आ	इ	इर्	उ	ऊ	ऋ	ए	ऐ	ओ	औ
a	ah	i	i	u	u	ri	e	ai	o	au

Consonants

क	ख	ग	घ	ङ
k	kh	g	gh	ng
च	छ	ज	झ	ञ
c	ch	j	jh	ny
ट	ठ	ड	ढ	ण
ṭ	ṭh	ð	ðh	ṇ
त	थ	द	ध	न
t	th	d	dh	n
प	फ	ब	भ	म
p	ph	b	bh	m
य	र	ल	व	
y	r	l	w	
श	ष	स	ह	
sh	s	s	h	

In the Devanagari script, nasal vowels are indicated by either a dot or half circle and dot above the letter, as shown below:

here	*ya*·hãh	यहाँ
finger	*aũ*·lah	औंला

vowels

Vowels, other than a, have two forms: a full one when written alone or at the beginning of a word, and an abbreviated form when attached to a consonant. The abbreviated form is written above, below or beside the consonant, as indicated below:

Vowel	ah	o	e	i	u
Symbol	ा	ो	े	ि/ी	ु/ू
Position	after	after	above	before/after	below

To illustrate, we've taken the first consonant k (क) as an example:

Script	Pronunciation
का	kah
को	ko
के	ke
कि/की	ki
कु/कू	ku

Note that the two different forms of i and u are pronounced identically.

Grammar

This chapter contains basic information to help you make your own sentences. There are plenty of examples, including a pronunciation guide for each. This will increase your ability to communicate simply – just insert different vocabulary items into the basic sentences provided.

word order

Nepali word order is usually subject-object-verb, rather than subject-verb-object, as it is in English:

Anita read the book. a·*ni*·ta ki·*tahb lekh*·yo
(lit: Anita book read)

The Nepali verb comes at the end of the sentence, with any objects or locations before it. In spoken Nepali, information that's clear from context, or not relevant in a particular situation, will generally be left out. This includes subject pronouns, particularly 'I':

I'm a traveller. *yah*·tri hũ
(lit: traveller am)

articles & demonstratives

In Nepali, there are no articles like the English 'the' or 'a/an'. Whether the speaker is referring to 'a market', 'the market' or 'market' is clear from context:

Where's the market? ba·*jahr ka*·hãh cha?
(lit: market where is?)

after the fact

Keep in mind that Nepali has postpositions that come after the noun, instead of prepositions as in English.

The book is on the table. ki·*tahb* ṭe·bul·mah cha (lit: book table-on is)

For more, see page 33.

To be specific, the demonstratives 'this', yo, or 'that', tyo, can be used:

I see the old building. ma tyo pu·*rah*·no ghar *her*·chu (lit: I that old building see)

The plural forms 'these', yi, and 'those', ti, may be used in a similar way. In everyday speech, however, singular forms are often used even with plural subjects:

those people tyo *mahn*·che·ha·ru (lit: that people)

The demonstratives yo and tyo are also used as third-person pronouns to mean 'he', 'she' and 'it' (see Pronouns, page 19).

nouns

To make a noun plural, the ending -ha·ru is added, although in speech it's often left out when plurality is clear from context or unimportant.

friend	*sah*·thi
friends	*sah*·thi·ha·ru

Spoken Nepali is also sometimes grammatically simplified. In everyday speech, singular forms are often used with a plural meaning.

Where are the books?	ki·*tahb* *ka*·hãh cha? (lit: book where is?)

instead of:

Where are the books?	ki·*tahb*·ha·ru *ka*·hãh chan? (lit: books where are?)

Nepali nouns have no grammatical gender (such as masculine/feminine/neuter), but they can have different endings, depending on how they're used in a sentence (see **Pronouns**, pages 19 - 21).

pronouns

Nepali pronouns have both formal and informal variations – you should use the formal ones, except with intimate friends, children and animals. Formal forms are used throughout this book, unless indicated otherwise.

subject pronouns

Like nouns, pronouns have no grammatical gender. There are three informal third-person singular pronouns commonly used, two of which (tyo/yo) can mean 'he', 'she' or 'it', and a third, *u*·ni, which can only mean 'he' or 'she'. Apart from *u*·ni, the pronouns are interchangeable and are often omitted in speech when they can be understood from context (for example, when they're the subject of the sentence, see page 17).

subject pronouns

SINGULAR		PLURAL	
I	ma	**we**	*hah*·mi(·ha·ru)
you (inf)	*ti*·mi	**you** (inf)	*ti*·mi·ha·ru
you (pol)	ta·*paĩ*	**you** (pol)	ta·*paĩ*·ha·ru
he/she (inf)	*u*·ni (ani)	**they** (inf)	*u*·ni·ha·ru (ani)
he/she/it (inf)	tyo/yo (inani)	**they** (inf)	ti/yi (inani)
he/she (pol)	*wa*·hãh	**they** (pol)	*wa*·hãh·ha·ru

Note that for 'we', the short form *hah*·mi is often used instead of the full form *hah*·mi·ha·ru. Remember also that *u*·ni and *u*·ni·ha·ru are used only for animate (living) objects. For inanimate (not living) objects, use tyo/yo (sg) and ti/yi (pl).

Pronouns (like nouns) take different endings according to their function in the sentence (whether they're the subject or object, or indicate possession or location). These endings generally translate as prepositions like 'to', 'of ' and 'with' in English. For subjects of sentences without objects, however, the basic pronouns are used without any additional endings:

He/She sleeps.	*u*·ni *sut*·cha **(inf)** (lit: he/she sleeps)

Where sentences do contain objects, the ending -le is generally added to the basic subject pronoun. This ending is a grammatical requirement but makes no difference to the meaning. There are some irregular forms to note. The first-person singular ma becomes *mai*·le and the third-person singular forms tyo and yo become tyas·le and yas·le:

typical endings

A challenge for English speakers may be to remember to add the Nepali noun/pronoun endings -le (for subjects), -lai (for objects) and -ko (for possessives), which generally translate as prepositions – (such as 'by', 'to' and 'of') in English.

I cooked rice.	*mai*·le bhaht pak·*ah*·ẽ (lit: I-le rice cooked)
He/She gives me tea.	*wa*·hãh·le *ma*·lai *ci*·yah *di*·nu·hun·cha (lit: he/she-le I-lai tea gives)
This is Rita's book.	yo *ri*·ta·ko ki·*tahb* ho (lit: this Rita-ko book is)

However, don't worry if you find the endings hard to master – context will often make it clear.

I understand this. *mai*·le yo *bujh*·chu (lit: I-le this understand)

When used with nouns, the ending -le translates as 'by', 'with', 'from', 'of 'or 'in', according to context:

In the opinion of the government ... sar·*kahr*·ko *rah*·ya·le ... (lit: government-ko opinion-le)

Sentences can contain two instances of -le – one attached to the subject pronoun and one attached to the instrument (in this example, 'the broom'):

He/She swept the floor with the broom. *wa*·hãh·le *ku*·co·le bhui la·*gah*·yo (lit: he/she-le broom-le floor swept)

object pronouns

Pronouns and nouns used as objects (whether direct or indirect objects) normally take the grammatical ending -lai, particularly if the object is a name or refers to a person:

I see Anita. ma a·*ni*·ta·lai *her*·chu (lit: I Anita-lai see)

The ending -lai often translates as 'to' or 'for', as in the following example:

I give it to you. ma yo ta·*paĩ*·lai *din*·chu (lit: I it you-lai give)

If an object is inanimate, -lai is usually left out.

He/She made a chair. *wa*·hãh mec ba·*nah*·yo (lit: he/she chair made)

Sometimes, subject nouns and pronouns also take the ending -lai. These are really grammatical objects in Nepali, but translate as subjects in English:

I feel tired. *ma*·lai *tha*·kai *lahg*·yo (lit: I-lai tired feel)

possessives

The possessive ending for both nouns and pronouns is -ko, 'of'. Since several possessive pronouns are irregular, they're all listed below.

possessives			
SINGULAR		**PLURAL**	
my	*me*·ro	**our**	*hahm*·ro
your (inf)	*tim*·ro	**your** (inf)	*ti*·mi·ha·ru·ko
your (pol)	ta·*paĩ*·ko	**your** (pol)	ta·*paĩ*·ha·ru·ko
her/his (inf)	*u*·ni·ko	**their** (inf)	*u*·ni·ha·ru·ko
her/his/its (inf)	*tyas*·ko/*yas*·ko	**their** (pol)	*wa*·hãh·ha·ru·ko
her/his/its (pol)	*wa*·hãh·ko		

This is our baby. yo *hahm*·ro *bac*·cah ho (lit: this our baby is)

Where's the tiger's lair? *bahgh*·ko ghar *ka*·hãh cha? (lit: tiger-ko lair where is?)

As in English, possessives come before the nouns they refer to.

my cat *me*·ro bi·*rah*·lo (lit: my cat)

Ram's shirt *rahm*·ko ka·*mij* (lit: Ram-ko shirt)

Possessive pronouns can also stand alone, in which case they translate as 'mine, ours, yours, his, hers, its, theirs'.

Is this hat yours? yo *ṭo*·pi ta·*paĩ*·ko ho? (lit: this hat yours is?)

This room is ours. yo *ko*·ṭhah *hahm*·ro ho (lit: this room ours is)

adjectives & demonstratives

As in English, Nepali adjectives precede the nouns they refer to:

expensive shop	ma·*hã*·go *pa*·sal (lit: expensive shop)
tall woman	*a*·glo *ai*·mai (lit: tall woman)

To compare two things, attach -bhan·dah, 'than', to the noun that would follow 'than' in English:

Ram is bigger than Anita.	rahm a·*ni*·ta·bhan·dah *ṭhu*·lo cha (lit: Ram Anita-than big is)

To create a superlative, insert *sab*·bhan·dah 'than all' before the adjective:

Mt Everest is Nepal's highest mountain.	*sa*·gar·mah·thah ne·*pahl*·ko *sab*·bhan·dah *u*·co pa·*hahḍ* ho (lit: Mt-Everest Nepal-ko than-all high mountain is)

verbs

Verb formation in Nepali is fairly straightforward, except with the verb 'to be' (see page 27). There are quite a few tenses, but you really only need to know the present and past tense forms and their negatives. Simple additions to these give you the continuous, future and imperative verb forms. Each section includes a list of tense endings, with an example, so you can easily look up the verb form you need at the time.

Nepali verbs are made up of two parts: the stem and the tense ending. The stem stays the same, while the ending changes according to person (first/second/third) and number (singular/plural). Infinitives (the dictionary form of a verb) end in -nu:

to do	*gar*·nu	**to eat**	*khah*·nu	**to go**	*jah*·nu

negation

There's no single negative form in Nepali that corresponds to 'not' in English. Instead, the verb forms for each person and number take a different ending to form the negative. They do follow a pattern, however, and are not difficult to learn alongside the positive ones. For this reason, positive and negative forms are listed together in the following verb sections.

the neutral verb

In conversation, the Nepalese commonly use a versatile neutral verb form for present and, especially, future tenses. It's used mainly in short statements and questions, and pronouns are usually left out. This is the simplest verb form to use when you get stuck!

The ending -ne replaces the infinitive ending -nu to form this neutral verb, and its negative is formed with the prefix na-:

Let's go out.	*bah*·hi·ra *jah*·ne (lit: outside to-go)
Let's not go out.	*bah*·hi·ra na·*jah*·ne (lit: outside not-to-go)

present tense

The present tense is used for regular actions and corresponds to the present in English:

I work every day.	ma *din*·hũ kahm *gar*·chu (lit: I daily work do)

As in English, it can also be used to indicate the future:

Next week we go to Nepal.	*au*·ne *hap*·tah *hah*·mi ne·*pahl jahn*·chaũ (lit: next week we Nepal go)

informal

To make the informal forms of the present tense, the following endings are added to the infinitive:

ABOUT NEPALI

essential verbs

to arrive	*pug*·nu	**to leave**	*choḍ*·nu
to ask	*sodh*·nu	**to look/watch**	*her*·nu
to be	*hu*·nu	**to make**	ba·*nau*·nu
to be able	*sak*·nu	**to read**	*paḍh*·nu
to call	bo·*lau*·nu	**to remember**	sam·*jha*·nu
to carry	*bok*·nu	**to say**	*bhan*·nu
to come	*au*·nu	**to see**	*dekh*·nu
to die	*mar*·nu	**to speak**	*bol*·nu
to do	*gar*·nu	**to stay/sit/live**	*bas*·nu
to drink	pi·*u*·nu	**to stop**	*rok*·nu
to eat	*khah*·nu	**to take**	*li*·nu
to forget	*bir*·sa·nu	**to tell**	*bhan*·nu
to give	*di*·nu	**to understand**	*bujh*·nu
to go	*jah*·nu	**to want/need**	*cah*·ha·nu
to hear/listen	*sun*·nu	**to write**	*lekh*·nu

polite

In the present tense, the polite verb forms all add the same endings to the infinitive: -hun·cha in the positive, and -hun·na in the negative:

you (sg) **do/don't**	ta·*paĩ*
you (pl) **do/don't**	ta·*paĩ*·ha·ru *gar*·nu·hun·cha/
he/she does/doesn't	*wa*·hãh *gar*·nu·hun·na
they do/don't	*wa*·hãh·ha·ru

Verbs whose stems end in a vowel keep the n – remember that ah is a vowel (see Pronunciation, page 11):

to go	*jah*·nu	**I go**	ma *jahn*·chu
to come	*au*·nu	**I come**	ma *aun*·chu

continuous tense

The present continuous is common in spoken Nepali, and corresponds to the English present continuous – the '-ing' form. The continuous tense can be applied to the present, past and future tenses. It's formed by inserting -dai- between the verb stem and the ending. Like the simple present, it may also be used to indicate future (see page 27). The present continuous for the verb 'to eat', *khah*·nu, is listed below:

informal

I am eating	ma *khahn*·dai·chu
you (sg) are eating	*ti*·mi *khahn*·dai·chau
he/she/it is eating	*u*·ni/tyo/yo *khahn*·dai·cha
we are eating	*hah*·mi(·ha·ru) *khahn*·dai·chaũ
you (pl) are eating	*ti*·mi·ha·ru *khahn*·dai·chau
they are eating	*u*·ni·ha·ru *khahn*·dai·chan

polite

you (sg) are/aren't eating	ta·*paĩ khahn*·dai·hu·nu·hun·cha
he/she is/isn't eating	*wa*·hãh*khahn*·dai·hu·nu·hun·na
you (pl) are/aren't eating	ta·*paĩ*·ha·ru *hahn*·dai·hu·nu·hun·cha
they are/aren't eating	*wa*·hãh·ha·ru *khahn*·dai·hu·nu·hun·na

past tense

The past tense is used for completed past actions, and corresponds to the English past tense.

informal

Below are the informal positive and negative forms for the verb 'to do', *gar*·nu:

I did/didn't	ma	*ga*·rẽ/*ga*·ri·nã
you (sg) did/didn't	*ti*·mi	*gar*·yau/*ga*·re·nau
he/she/it did/didn't	*u*·ni/tyo/yo	*gar*·yo/*ga*·re·na
we did/didn't	*hah*·mi(·ha·ru)	*gar*·yaũ/*ga*·re·naũ
you (pl) did/didn't	*ti*·mi·ha·ru	*gar*·yau/*ga*·re·nau
they did/didn't	*u*·ni·ha·ru	*ga*·re/*ga*·re·nan

polite

For the polite forms, attach -bha·yo (for positive past tense) and -bha·e·na (for negative past tense) after the infinitive:

you did/didn't (sg)	ta·*paĩ*
you did/didn't (pl)	ta·*paĩ*·ha·ru *gar*·nu·bha·yo/
he/she did/didn't	*wa*·hãh *gar*·nu·bha·e·na
they did/didn't	*wa*·hãh·ha·ru

When a past tense sentence contains an object, the subject always takes the ending -le (see page 20):

I did it.	*mai*·le yo *ga*·rẽ (lit: I-le it did)
I didn't do it.	*mai*·le yo *ga*·ri·nã (lit: I-le it didn't)

future tense

The simplest and most common future tense used in spoken Nepali is formed with a positive or negative verb in the present tense followed by *ho*·lah (the third-person singular future form of 'to be', see page 28):

I will go.	ma *jahn*·chu *ho*·lah (lit: I go will-be)
They will not go.	*wa*·hãh·ha·ru *jah*·nu·hun·na *ho*·lah lit: they not-go will-be)

to be

The Nepali verb 'to be', *hu*·nu, is complex – it's explained below in full detail. There are three alternate present tense forms of *hu*·nu: cha, ho and *hun*·cha, each used in a different way. The most common forms cha and ho both translate as 'is' and they're sometimes interchangeable. Generally cha is used for location (indicating where) and ho for defining (indicating who and what):

My house is in Nepal.	*me*·ro ghar ne·*pahl*·mah cha (lit: my house Nepal-in is)

My mother is a doctor.	*me*·ro *ah*·mah *ḍahk*·ṭar ho (lit: my mother doctor is)

Although *hun*·cha also translates as 'is', it refers to general facts or events, unlike cha or ho:

This mango is sweet.	yo ãhp *gu*·li·yo cha (lit: this mango sweet is)
Mangoes are sweet.	ãhp *gu*·li·yo *hun*·cha (lit: mango sweet is)

present tense

informal

cha

I am/am not	ma	chu/*chai*·na
you (sg) are/are not	*ti*·mi	chau/*chai*·nau
he/she/it is/is not	*u*·ni/tyo/yo	cha/*chai*·na
we are/are not	*hah*·mi(·ha·ru)	chaũ/*chai*·naũ
you (pl) are/are not	*ti*·mi·ha·ru	chau/*chai*·nau
they are/are not	*u*·ni·ha·ru	chan/*chai*·nan

ho

I am/am not	ma	hũ/*hoi*·na
you (sg) are/are not	*ti*·mi	hau/*hoi*·nau
he/she/it is/is not	*u*·ni/tyo/yo	ho/*hoi*·na
we are/are not	*hah*·mi(·ha·ru)	haũ/*hoi*·naũ
you (pl) are/are not	*ti*·mi·ha·ru	hau/*hoi*·nau
they are/are not	*u*·ni·ha·ru	hun/*hoi*·nan

huncha

As well as the irregular present tense forms of cha and ho, *hu*·nu has a set of regular present tense forms, made from the stem hu- and the usual present tense endings (see page 23):

I am/am not	ma	*hun*·chu/*hun*·di·na
you are/are not (sg)	*ti*·mi	*hun*·chau/*hun*·dai·nau
he/she/it is/is not	*u*·ni/tyo/yo	*hun*·cha/*hun*·dai·na
we are/are not	*hah*·mi(·ha·ru)	*hun*·chaũ/*hun*·dai·naũ

you are/are not (pl)	*ti*·mi·ha·ru	*hun*·chau/*hun*·dai·nau
they are/are not	*u*·ni·ha·ru	*hun*·chan/*hun*·dai·nan

polite

The polite versions are the same for cha, ho and *hun*·cha:

you (sg) are/are not	ta·*paĩ*
you (pl) are/are not	ta·*paĩ*·ha·ru *hu*·nu·hun·cha/
he/she is/is not	*wa*·hãh *hu*·nu·hun·na
they are/are not	*wa*·hãh·ha·ru

past tense

cha & ho

informal

In the past tense, cha and ho are identical:

I was/was not	ma *thi*·ẽ/*thi*·e·nã
you (sg) were/were not	*ti*·mi *thi*·yau/*thi*·e·nau
he/she/it was/was not	*u*·ni/tyo/yo *thi*·yo/*thi*·e·na
we were/were not	*hah*·mi(·ha·ru) *thi*·yaũ/*thie*·naũ
you (pl) were/were not	*ti*·mi·ha·ru *thi*·yau/*thi*·e·nau
they were/were not	*u*·ni·ha·ru *thi*·e/*thi*·e·nan

polite

The positive and negative polite forms are as follows:

you (sg) were/were not	ta·*paĩ*
you (pl) were/were not	ta·*paĩ*·ha·ru *hu*·nu·hun·thyo/
he/she was/was not	*wa*·hãh *hu*·nu·hun·na·thyo
they were/were not	*wa*·hãh·ha·ru

huncha

informal

I was/was not	ma *bha*·ẽ/*bha*·i·nã
you (sg) were/were not	*ti*·mi *bha*·yau/*bha*·e·nau
he/she/it was/was not	*u*·ni/tyo/yo *bha*·yo/*bha*·e·na
we were/were not	*hah*·mi(·ha·ru) *bha*·yaũ/*bha*·e·naũ
you (pl) were/were not	*ti*·mi·ha·ru *bha*·yau/*bha*·e·nau
they were/were not	*u*·ni·ha·ru *bha*·e/*bha*·e·nan

more of the other

There are two words in Nepali meaning 'other': *ar*·ko 'the other of two' is generally used with singular nouns, while *a*·ru 'other, else, more' is used with plural nouns and objects that can't be counted:

I'll give you the other book.	ma ta·*paĩ*·lai *ar*·ko ki·*tahb din*·chu (lit: I you-to other book give)
Please drink more tea.	*a*·ru *ci*·yah *piu*·nu·hos (lit: more tea drink-hos)

polite

you (sg) were/were not	ta·*paĩ*
you (pl) were/were not	ta·*paĩ*·ha·ru *hu*·nu·bha·yo/
he/she was/was not	*wa*·hãh*hu*·nu·bha·e·na
they were/were not	*wa*·hãh·ha·ru

to have

There's no verb equivalent to the English 'to have'. The idea of possession is expressed using a form of cha, 'to be', plus a possessive noun or pronoun:

He/She has five children.	*wa*·hãh·ko pahnc *ja*·nah cho·rah·*cho*·ri chan (lit: his/her five people children are)

If the possession is portable, one of the 'with' postpositions, -sã·ga or -si·ta (see page 33), is added to the possessor:

Do you have some money?	ta·*paĩ*·sã·ga *pai*·sah cha? (lit: you-with money is?)
I don't have a pen.	*ma*·sã·ga *ka*·lam *chai*·na (lit: I-with pen is-not)

modals

Nepali, particularly in its spoken form, almost always makes use of two or more verbs, including a modal (such as 'can', 'must' or 'should' in English) which comes after the main verb. The most common modals are (man) *lahg*·nu, 'to be felt/ to seem', and (man) *par*·nu, 'to like/to be necessary'.

The present tense verb forms (*lahg*·cha and *par*·cha) are used for general situations and the past tense forms (*lahg*·yo and *par*·yo) are used for particular situations (as well as events that happened in the past), as reflected in the examples below:

Women like to dance.	*ai*·mai·ha·ru *nahc*·na (man) *lahg*·cha (lit: women to-dance feels)
Today I feel like eating spicy food.	*ah*·ja *ma*·lai *pi*·ro *khah*·nah *khah*·lai·na (man) *lahg*·yo (lit: today me spicy food to-eat felt)

Both verbs are also commonly used in a non-modal context – (man) *lahg*·nu 'to be felt' and (man) *par*·nu 'to fall':

I'm hungry.	*ma*·lai bhok *lahg*·yo (lit: me hunger felt)
Today it rains/will rain.	*ah*·ja *pah*·ni *par*·cha (lit: today rain falls)
Yesterday it rained.	*hi*·jo *pah*·ni *par*·yo (lit: yesterday rain fell)

necessity

To express necessity, use the infinitive form of the main verb, plus a third-person singular form of the modal verb *par*·nu (see above).

to be

The verb *hu*·nu 'to be' has a complex conjugation with three present-tense forms, each used differently. You may need to keep referring back to this section (page 27 - 30) for a while.

It's necessary to walk there.	*tya*·hãh *hĩḍ*·nu·par·cha (lit: there walk-must)
It isn't necessary to come to this office.	yo kahr·*yah*·la·ya·mah *au*·nu·par·dai·na (lit: this office-to come-must-not)

The subject is usually omitted; if expressed, it takes -lai where there is no object and -le where there is an object.

I need to sleep.	*ma*·lai *sut*·nu·par·cha (lit: I-lai sleep-must)
I have to wash these clothes.	*mai*·le yo *lu*·gah *hu*·nu·par·cha (lit: I-le this clothing wash-must)

imperative

The imperative form is used for giving orders or making requests. To make a polite imperative, add the suffix -hos to the infinitive ending -nu. To negate this, use the prefix na-:

Please eat.	*khah*·nu·hos (lit: to-eat-hos)
Please don't tell me.	*ma*·lai na·*bhan*·nu·hos (lit: I-to na-to-tell-hos)
Could you tell me where my room is?	*ma*·lai *bhan*·nu·hos, *me*·ro *ko*·ṭhah *ka*·hãh cha? (lit: I-to tell-to-hos, my room where is)

questions

'yes/no' questions

In Nepali, the simplest way to ask a question is to raise the tone of your voice at the end of the sentence. To answer a 'yes/no' question, repeat the main verb in the affirmative or negative:

Are you Nepalese?	ta·*paĩ* ne·*pah*·li *hu*·nu·hun·cha? (lit: you Nepali are?)
Yes (I am).	*hu*·nu·hun·cha
No (I'm not).	*hu*·nu·hun·na

information questions

Question words, which normally precede the verb, are used to form information questions:

How? (by what means)	*ka*·sa·ri?
How? (quality)	*kas*·to?
How much/many?	*ka*·ti?
What?	ke?
When?	*ka*·hi·le?
Where?	*ka*·hãh?
Which?	kun?
Who?	ko?
Whose?	*kas*·ko?
Why?	*ki*·na?

Where's the tiger?	bahgh *ka*·hãh cha? (lit: tiger where is?)
Whose book is this?	yo *kas*·ko ki·*tahb* ho? (lit: this whose book is?)

postpositions

In Nepali, 'prepositions' follow the noun they refer to and so are usually called postpositions.

about	-*ti*·ra
after	-*pa*·chi
at/in/on/to	-mah
behind	-pa·*chah*·ḍi
between	-bic
by/with	-le

far	-*ṭah*·ḍhah
for (the sake of)	-ko *lah*·gi
from (time)	-*de*·khi
from (place)	-*bah*·ṭa

I live near the market.	ma ba·*jahr*·na·jik *bas*·chu (lit: I market-near live)
What's in the bag?	*jho*·lah·mah ke cha? (lit: bag-in what is?)

Postpositions are also used with personal pronouns and, occasionally, adverbs:

Please come with me.	*ma*·sã·ga *au*·nu·hos (lit: I-with come-hos)
Please come in from outside.	*bah*·hi·ra·bah·ṭa *bhi*·tra *au*·nu·hos (lit: outside-from inside come hos)

conjunctions

Conjunctions in Nepali are used pretty much as they are in English. Here's a list of the most common ones:

and	ra	**but**	*ta*·ra
and then	*a*·ni	**or**	ki
because	*ki*·na·bha·ne	**otherwise**	*na*·tra

Is the water hot or cold?	*pah*·ni *tah*·to cha ki *ci*·so cha? (lit: water hot is or cold is?)

The Nepalese counting system measures quantities using different base units to those used in English. For example, 'one million' in Nepali is das lahkh (दस लाख), '10 hundred thousand'. The pattern is a little irregular. If you're unsure of the correct form for a number, say the larger number followed by 'and', ra (र), and then the smaller number, for example, tis ra pāhc (तीस र पाँच), '30 and 5' to mean '35', *paĩ*·tis (पैंतीस).

cardinal numbers

सङ्ख्याहरू

0	*sun*·ya	शून्य
1	ek	एक
2	*du*·i	दुइ
3	tin	तीन
4	cahr	चार
5	pãhc	पाँच
6	cha	छ
7	saht	सात
8	ahṭh	आठ
9	nau	नौ
10	das	दस
11	e·*ghah*·ra	एघार
12	*bah*·hra	बाह्र
13	*te*·hra	तेह्र
14	*cau*·dha	चौध
15	*pan*·dhra	पन्ध्र
16	*so*·hra	सोह्र
17	*sa*·tra	सत्र
18	a·*ṭhah*·ra	अठार
19	un·*nais*	उन्नाईस
20	bis	बीस

21	ek·*kais*	एक्काईस
22	bais	बाईस
23	teis	तेईस
24	*cau*·bis	चौबीस
25	pac·*cis*	पच्चीस
26	*chab*·bis	छब्बीस
27	sat·*tais*	सत्ताईस
28	aṭ·*ṭhais*	अठ्ठाईस
29	u·*nan*·tis	उनन्तीस
30	tis	तीस
40	*cah*·lis	चालीस
50	pa·*cahs*	पचास
60	*sah*·ṭhi	साठी
70	*sat*·ta·ri	सत्तरी
80	*a*·si	असी
90	*nab*·be	नब्बे
100	ek say	एक सय
1000	ek ha·*jahr*	एक हजार
10,000	das ha·*jahr*	दस हजार
100,000	ek lahkh	एक लाख
200,000	*du*·i lahkh	दुई लाख
one million	das lahkh	दस लाख
ten million	ek *ka*·roḍ	एक करोड
one billion	ek *a*·rab	एक अरब

ordinal numbers

क्रमसूचक संख्याहरु

Ordinal numbers are formed by adding the suffix -aŭ to the relevant cardinal number. The first four are irregular, however, and should be learnt individually:

1st	*pa*·hi·lah	पहिला
2nd	*dos*·rah	दोस्रा
3rd	*tes*·rah	तेस्रा
4th	*caũ*·ṭho	चौंठो

5th	*pãh*·caũ	पाँचौं
10th	*da*·saũ	दसौं
20th	*bi*·saũ	बीसौं

fractions

भागहरू

a quarter	*cau*·thai	चौथाइ
a third	*ti*·hai	तीहाइ
a half	*ah*·dhah	आधा
three-quarters	*pau*·ne	पौने
one-and-a-half	*ḍe*·ḍha	डेढ
two-and-a-half	*a*·ḍhai	अढाई

counters

जना र वटा

When counting people or objects in Nepali, remember to use a counter (or classifier) after the number and before the noun. The counter for objects is *wa*·ṭah (वटा) and for people *ja*·nah (जना), but informally *wa*·ṭah is also used for people. It's a bit like saying 'two *sheets* of paper' or 'two *slices* of bread'. The system is regular after the number three, but the first three should be learnt individually:

one	ek	एक
one (thing)	*eu*·ṭah	एउटा
one (person)	*ek*·ja·nah	एकजना
two	*du*·i	दुइ
two (things)	*du*·i·ṭah	दुइवटा
two (people)	*du*·i·ja·nah	दुइजना
three	tin	तीन
three (things)	*tin*·ṭah	तीनवटा
three (people)	*tin*·ja·nah	तीनजना
five	pãhc	पाँच
five (things)	pãhc *wa*·ṭah	पाँचवटा
five (people)	pãhc *ja*·nah	पाँचजना

ten	das	दस
ten (things)	das *wa*·ṭah	दसवटा
ten (people)	das *ja*·nah	दसजना

How many? (things)
ka·ti *wa*·ṭah? कतिवटा ?
How many? (people)
ka·ti *ja*·nah? कतिजना ?

apple	syau	स्याउ
two apples	*du*·i·ṭah syau	दुइटा स्याउ
sister	*ba*·hi·ni	बहिनी
three sisters	tin *ja*·nah *ba*·hi·ni	तीनजना बहिनी

To make a multiple, place *pal*·ṭa (पल्ट) after the number:

two times	*du*·i *pal*·ṭa	दुइपल्ट
three times	tin *pal*·ṭa	तीनपल्ट

useful amounts

उपयोगी परिमाणहरु

How much?	*ka*·ti?	कति ?
Please give me ...	*ma*·lai ... *di*·nu·hos	मलाई ... दिनुहोस
I need ...	*ma*·lai ... *cah*·hi·yo	मलाई ... चाहियो
double	*do*·bar	दोब्बर
a dozen	ek *dar*·jan	एक दर्जन
enough	pra·*shas*·ta	प्रशस्त
many/much/a lot	*thup*·rai	थुप्रै
a bottle of ...	ek *si*·si ...	एक सिसी ...
half a kg of ...	*ah*·dhah *ki*·lo ...	आधा किलो ...
100 grams	ek say grahm	एक सय ग्राम
a cup of ...	ek kap ...	एक कप ...
a glass of ...	ek gi·*lahs* ...	एक गिलास ...
a kg	ek *ki*·lo	एक किलो
a packet of ...	ek *po*·ko ...	एक पोको ...
a slice of ...	ek *ṭuk*·rah ...	एक टुक्रा ...

Time, Dates & Festivals
समय, मितिहरु र चाडबाड

telling the time

समय भन्नु

Telling the time in Nepali is similar to English, using phrases equivalent to quarter past, half past and quarter to the hour (rather than 9.15, 9.30, 9.45 and so on). The 24-hour clock is not often employed, so bi·*hah*·na (बिहान), 'morning', and *be*·lu·kah (बेलुका), 'evening', indicate am and pm.

What time is it?
ka·ti *ba*·jyo? — कति बज्यो ?
(lit: how-much clock-of?)

It's two o'clock.
du·i *ba*·jyo — दुइ बज्यो
(lit: two clock-of)

At what time?
ka·ti *ba*·je·ti·ra? — कति बजेतिर ?
(lit: how-much clock-at?)

At two o'clock.
du·i *ba*·je·ti·ra — दुइ बजेतिर
(lit: two clock-at)

At ten o'clock in the morning.
bi·*hah*·na das *ba*·je·ti·ra — बिहान दस बजेतिर
(lit: morning ten clock-at)

quarter past — *sa*·wah — सवा
(lit: plus-a-quarter)

half past — *sah*·ḍhe — साढे
(lit: plus-a-half)

quarter to — *pau*·ne — पौने
(lit: minus-a-quarter)

It's early.	*sa*·be·rai ho	सबेरै हो
It's late.	*ḍhi*·lo cha	ढिलो छ

Quarter to two.
pau·ne *du*·i *ba*·jyo — पौने दुइ बज्यो
(lit: quarter-to two clock-of)

Quarter past two.
sa·wah *du*·i *ba*·jyo — सवा दुइ बज्यो
(lit: quarter-past two clock-of)

Half past two.
sah·ḍhe *du*·i *ba*·jyo — साढे दुइ बज्यो
(lit: half-past two clock-of)

Twenty to one.
ek *baj*·na·lai bis *mi*·naṭ *bãh*·ki cha — एक बज्नलाई बीस मिनेट बाकि छ
(lit: one clock-to twenty minute remain is)

days of the week

बारहरू

What day is it today?
ah·ja ke bahr? — आज के बार ?

Monday	*som*·bahr	सोमबार
Tuesday	*mang*·gal·bahr	मङ्गलबार
Wednesday	*bu*·dha·bahr	बुधबार
Thursday	*bi*·hi·bahr	बिहिबार
Friday	*su*·kra·bahr	शुक्रबार
Saturday	*sa*·ni·bahr	शनिबार
Sunday	*ai*·ta·bahr	आईतबार

the nepalese calendar

बिक्रम सम्बत्

The Hindu calendar *Bikram Sambat* is used in Nepal. It's a lunar-solar system, 57 years ahead of the Gregorian calendar, *Isvi Sambat*, so that 2002 AD is 2059 BS. Both have 365 days and 12 months, but the number of days in a Nepalese month varies from 29 to 32.

the nepalese calendar	
bai·sahkh mid-April to mid-May	बैशाख
jeṭh mid-May to mid-June	जेठ
a·*sahr* mid-June to mid-July	असार
saun mid-July to mid-August	साउन
bha·dau mid-August to mid-September	भदौ
a·soj mid-September to mid-October	असोज
kaht·tik mid-October to mid-November	कार्तिक
mang·sir mid-November to mid-December	मङ्सिर
pus mid-December to mid-January	पुस
mahgh mid-January to mid-Februray	माघ
phah·gun mid-February to mid-March	फागुन
cait mid-March to mid-April	चैत

There are three other calendars which are less widely used: the *Shakya Sambat* for astrology, the Newars' *Nepal Sambat*, of the Kathmandu Valley and the Tibetan 60-year cyclical calendar. The first Nepalese month begins in mid-April.

Each lunar month is divided into two fortnights, and each of the fourteen days has a name; e·*kah*·da·si (एकादशी) is the eleventh day, an inauspicious day when meat is to be avoided.

ma·*sahn*·ta last day of a Nepalese month	मसान्त
sang·*krahn*·ti first day of a Nepalese month	संक्रान्ति

dates

मितिहरु

The Hindu calendar uses the word *ga*·te (गते) to indicate the date:

What Nepali date is it today?
ah·ja *ka*·ti *ga*·te? — आज कति गते ?

The first of the Nepali month.
ek *ga*·te — एक गते

It's 1 *Magh*.
mahgh ek *ga*·te ho — माघ एक गते हो

The Gregorian calendar uses the word *tah*·rikh (तारिख) to indicate the date. Like *ga*·te, *tah*·rikh follows the number:

What date is it today?
ah·ja *ka*·ti *tah*·rikh? — आज कति तारिख ?

The third of the month.
tin *tah*·rikh — तीन तारिख

It's 18 October.
ok·*ṭo*·bar a·*ṭhah*·ra *tah*·rikh ho — अक्टोबर अठार तारिख हो

day	din	दिन
fortnight	*pan*·dhra din	पन्ध्र दिन
hour	*ghaṇ*·ṭah	घण्टा
minute	*mi*·naṭ	मिनेट
month	*ma*·hi·nah	महीना
public holiday	sar·*kah*·ri *bi*·dah	सरकारी बिदा
week	*hap*·tah	हप्ता
year	*bar*·sa/sahl	बर्ष/साल

present

बर्तमान

now	*a*·hi·le	अहिले
nowadays	hi·jo·*ah*·ja	हिजोआज
this morning	*ah*·ja bi·*hah*·na	आज बिहान
this evening	*ah*·ja *be*·lu·kah	आज बेलुका
this month	yo *ma*·hi·nah	यो महिना
this week	yo *hap*·tah	यो हप्ता
this year	yo *bar*·sa	यो बर्ष
today	*ah*·ja	आज
tonight	*ah*·ja *rah*·ti	आज राति

past

भूतकाल

a while ago	*ek*·chin *bha*·yo	एकछिन भयो
after	*pa*·chi	पछि
(five) years ago	(pãhc) *bar*·sa *bha*·yo	(पाँच) बर्ष भयो
(three) days ago	(tin) din *bha*·yo	(तीन) दिन भयो
(half an hour) ago	*(ah*·dhah *ghaṇ*·ṭah) *bha*·yo	(आधा घण्टा) भयो
last Friday	*ga*·ya·ko *su*·kra·bahr	गएको शुक्रबार
last night	*hi*·jo *rah*·ti	हिजो राति
last week	*ga*·ya·ko *hap*·tah	गएको हप्ता
last month	*ga*·ya·ko *ma*·hi·nah	गएको महीना
last year	*ga*·ya·ko *bar*·sa	गएको बर्ष
long ago	*dhe*·rai sa·*ma*·ya *bha*·yo	धेरै समय भयो

recently	*hahl*·sah·lai	हालसालै
since (May)	*(mai)*·de·khi	(मे)देखि
the day before yesterday	*as*·ti	अस्ति
yesterday	*hi*·jo	हिजो
yesterday evening	*hi*·jo *be*·lu·kah	हिजो बेलुका
yesterday morning	*hi*·jo bi·*hah*·na	हिजो बिहान

future

भबिष्य

coming year	*au*·ne *bar*·sa	आउने बर्ष
in (five) minutes	(pãhc) *mi*·naṭ *pa*·chi	(पाँच) मिनेट पछि
in (six) days	(cha) din *pa*·chi	(छ) दिन पछि
next week	*ar*·ko *hap*·tah	अर्को हप्ता
next month	*ar*·ko *ma*·hi·nah	अर्को महीना
next year	*ar*·ko *bar*·sa	अर्को बर्ष
soon	*cãh*·ḍai	चाँडै
the day after tomorrow	*par*·si	पर्सि
tomorrow	*bho*·li	भोलि
tomorrow morning	*bho*·li bi·*hah*·na	भोलि बिहान
tomorrow afternoon	*bho*·li *diũ*·so	भोलि दिउँसो
tomorrow night	*bho*·li *rah*·ti	भोलि राति
until (June)	*(jun)*·sam·ma	(जुन)सम्म
within an hour/ month	ek *ghaṇ*·ṭah·bhi·tra/ *ma*·hi·nah·bhi·tra	एक घण्टाभित्र/ महिना भित्र

during the day

दिनमा

afternoon	*diũ*·so	दिउँसो
all day	*din*·bha·ri	दिनभरि
dawn	bi·*hahn*	बिहान्

dusk	*san*·dhyah·kahl	सन्ध्याकाल
early	*sa*·be·rai	सबेरै
evening	*be*·lu·kah	बेलुका
late	*ḍhi*·lo	ढिलो
lunchtime	*ca*·me·nah·ko *be*·lah	चमेनाको बेला
midday	ma·*dhyahn*·ha	मन्ध्यान्ह
midnight	ma·*dhya*·raht	मध्यरात
morning	bi·*hah*·na	बिहान
night	raht	रात
noon	ma·*dhyahn*·ha	मन्ध्यान्ह
sunrise	*sur*·yo·da·ya	सुर्योदय
sunset	sur·*yahs*·ta	सुर्यास्त

festivals

चाडबाडहरू

Hundreds of festivals, celebrating the many gods and religious deities, are held every year within Nepal. The official state religion is Hinduism, but it mingles harmoniously with Buddhism, and many religious festivals are celebrated together by Hindus and Buddhists. Festivals are held according to the ancient lunar calendar and fall on the days of full or new moons, so the date and month in which they fall changes each year.

ba·sant *pãn*·ca·mi बसन्त पञ्चमी
January/February – celebration of spring; in honour of Saraswati, the goddess of learning

shi·va·*rah*·tri शिवरात्रि
February – Shiva's birthday

ho·li होली
February/March – Festival of Colours

lo·sahr ल्होसार
February/March – two-week festival for Tibetan New Year

gods & prominent beings

Religion is a significant part of Nepalese culture and you'll find it easier to gain some cultural understanding if you're familiar with religious terminology. Most temples are dedicated to one or other of a multitude of gods, each known by various names or forms. There are said to be 300 million Hindu deities!

Brahma *brah*·ma ब्रम्हा
Supreme Being of the Hindu Trinity, Great Creator of all worldly things. His consort is Saraswati and his animal is a swan or goose.

Buddha *bud*·dhah बुद्ध
The Enlightened One of Buddhism; for Hindus, the ninth incarnation of Vishnu.

Ganesh *ga*·ṇesh गणेश
Elephant-headed god of wisdom, prosperity and success, and the remover of obstacles. Elder son of Shiva and Pahrvati, and easily the most popular god in Nepal. His animal is the shrew, a symbol of wisdom. Ganesh is also called Vinayak.

Laxmi *lach*·mi लक्ष्मी
goddess of wealth and prosperity, consort of Vishnu

Manjushri *mahn*·jush·ri मन्जुश्री
god of divine wisdom, founder of Nepalese civilisation and creator of the Kathmandu Valley

Pahrvati *pahr*·va·ti पार्वती
peaceful consort of Shiva representing his female and, through Kahli and Durga, his fearsome side. Pahrvati's symbol is the yoni, which complements Shiva's lingam.

Kumari ku·*mah*·ri कुमारी
young virgin Newar girl who's worshipped by the Nepalese as a living goddess

Pashupati pa·shu·*pa*·ti पशुपती
a benevolent form of Shiva. Lord of Beasts and keeper of all living things. Supreme god of Nepal.

Shiva *shi*·va शिव
second member of the Hindu Trinity. The destroyer and regenerator who represents time and procre-ation. The most important god in Nepal, he's often represented by a lingam, his shakti is Pahrvati, his animal is the bull Nandi and his common symbols are the trident and drum. His home is Mt Kailash in Tibet. He is supposed to have thousands of forms. Mahhahdev, the Great God, is also a manifestation of Shiva, and so is Natarahj the god of cosmic dancing. He's supposed to smoke hashish.

Tara *tah*·rah तारा
represents the principle of 'femaleness' for both Hindus and Buddhists, and takes various forms, (Green Tara and White Tara are among them).

Vishnu *vish*·ṇu विष्णु
third member of the Hindu trinity; the Preserver. He appeared on earth in nine incarnations, including the Buddha and Krishna, with the tenth yet to come. His vehicle is the Garuda, a mythical bird.

(See pages 107 for more religious terms.)

cait da·*saĩ* चैते दशैं
March/April – festival dedicated to Durga (the wrathful form of Pahrvati), six months before the biggest festival Dasain

bis·kat *jah*·trah बिस्का जात्रा
April – feast of the death of the Snake Demons; part of the Nepalese New Year

bud·dha *ja*·yan·ti बुद्ध जयन्ती
April/May – Buddha's birthday

rah·to ma·*chen*·dra·nahth *jah*·trah रातो मछेन्द्रनाथ जात्रा
April/May – Festival of Red Machendranahth, also known as Bhota Jahtrah (Festival of the Sacred Vest)

ku·mahr·*sah*·sthi कुमार षष्ठी
May/June – birthday of Kahttikayah, god of war, son of Shiva

nahg *pãn*·ca·mi नाग पञ्चमी
July/August – day of the Snake Gods, who are rain-givers and guardians of water. Snakes are honoured.

ra·chah·*ban*·dhan रक्षा बन्धन
August – yellow thread is given out by Hindu priests and worn for good luck up until Tihahr or for at least a week. Unlike sacred thread, it's available to women and non-Hindus.

gũ·lah गुँला
August/September – month of Newar Buddhist ceremonies

krish·ṇa *ja*·yan·ti कृष्ण जन्माष्टमी
August/September – birthday of Krishna, epic hero

tij तीज
August/September – three-day Festival of Women

in·dra *jah*·trah ईन्द्र जात्रा
September – festival honouring Indra, the rain god

da·*saĩ (dur*·gah *pu*·jah) दशैं (दुर्गा पूजा)
September/October – Nepal's biggest annual festival. Celebrated in honour of Durga's slaying of the demons. On the

eighth day of Dasain, sacrifices and offerings to Durga begin. The ninth day is the main day of sacrifice, on which all Nepalese eat meat. The tenth day is for family celebration.

kaht·tik *pur*·ṇi·mah कार्तिक पुर्णिमा
September/October – full moon day of Kartik, marking the end of Dasain and celebrated by gambling

di·*pah*·wa·li दिपावली
October/November – the Festival of Lights, on the third and most important day of Tihahr, dedicated to Laxmi

mha *pu*·jah म्ह पूजा
October/November – Newar New Year; day of selfworship

ti·hahr तिहार
October/November – second-most important Hindu festival in Nepal (after Dasain), honouring certain animals.

mah·hah·*lax*·mi *pu*·jah महालक्ष्मी पूजा
November – harvest festival

mah·ni rim·du मानी रीमदु
November – three-day Sherpa festival, held at Thyangpoche monastery in the Solu Khumbu region

useful words

उपयोगी शब्द

aũ·si	**the dark moon**	औंसी
cahḍ·bahḍ	**festival**	चाडबाड
cai·tya	**lotus-shaped stupa**	चैत्य
ci·rahg	**ceremonial oil lamp or torch**	चीराग
ghahṭ	**platform for cremation; riverside steps**	घाट
ji·van	**life**	जीवन
jin·da·gi	**lifetime**	जिन्दगी
kahl	**death**	काल
lah·mah	**Buddhist spiritual teacher**	लामा

mah·ni	**stone carved with Buddhist**	मानि
maṇ·dap	**pavilion**	मण्डप
man·tra	**prayer; religious incantation**	मन्त्र
pahp	**sin**	पाप
pra·*sahd*	**sacred food**	प्रसाद
pu·jah	**prayer/worship/ceremony**	पूजा
pur·ṇi·mah	**night of the full moon**	पुर्णिमा
rah·*mah*·yahṇ	**popular Hindu epic**	रामायण
rath	**vehicle of the gods**	रथ
sang·gha	**community of Buddhists**	संघ
stu·pah	**Buddhist temple or sanctuary**	स्तुपा
va·*hah*·nah	**animal of a Hindu god**	बहान
vaj·rah·*cahr*·ya	**Newar Buddhist priest**	बज्राचार्य
yah·nah	**way to Buddhist enlightenment**	याना
yo·gi	**holy man**	योगि

religious terms

dhar·ma धर्म
religious teaching, law and doctrine defining the path to universal harmony via individual morals

gu·ru गुरु
spiritual guide who teaches by inspiring people to follow his or her example

kar·ma कर्म
the law of cause and effect: the cumulative actions of all previous lives determine the soul's next rebirth

ling·gam लीङ्गम
phallic symbol of Shiva; a symbol of Shiva's creative role

ma·hah·*bhah*·rat महाभारत
Hindu epic of the battle between two families

maṇ·da·lah मण्डला
mystic circular design used as a meditation device

mokh·sah मोक्ष
Hindu equivalent of nir·*bhah*·nah

nir·*bhah*·nah निर्भाना
the achievement of a state of enlightenment and spiritual peace via the annihilation of individuality and the end of misery and pain (caused by desires): the eventual aim of Buddhists

sah·dhu साधु
a Hindu ascetic on a spiritual search, usually a follower of Shiva, carrying a trident

sam·*sahr* समसार
Hindu cycle of transmigration and reincarnation

swas·ti·kah स्वस्तीका
for Hindus, a sign of law (*swas*·ti means 'wellbeing'); for Buddhists, a symbol of the esoteric doctrine of the Buddha

tan·tra तन्त्र
psycho-sexual mystic philosophy which leads to enlightenment; a major influence on Nepalese Hinduism and Buddhism

ti·kah टिका
mark of red *sindur* (vermilion) paste, placed on the forehead

vaj·ra बज्र
thunderbolt or diamond, the symbol of Tantric Buddhism; represents nir·*bhah*·nah

yo·ni योनी
symbol of Pahrvati, representing the female sexual organ

never ever leather

You may not be allowed inside Hindu temples, but if you are, always remove shoes and any leather items such as belts.

Always walk around Buddhist shrines and stupas clockwise. It's customary to present the head lama with a white scarf *(khata)* as a mark of respect.

birthdays

जन्मदिनहरु

When's your ...?	ta·*paĩ*·ko ... *ka*·hi·le ho?	तपाईको ... कहिले हो ?
birthday	*jan*·ma·din	जन्मदिन
birthday cake	*jan*·ma·din·ko kek	जन्मदिनको केक
birthday celebration	*jan*·mot·sab	जन्मोत्सब
candles	*main*·bat·ti	मैनबत्ती

My ... is on (25 January).
me·ro ... (pac·*cis* *ja*·na·wa·ri)·mah ho
मेरो ... (पच्चीस जनवरी)मा हो

Happy Birthday!
jan·ma·din·ko shu·bha·*kah*·ma·nah!
जन्मदिनको शुभकामना !

Blow out the candles!
main·bat·ti *phuk*·nu·hos!
मैनबत्ती फुक्नुहोस !

weddings

विवाहहरु

For women, marriage means leaving their families and accepting the authority of their in-laws. Wives may return home to visit their own families, but only with their mother-in-law's permission. Most marriages are still arranged between the two families, although love matches are becoming more common. It's no longer unusual for young Nepalese to have a boyfriend or girlfriend, but these are rarely sexual relationships.

In urban communities the typical marrying age is mid-20s or older, even for women, but it's often younger among rural people. Child marriage still exists.

Best wishes!
shu·bha·*kah*·ma·nah!
शुभकामना !

Congratulations!
ba·dhai! बधाइ !

To the bride and groom!
du·la·hi ra *du*·la·hah·lai! दुलही र दुलहालाई !

engagement	*vahg*·dahn	वाग्दान
honeymoon	pra·*mod*·kahl	प्रमोदकाल
rice-feeding ceremony	bhaht khu·*wau*·ne	भात खुवाउने
wedding/marriage	bi·*hah*	विवाह
wedding anniversary	bi·*hah*·ko bahr·si·*kot*·sab	विवाहको वार्षिक उत्सोव
wedding cake	bi·*hah*·ko kek	विवाहको केक
wedding guests	*jan*·ta	जन्त
wedding present	bi·*hah*·ko *u*·pa·hahr	विवाहको उपहार

newar traditional culture

The Newars are the ethnic group indigenous to the Kathmandu Valley, with a history that goes back at least one millennium. They have a unique language, Newari. Newar life is centred on the family and local community, and the people traditionally live in extended family homes around communal courtyards.

The Newars have a rich cultural, social and spiritual lifestyle. Their traditional occupations are trade and agriculture, and they were originally Buddhist until Hinduism came to Nepal; many follow both philosophies. Ceremonies, feasts and festivals are an important part of everyday life and it's said there's a Newar festival for every day of the year! These are usually organised by community organisations called guthi which take care of most communal business.

Newars are famous for their food (see page 168) and the vast number of different dishes. There are a hundred ways to prepare buffalo meat alone! They're also renowned for their art and architecture – woodcarving and pagodas are two Newar specialisties.

toasts & condolences

शुभकामना र समबेदनाहरू

Bon appetit!	*rahm*·ro·sã·ga *khah*·nu·hos!	राम्रोसँग खानुहोस !
Bon voyage!	*rahm*·ro·sã·ga *yah*·trah *gar*·nu·hos!	राम्रोसँग यात्रा गर्नुहोस !
Get well soon!	*chi*·ṭo *ni*·ko·hu·nu·hos!	छिटो निको हुनुहोस !
God protect you!	*bha*·ga·bahn·le	भगबानले

घुम्न

There are no trains in Nepal (except right on the Indian border) and much of the country can only be reached by walking or flying. In towns, rickshaws, tempos (three-wheeled auto-rickshaws) and taxis are cheap and readily available. Rickshaws are usually the cheapest form of transport, but you should always bargain over the cost of the journey beforehand.

For longer trips, you have the option of a bus, taxi, or chauffeur-driven car.

finding your way

बाटो खोज्नु

The Nepalese are happy to help with directions and may even offer to escort you to your destination. It can be easy to get lost as you walk along the country's winding alleys and trails, but it's often the best way to see the country, and meet and interact with locals.

Where's the ...?	... *ka*·hãh cha?	... कहाँ छ ?
bus station	bas is·*ṭe*·san	बस स्टेसन
bus stop	bas bi·*sau*·ni	बस बिसौनी
road to ...	... *jah*·ne *bah*·ṭo	... जाने बाटो

What time does the ... leave/arrive?	... *ka*·ti ba·*je*·ti·ra *choḍ*·cha/*pug*·cha?	... कति बजेतिर छोड्छ/पुग्छ ?
aeroplane	*ha*·wai·ja·hahj	हवाईजहाज
boat	*ḍung*·gah	डुङ्गा
bus	bas	बस

How do I get to ...?
... *ka*·sa·ri *jah*·ne? ... कसरी जाने ?

Could you tell me where ... is?
ma·lai *bhan*·nu·hos,
... *ka*·hãh cha? — मलाई भन्नुहोस्, ... कहाँ छ ?

Is this the way to ...?
yo *bah*·ṭo ... *jah*·ne *bah*·ṭo ho? — यो बाटो ... जाने बाटो हो ?

Is it nearby?
na·jik cha? — नजिक छ ?

Is it far from here?
ya·hãh·bah·ṭa *ṭah*·ḍhah cha? — यहाँबाट टाढा छ ?

Is it difficult to get there?
jah·na *gah*·hro cha? — जान गाह्रो छ ?

Can I walk there?
hĩ·*ḍe*·ra *jah*·na *sa*·kin·chu? — हिंडेर जान सक्छु ?

It's near.
na·jik cha — नजिक छ

Please show me (on the map).
(*nak*·sah·mah) *ma*·lai
de·*khau*·nu·hos — (नक्सामा) मलाई देखाउनुहोस

Are there other means of getting there?
tya·hãh *jah*·ne *ar*·ko
u·*pah*·ya cha? — त्यहाँ जाने अर्को उपाय छ ?

Thank you for showing us the way.
hah·mi·lai *bah*·ṭo
de·*khah*·ya·ko·mah
dhan·ya·bahd — हामीलाईर् बाटो देखाएकोमा धन्यबाद

What ... is this?	yo kun ... ho?	यो कुन ... हो ?
city	*sha*·har	शहर
place	ṭhaũ	ठाउँ
road	*bah*·ṭo	बाटो
village	gaũ	गाउँ

directions

निर्देशन

Turn at the ...	... *moḍ*·nu·hos	... मोड्नुहोस
next corner	*au*·ne *ku*·nah	आउने कुना
street on the (right)	(*dah*·yãh) *bah*·ṭo·mah	(दायाँ) बाटोमा
across	*pah*·ri	पारी
along	*hun*·dai	हुँदै
behind	pa·*chah*·ḍi	पछाडि
below	*ta*·la	तल
beside	*cheu*·mah	छेउमा
down	*ta*·la	तल
far	*ṭah*·ḍhah	टाढा
here	*ya*·hãh	यहाँ
in front of	a·*gah*·ḍi	अगाडि
inside	*bhi*·tra	भित्र
left	*bah*·yãh	बायाँ
middle	bic	बीच
near	*na*·jik	नजिक
on	mah	मा
on top of	*mah*·thi	माथि
opposite	*pah*·ri	पारी
outside	*bah*·hi·ra	बाहिर
over	*mah*·thi	माथि
over there	u *tya*·hãh	उ त्यहाँ
right	*dah*·yãh	दायाँ
side	cheu	छेउ
there	*tya*·hãh	त्यहाँ
towards	*ti*·ra	तिर
up here/there	u *mah*·thi	उ माथि
north	*ut*·tar	उत्तर
south	*da*·chiṇ	दक्षिण
east	*pur*·ba	पूर्व
west	*pash*·cim	पश्चिम

addresses

ठेगानाहरू

Addresses in Nepal are written in the Devanagari script and can be found on a metal plaque (usually blue) near the front door. The first line is a letter-number combination indicating the block, the second line is the suburb (if any), and the third line mentions the town plus the one-digit national zone number:

छ ४ – ९३८ – ३	Cha 4 - 938 - 3
नयाँ बजार	Naya Bazaar
काठमाडौं – ४	Kathmandu - 4

Unfortunately, block numbers aren't chronological and most streets don't have names, so trying to find someone's home can be quite a challenge. Most people are known by name in their neighbourhood, however, so ask around.

tempo, taxi & rickshaw

ट्याम्पु, ट्याक्सी र रीक्सा

Tempos and taxis all have meters and are required to use them, but the drivers may refuse or ask to 'double the meter' at peak times, during rain and after dark, so bargain hard! Drivers are also notorious for being unable to change large bills (100 rupees or more) and not carrying any small change, so try to keep some with you.

Is this taxi available?
ṭyahk·si *khah*·li ho? — ट्याक्सी खाली हो ?

Please take me to ...
ma·lai ...·mah *lah*·nu·hos — मलाई ...मा लानुहोस

How much is it to go to ...?
... *jah*·na·lai *ka*·ti *pai*·sah *lahg*·cha? — ... जानलाई कति पैसा लाग्छ ?

PRACTICAL

How much is the fare?
bhah·ḍah *ka*·ti *par*·cha? — भाडा कति पर्छ ?

For two people?
du·i *ja*·nah·ko *lah*·gi? — दुइ जनाको लागि ?

Does that include the luggage?
sah·mahn *sa*·met *ga*·re·ra? — सामान समेत गरेर ?

instructions — निर्देशन

Go straight ahead.
si·dhah *jah*·nu·hos — सिधा जानुहोस

Please drive slowly.
bi·*stah*·rai *hãhk*·nu·hos — बिस्तारै हाक्नुहोस

Please hurry.
chi·ṭo *gar*·nu·hos — छिटो गर्नुहोस

Be careful!
hos *gar*·nu·hos! — होस गर्नुहोस !

Stop!
rok·nu·hos! — रोक्नुहोस !

Continue!
jahn·dai *gar*·nu·hos! — जादै गर्नुहोस !

The next street to the left/right.
au·ne *bah*·ṭo *bah*·yãh·mah/ *dah*·yãh·mah — आउने बाटो बायाँमा/ दायाँमा

Please wait here.
ya·hãh *par*·kha·nu·hos — यहाँ पर्खिनुहोस

Stop at the corner.
ku·nah·mah *rok*·nu·hos — कुनामा रोक्नुहोस

buying tickets — टिकट किन्नु

Where do they sell (bus) tickets?
(bas)·ko *ṭi*·kaṭ *ka*·hãh *bec*·cha? — (बस्)को टिकट कहाँ बेच्छ ?

I want to go to ...
ma ...·mah *jahn*·chu — म ...मा जान्छु

I'd like ...	*ma*·lai ... *di*·nu·hos	मलाई ... दिनुहोस
a one-way ticket	*jah*·ne *ṭi*·kaṭ	जाने टिकट
a return ticket	jah·ne·*au*·ne *ṭi*·kaṭ	जानेआउने टिकट
two tickets	*du*·i·wa·ṭah *ṭi*·kaṭ	दुइवटा टिकट

What time does it ...?	*ka*·ti *ba*·je ...?	कति बजे ... ?
arrive	*pug*·ne	पुग्ने
leave	*jah*·ne	जाने
return	*phar*·ka·ne	फर्कने

Do I need to book (a ticket)?
ma·lai (*ṭi*·kaṭ) *sany*·cit *gar*·nu·par·cha? — मलाई (टिकट) सञ्चित गर्नुपर्छ ?

I'd like to book a seat to ...
ma·lai ...·mah ek ṭhaũ *sany*·cit *gar*·nu·par·yo — मलाई ... मा एक ठाउँ सञ्चित गर्नुपर्यो

The bus/flight is full.
bas/u·*ḍahn bhar*·yo — बस/उडान भयो

Can I have a stand-by ticket?
ma·lai is·*ṭaiṇḍ*·bai *ṭi*·kaṭ *pain*·cha? — मलाई स्ट्याड बाइ टिकट पाइन्छ ?

How long does the trip take?
sa·phar *ka*·ti sa·*ma*·ya *lin*·cha? — सफर कति समय लिन्छ ?

air

हवाई

Many tourist destinations in Nepal are only, or most easily, reached by air. Domestic flights should be booked at least a week in advance. It's essential to reconfirm your flight at least once beforehand, particularly if it's a busy time of year or a popular destination.

Is there a flight to ...?
...·ko u·*ḍahn* cha? — ...को उडान छ ?

When's the next flight to ...?
...·ko *ar*·ko u·*ḍahn* *ka*·hi·le *jahn*·cha? — ...को अर्को उडान कहिले जान्छ ?

How long does the flight take?
u·*ḍahn* *ka*·ti sa·*ma*·ya *lin*·cha? — उडान कति समय लिन्छ ?

What time do I have to check in at the airport?
bi·mahn·sthal·mah *ka*·ti *ba*·je·ti·ra cek in *gar*·nu·par·cha? — विमानस्थलमा कति बजेतिर चेक इन गर्नुपर्छ ?

Where's the landing strip?
ha·wai *grau*·na *ka*·hãh cha? — हवाई ग्राउन कहाँ छ ?

Where's the baggage claim?
mahl·sah·mahn *li*·ne ṭhaũ *ka*·hãh cha? — मालसामान लिने ठाउँ कहाँ छ ?

My luggage hasn't arrived.
me·ro *mahl*·sah·mahn *pu*·ge·na — मेरो मालसामान पुगेन

at customs — भन्सारमा

I have nothing to declare.
ma·sã·ga ḍi·*klair* *gar*·nu·par·ne *ke*·hi *pa*·ni *chai*·na — म सँग डिक्लिएर गर्नु पर्ने केहि पनि छैन

I have something to declare.
ma·sã·ga ḍi·*klair* *gar*·nu·par·ne cha — म सँग डिक्लिएर गर्नु पर्ने छ

Do I have to declare this?
yo ḍi·*klair* *gar*·nu·par·cha? — यो डिक्लिएर गर्नुपर्छ?

This is all my luggage.
me·ro *sa*·bai *mahl*·sah·mahn *ya*·hãh cha — मेरो सबै मालसामान यहाँ छ

That's not mine.
tyo *me*·ro *hoi*·na — त्यो मेरो होइन

I didn't know I had to declare it.
ma·lai ḍi·*klair* *gar*·nu·par·cha *bhan*·ne *ku*·rah *thah*·hah *thi*·e·na — मलाई डिक्लिएर गर्नुपर्छ भन्ने कुरा थाहा थिएन

bus

बस

Town buses are cheap but often crowded and slow, although riding on the roof can be a good option for sightseeing and watching your bags. It can be difficult to find the right bus and get off at the right spot. Women may also experience unwanted physical attention in the crush. Long-haul buses, especially tourist ones, aren't so bad, although they do travel at hair-raising speeds on narrow, winding roads.

When's the ... bus?	... bas *ka*·hi·le *jahn*·cha?	... बस कहिले जान्छ?
first	*pa*·hi·lah	पहिला
last	*an*·tim	अन्तिम
next	*ar*·ko	अर्को

How often do buses come?
bas *ka*·ti *ak*·sar *aun*·cha? बस कति अक्सर आउँछ?

Where do I get the bus for ...?
... *jah*·ne bas *ka*·hãh *li*·ne? ... जाने बस कहाँ लिने ?

Which bus goes to ...?
...·mah kun bas *jahn*·cha? ...मा कुन बस जान्छ ?

Does this bus stop at (Mugling)?
yo bas *(mug*·ling)·mah *rok*·cha? यो बस (मुग्लीङ्ग)मा रोक्छ ?

Where does this bus go?
yo bas *ka*·hãh *jahn*·cha? यो बस कहाँ जान्छ ?

Is the bus full?
bas *bhar*·yo? बस भर्यो ?

Are there any stops?
ka·tai *rok*·cha? कतै रोक्छ ?

Will it be on time?
sa·*ma*·ya·mah *pug*·cha? समयमा पुग्छ ?

Is this seat taken?
ya·hãh *ko*·hi *mahn*·che cha? यहाँ कोहि मान्छे छ ?

Please stop the bus when we get to ...

... *ah*·ye *pa*·chi bas *ro*·ki·di·nu·hos — ... आएपछि बस रोकिदिनुहोस

The bus is delayed/cancelled.

bas *ḍhi*·lo/*rad*·da *bha*·yo — बस ढिला/रद्द भयो

How long will the bus be delayed?

bas *ka*·ti sa·*ma*·ya a·*be*·lah *hun*·cha? — बस कति समय अबेला हुन्छ ?

Is it a direct route?

si·dhah *jahn*·cha? — सिधा जान्छ ?

I want to get off at ...

ma ...·mah *or*·lin·chu — म ...मा ओर्लिन्छु

I want to get off here.

ma *ya*·hãh *or*·lin·chu — म यहाँ ओर्लिन्छु

boat

डुङ्गा

Rowing boats can be hired, with or without boatmen, on Phewa Lake in Pokhara and boats and canoes can be taken out on some rivers, such as the Rapti River in the Royal Chitwan National Park. There are also many rafting and kayaking trips available through travel companies.

Where does the boat leave from?

ḍung·gah ka·hãh·*bah*·ṭa *choḍ*·cha? — डुङ्गा कहाँबाट छोड्छ ?

What time does the boat arrive?

ḍung·gah *ka*·ti ba·*je*·ti·ra *pug*·cha? — डुङ्गा कति बजेतिर पुग्छ ?

How much to hire a boat for (one day)?

ḍung·gah (ek *din*)·ko *lah*·gi *bha*·ḍah·mah *ka*·ti ho? — डुङ्गा (एक दिन)को लागि भाडामा कति हो ?

Is that with a boatman?

mah·jhi·sã·ga ho? — माझिसँग हो ?

car

मोटर

In Nepal, you're unlikely to drive a rental vehicle yourself: hiring a car, jeep or minibus typically means hiring a driver too. This is the most expensive type of road transport. However, the driver adds little to the overall cost and generally makes the trip easier and more enjoyable. The driver can also help to negotiate accommodation and other costs.

The hire charge is usually calculated by distance and whether the trip is one-way or return. It may or may not include the cost of petrol or the driver's expenses, so be sure to check. Insurance should also be checked out, and it may be worth asking to see the vehicle and meet the driver beforehand.

Where can I hire a car (and driver)?
mo·ṭar (ra *ḍrai*·bhar) *ka*·hãh *bha*·ḍah·mah *li*·ne? — मोटर (र चलक) कहाँ भाडामा लिने ?

How much is it daily/weekly?
din·ko/*hap*·tah·ko *ka*·ti ho? — दिनको/हप्ताको कति हो ?

How much is it to ...?
... *ka*·ti ho? — ... कति हो ?

Does that include insurance/mileage?
bi·mah/*ṭah*·ḍhah *sa*·met ho? — बिमा/टाढा समेत हो ?

I'll pay half now and half at the end of the trip.
ma *ah*·dhah *pai*·sah *a*·hi·le *tir*·chu ra *bah*·ki *pai*·sah *sa*·phar *pa*·chi *tir*·chu — म आधा पैसा अहिले तिर्छु र बाकि पैसा सफर पछि तिर्छु

I'd like to meet the driver.
ma·lai *ḍrai*·bhar *bheṭ*·na man *lahg*·yo — मलाई चालक भेट्न मन लाग्यो

I'd like to see the vehicle.
ma·lai *gah*·ḍi *her*·na man *lahg*·yo — मलाई गाडि हेर्न मन लाग्यो

Where's the next stop?
ar·ko *ro*·kai *ka*·hi·le *aun*·cha? — अर्को रोकाइ कहिले आउँछ ?

Please stop here/somewhere for a while.
ya·hãh/*ka*·tai *ek*·chin *rok*·nu·hos यहाँ/कतै एकिछन रोक्नुहोस

How long can we park here?
gah·ḍi *ya*·hãh *ka*·ti *rok*·nu·hun·cha? गाडि यहाँ कति रोक्नुहुन्छ ?

Does this road lead to ...?
yo *bah*·ṭo ...·mah *jahn*·cha? यो बाटो ...मा जान्छ ?

bicycle

साइकल

Bicycles are a cheap form of urban transport and often the most convenient, as taxis can be difficult to find after dark. You can also hire mountain bikes.

Is there a bike path?
sai·kal·ko *bah*·ṭo cha? साइकलको बाटो छ ?

Where can I hire a bicycle?
sai·kal *ka*·hãh *bhah*·dah·mah *li*·ne? साइकल कहाँ भाडामा लिने ?

Where can I find (second-hand) bikes for sale?
(pu·*rah*·no) *sai*·kal *ka*·hãh *kin*·ne? (पुरानो) साइकल कहाँ किन्ने ?

How much is a bicycle per hour/day?
sai·kal *ghan*·ṭah·ko/ *din*·ko *ka*·ti ho? साइकल घण्टाको/ दिनको कति हो ?

I'd like to hire a bicycle for ...	*ma*·lai ...·ko *lah*·gi *eu*·ṭah *sai*·kal *bhah*·dah·mah *cah*·hi·yo	मलाई ...को लागि एउटा साइकल भाडामा चाहियो
one day	ek din	एक दिन
two days	*du*·i din	दुइ दिन
one week	ek *hap*·tah	एक हप्ता

Is it within cycling distance?
sai·kal·bah·ṭa *jah*·na *sak*·in·cha? साइकलबाट जान सकिन्छ ?

I have a flat tyre.
me·ro *cak*·kah·mah pwahl *bha*·yo मेरो चक्कामा प्वाल भयो

bicycle	*sai*·kal	साइकल
bicycle path	*sai*·kal·ko *bah*·ṭo	साइकलको बाटो
brakes	brek	ब्रेक
handlebars	*hen*·ḍal	हेन्डल
helmet	pha·*lah*·me *ṭo*·pi	फलामे टोपी
inner tube	ṭyub	टयुब
lights	*sai*·kal *bat*·ti	साइकल बत्ती
mountain bike	*maun*·ṭen baik	माउन्टेन बाइक
padlock	*tahl*·cah	ताल्चा
pump	pamp	पम्प
puncture	pwahl	प्वाल
racing bike	*re*·sing baik	रेसिङ्ग बाइक
saddle	siṭ	सीट
wheel	*cak*·kah	चक्का

Accommodation
डेरा

The Nepalese tourism sector has become more up-market in recent years, but there are still plenty of inexpensive places to stay. In Kathmandu, there's a huge choice of accommodation, ranging from five-star hotels to small guesthouses with picturesque roof gardens and tiny lodges with basic facilities and rock-bottom prices.

Outside Kathmandu, in towns and tourist centres, the range and prices are similar. Hotels and lodges are generally modestly priced, but standards differ so it's worth checking a few places in the same location. On trekking routes, accommodation can be particularly basic, especially in remote areas, although this is changing rapidly.

finding accommodation
डेरा खोज्नु

See Trekking, page 145, for words and phrases on Camping.

I'm looking for a/the ...	ma ... *kho*·je·ko	म ... खोजेको
camp site	*shi*·bir	शिविर
guesthouse	*pah*·hu·nah ghar	पाहुना घर
hotel	*ho*·ṭel	होटेल
lodge	laj	लज
youth hostel	yuṭh *hos*·ṭel	युथ होस्टेल

go green

Keep in mind that staying in a place that uses solar energy, kerosene or gas for cooking and hot water, instead of a wood stove, puts far less stress on the local forests.

Where's a ... hotel?	... *ho*·ṭel *ka*·hãh cha?	... होटेल कहाँ छ ?
cheap	*sas*·to	सस्तो
clean	sa·*phah*	सफा
good	*rahm*·ro	राम्रो
nearby	*na*·jik	नजिक
Where's the ... hotel?	... *ho*·ṭel *ka*·hãh cha?	... होटेल कहाँ छ ?
best	ek *nam*·bar	एक नम्बर
cheapest	sab·*bhan*·dah *sas*·to	सबभन्दा सस्तो

What's the address?
ṭhe·*gah*·nah ke ho? — ठेगाना के हो ?

Please write down the address.
ṭhe·*gah*·nah *lekh*·nu·hos — ठेगाना लेख्नुहोस

Also see **Addresses**, page 58.

booking ahead

सञ्चित राख्नु

I'd like to book a room.
ma·lai *ko*·ṭhah *sany*·cit *gar*·nu·par·yo — मलाई कोठा सञ्चित गर्नुपर्यो

Do you have any rooms/ beds available?
ko·ṭhah/khahṭ *pain*·cha? — कोठा/खाट पाइन्छ ?

Do you have a room with ...?	... *khahṭ*·ko *ko*·ṭhah *pain*·cha?	... खाटको कोठा पाइन्छ ?
two beds	*du*·i·wa·ṭah	दुइवटा
a double bed	*du*·i·ja·nah·ko	दुइजनाको
a single bed	*ek*·ja·nah·ko	एकजनाको
How much for ...?	...·ko *ka*·ti ho?	...को कति हो ?
one night	ek raht	एक रात
a week	ek *hap*·tah	एक हप्ता
two people	*du*·i *ja*·nah	दुइ जना

I'd like to share a dorm.
ma·lai *chah*·trah·bahs *bãhḍ*·nu man *lahg*·yo — मलाई छात्राबास बाध्नु मन लाग्यो

they may say

mahph *gar*·nu·hos, *ho*·ṭel *bhar*·yo
Sorry, the hotel's full:

For (three) nights.
(tin) *raht*·ko *lah*·gi — (तीन) रातको लागि

I'll be arriving at ... o'clock.
ma ... *ba*·je·ti·ra *pug*·chu — म ... बजेतिर पुग्छु

My name's ...
me·ro nahm ... ho — मेरो नाम ... हो

Can I pay by credit card?
kre·ḍiṭ *kahrḍ*·le *tir*·nu·hun·cha? — क्रेडिट कार्डले तिर्नुहुन्छ?

checking in

चेक इन गर्नु

I have a (room) reservation.
mai·le (*ko*·ṭhah) *sany*·cit *ga*·re·ko — मैले (कोठा) सञ्चित गरेको

I/We want a room with (a) ...	*ma*·lai/*hah*·mi·lai ... *bha*·ya·ko *ko*·ṭhah *cah*·hi·yo	मलाई/हा मिलाई ... भएको कोठा चाहियो
bathroom	snahn *kak*·sha	स्नान कक्ष
hot water	*tah*·to *pah*·ni	तातो पानी
shower	snahn	स्नान
TV	*ṭe*·li·bhi·jan	टेलिभिजन
window	jhyahl	झ्याल

Can I see the room?
ko·ṭhah *her*·na *sak*·in·cha? — कोठा हेर्न सकिन्छ ?

Are there any other rooms?
ar·ko *ko*·ṭhah *pain*·cha? — अर्को कोठा पाइन्छ ?

Are there any cheaper rooms?
ar·ko *ku*·nai *sas*·to *ko*·ṭhah cha? — अर्को कुनै सस्तो कोठा छ ?

Where's the toilet?
shau·cah·la·ya/bahṭh·rum ka·hãh cha? — शैचालय/बथरुम कहाँ छ ?

Is there hot water (all day)?
(din·bha·ri) tah·to pah·ni aun·cha? — (दिनभरी) तातो पानी आउँछ ?

Is breakfast included?
bi·hah·na·ko khah·nah sa·met ho? — बिहानको खाना समेत हो ?

The room's fine. I'll take it.
ko·ṭhah ṭhik cha, ma lin·chu — कोठाठीक छ, म लिन्छु

requests & queries

अनुरोध र प्रश्न

I have a request.
eu·ṭah a·nu·rodh cha — एउटा अनुरोध छ

Please wake me up at ... o'clock tomorrow morning.
ma·lai bho·li bi·hah·na ... ba·je u·ṭhau·nu·hos — मलाई भोलि बिहान ... बजे उठाउनुहोस

Where's the bathroom?
bahṭh·rum ka·hãh cha? — बथरुम कहाँ छ ?

Does the hotel have a restaurant?
ho·ṭel·mah bho·ja·nah·la·ya cha? — होटेलमा भोजनालय छ ?

Where's breakfast served?
bi·hah·na·ko khah·nah ka·hãh din·cha? — बिहानको खाना कहाँ दिन्छ ?

Can we use the kitchen?
hah·mi·le bhahn·chah ca·lau·nu·hun·cha? — हामीले भान्छा चलाउनुहुन्छ ?

Is there a laundry nearby?
e·tah lu·gah·dhu·ne ṭhaũ na·jik cha? — एता लुगाधुने ठाउँ नजिक छ ?

Is there somewhere to wash clothes?
lu·gah·dhu·ne ṭhaũ pain·cha? — लुगाधुने ठाउँ पाइन्छ ?

Please wash/iron this clothing.
yo lu·gah (dhu·i di·nu·hos; is·ṭri la·gau·nu·hos) — यो लुगा (धोई दिनुहोस; इस्त्री लगाउनुहोस)

Is my laundry ready?
me·ro *lu*·gah *ta*·yahr *bha*·yo? मेरो लुगा तयार भयो ?

I need this clothing today/tomorrow.
me·ro *lu*·gah *ah*·ja/*bho*·li *cah*·hin·cha मेरो लुगा आज/भोलि चाहिन्छ

Please clean the room.
ko·ṭhah *sa*·phah *gar*·nu·hos कोठा सफा गर्नुहोस

Please change the sheets.
tan·nah *pher*·nu·hos तन्ना फेर्नुहोस

Do you have a safe?
ta·*paĩ*·ka·hãh su·*ra*·chit ṭhaũ cha? तपाईकहाँ सुरक्षित ठाउँ छ ?

Could I leave this to be stored?
yo *ya*·hãh *choḍ*·na *sa*·kin·cha? यो यहाँ छोड्न सकिन्छ ?

Could I have a receipt for it?
yas·ko bil *di*·nu·hun·cha? यस्को बिल दिनुहुन्छ ?

Do you change money here?
ya·hãh *pai*·sah *sahṭ*·nu·hun·cha? यहाँ पैसा साट्नुहुन्छ ?

Do you arrange tours?
ya·hãh *bhra*·maṇ ban·do·*bas*·ta *gar*·nu·hun·cha? यहाँ भ्रमण बन्दोबस्त गर्नुहुन्छ ?

Can I leave a message?
me·ro *kha*·bar *rahkh*·nu·hun·cha? मेरो खबर राख्नुहुन्छ ?

Is there a message board?
kha·bar·ko ṭhaũ cha? खबरको ठाउँ छ ?

Is there a message for me?
me·ro *lah*·gi *kha*·bar cha? मेरो लागि खबर छ ?

self-catering

If you're staying in one area for some time, most guesthouses don't mind if you prepare your own food in your room. Try to find a place near a local market, as fridges are still a luxury item in Nepal except in expensive accommodation. Also, there are no public laundrettes for washing your own clothes, but you'll find plenty of places to have laundry done cheaply, including most hotels.

Could I use the telephone?
ma phon *gar*·na *sak*·chu? म फोन गर्न सक्छु ?

Do I leave my key at reception?
sãh·co ri·*sep*·san·mah *choḍ*·ne? साँचो रीसेप्सनमा छोड्ने ?

I've locked myself out.
sãh·co *ko*·ṭhah·mah *par*·yo साँचो कोठामा पर्यो

We left the key at reception.
hah·mi·le *sãh*·co ri·*sep*·san·mah *cho*·ḍe·ko हामीले साँचो रीसेप्सनमा छोडेको

I need (a/another) ...	*ma*·lai ... *cah*·hi·yo	मलाई ...चाहियो
Could we have (a/another) ...?	*hah*·mi·lai ... *di*·nu·hun·cha?	हामीलाई ... दिनुहुन्छ ?
bedding	bi·*chyau*·nah	बिछयौना
blanket	*kam*·mal	कम्बल
breakfast	bi·*hah*·na·ko *khah*·nah	बिहानको खाना
candle	*main*·bat·ti	मैनबत्ती
chair	mec	मेच
curtain	*par*·dah	पर्दा
fan	*pã*·khah	पंखा
the key	*sãh*·co	साँचो

complaints

सिकायतहरू

Excuse me, there's a problem with my room.
sun·nu·hos, *me*·ro *ko*·ṭhah·mah sa·*mas*·yah *bha*·yo सुन्नुहोस, मेरो कोठामा समस्या भयो

I don't like this room.
ma·lai yo *ko*·ṭhah man *par*·dai·na मलाई यो कोठा मन पर्दैन

Can I change rooms?
ko·ṭhah *sahṭ*·nu·hun·cha? कोठा साट्नुहुन्छ ?

The window doesn't open/close.
jhyahl *khol*·na/*lau*·na *sa*·ke·na झ्याल खोल्न/लाउन सकेन

This room smells.
yo ko·ṭhah ga·naun·cha — यो कोठागनाउन्छ

The toilet won't flush.
bahṭh·rum kahm gar·dai·na — बथरुम काम गर्‌दैन

There's no (hot) water.
(tah·to) pah·ni chai·na — (तातो) पानी छैन

The ... doesn't work.
... kahm gar·dai·na — ... काम गर्दैन

Can you get it fixed?
yo ba·nau·na sa·kin·cha? — यो बनाउन सकिन्छ ?

It's too ...	*dhe·rai ... cha*	धेरै ... छ
bright	*u·jyah·lo*	उज्यालो
cold	*ci·so*	चिसो
dark	*ã·dhyah·ro*	अँध्यारो
expensive	*ma·hã·go*	महँगो
hot	*tah·to*	तातो
light	*u·jyah·lo*	उज्यालो
noisy	*hal·lah*	ह ल्ला
small	*sah·no*	सानो

This ... is not clean.	*yo ... sa·phah chai·na*	यो ... सफा छैन
bedding	*tan·nah*	तन्ना
blanket	*kam·mal*	कम्बल
pillow	*si·rah·ni*	सिरानी
pillowcase	*si·rah·ni·ko khol*	सिरानीको खोल
sheet	*tan·nah*	तन्ना

checking out

चेक आउट गर्नुहोसु

What time do we have to check out?
hah·mi·lai ka·ti ba·je cek auṭ gar·nu·par·cha? — हामीलाई कति बजे चेक आउट गर्नुपर्छ ?

I would like to check out ...	ma ... cek auṭ *gar*·chu	म ... चेक आउट गर्छु
now	*a*·hi·le	अहिले
at noon	*bah*·hra *ba*·je	बाह्र बजे
tomorrow	*bho*·li	भोलि

We had a great stay, thank you.
hah·mi·le *rahm*·ro·sã·ga *bas*·yaũ, *dhan*·ya·badh — हामीले राम्रोसँग बस्यौ, धन्यबाद

You've been wonderful.
ta·*paĩ ek*·dam *rahm*·ro *bha*·yo — तपाई एकदम राम्रो भयो

Thank you for all your help.
ta·*paĩ*·le *mad*·dat *di*·ye·ko·mah *dhan*·ya·bahd — तपाईले मद्दत दियेकोमा धन्यवाद

The room was perfect.
ko·ṭhah *ek*·dam *rahm*·ro *thi*·yo — कोठा एकदम राम्रो थियो

We hope we can return some day.
ek din *hah*·mi·lai *phar*·ka·na man *lahg*·cha — एक दिन हामीलाई फर्खन मन लाग्छ

I'd like to pay now.
ma *a*·hi·le *pai*·sah *tir*·chu — म अहिले पैसा तिर्छु

Can I pay with a travellers cheque?
ṭrah·bhlar *cek*·le *tir*·nu·hun·cha? — ट्याभलर चेकले तिर्नुहुन्छ ?

There's a mistake in the bill.
bil·mah *gal*·ti *bha*·yo — बिलमा गल्ती भयो

Can I leave my backpack here until tonight?
ma *ya*·hãh *jho*·lah *be*·lu·kah·sam·ma *choḍ*·na *sa*·kin·cha? — म यहाँ झोला बेलुकासम्म छोड्न सकिन्छ ?

Can you call a taxi for me?
me·ro *lah*·gi *ṭyahk*·si bo·*lau*·nu·hun·cha? — मेरो लागि टयाक्सी बोलाउनुहुन्छ ?

I'm coming back ...	ma ... *phar*·kin·chu	म ... पर्खिन्छु
in a few days	*ke*·hi din *pa*·chi	केहि दिन पछि
in two weeks	*du*·i *hap*·tah *pa*·chi	दुइ हप्ता पछि

Around Town
शहरमा

There's plenty to do around town in Nepal. Kathmandu, in particular, is a great place to hang out and is known to some as 'serendipity land'. As well as tourist information centres and a huge tourist industry awaiting you, there are also special tourist police to help out if needed. Most towns have decent banking and telecommunications facilities and a reasonable postal service.

looking for ...

... खोज्नु

I'm looking for a/the ...	ma ... *kho*·je·ko	म ... खोजेको
Where's a/the ...?	... *ka*·hãh cha?	... कहाँ छ ?
art gallery	ka·*lah*·ko ghar	कलाको घर
bank	baĩk	बैंक
cinema	*si*·ne·mah	सिनेमा
city centre	*sha*·har·ko bic	शहरको बीच
... consulate	... *rahj*·du·tah·vahs	... राजदूतावास
... embassy	... *rahj*·du·tah·vahs	... राजदूतावास
... hotel	... *ho*·ṭel	... होटेल
main square	pra·*mukh* cok	प्रमुख चोक
market	ba·*jahr*	बजार
museum	sã·gra·*hah*·la·ya	संग्रहालय
police	pra·*ha*·ri	प्रहरी
post office	*hu*·lahk *aḍ*·ḍah	हुलाक अड्डा
public toilet	shau·*cah*·la·ya	शौचालय
telephone centre	phon *aḍ*·ḍah	फोन अड्डा
tourist information office	par·*ya*·ṭan kahr·*yah*·la·ya	पर्यटन कार्यालय
town square	*sha*·har·ko cok	शहरको चोक

at the bank

बैंकमा

Changing money and travellers cheques is usually straightforward. International transfers are becoming less complicated and, in major centres, there are even some automatic teller machines (ATMs). With the exception of some expensive hotels and resorts, exchange counters and other places that accept foreign currency don't normally charge much more than the official bank rate.

Remember that it can be difficult to change large bills (100 rupees or more), especially in the countryside, so ask for and carry plenty of small change.

What time does the bank open?
baĩk *ka*·ti *ba*·je *khol*·cha? बैंक कति बजे खोल्छ ?

Where can I cash a travellers cheque?
ṭrah·bhlar cek *ka*·hãh *sahṭ*·nu·hun·cha? ट्याभलर चेक कहाँ साट्नुहुन्छ ?

I want to change (a) ...	... *sahṭ*·nu·par·yo	... साट्नुपर्यो
cheque	cek	चेक
some money	*pai*·sah *a*·li·ka·ti	पैसा अलिकति
travellers cheque	*ṭrah*·bhlar cek	ट्याभलर चेक

Please change this into Nepalese rupees.
yo ne·*pah*·li ru·*pi*·yãh·mah *sah*·ṭi *di*·nu·hos यो नेपाली रुपियाँमा साटी दिनुहोस

Can I exchange money here?
ya·hãh *pai*·sah *sahṭ*·nu·hun·cha? यहाँ पैसा साट्नुहुन्छ ?

What's the exchange rate today?
ah·ja *sahṭ*·ne reṭ *ka*·ti cha? आज साट्ने रेट कति छ ?

keep receipts

Be sure to keep all your exchange receipts if you want to extend your visa or re-exchange rupees into other currency when you leave the country.

What's your commission?
ta·*paĩ*·ko *ah*·yog *ka*·ti cha? — तपाईको कमिशन कति छ ?

How many rupees per US dollar?
ek *ḍa*·lar·ko *ka*·ti ho? — एक डलरको कति हो ?

Please write it down.
le·khi·*di*·nu·hos — लेखिदिनुहोस

Where do I sign?
ka·hãh *sa*·hi *gar*·ne? — कहाँ सही गनेर् ?

Please give me smaller notes.
khu·drah *pai*·sah *di*·nu·hos — खुद्रा पैसा दिनुहोस

Please give me smaller change for this note.
yas·lai *khu*·drah *pai*·sah *di*·nu·hos — यसलाई खुद्रा पैसा दिनुहोस

Can I have money sent here from my bank?
me·ro *baĩk*·bah·ṭa *pai*·sah *ya*·hãh *aun*·cha? — मेरो बैंकबाट पैसा यहाँ आउँछ ?

How long will it take to arrive?
pug·na *ka*·ti sa·*ma*·ya *lahg*·cha? — पुग्न कति समय लाग्छ ?

I'm expecting some money from ...
...·bah·ṭa *pai*·sah a·*pe*·chah *gar*·chu — ...बाट पैसा अपेक्षा गर्छु

Has my money arrived yet?
me·ro *pai*·sah *ah*·yo? — मेरो पैसा आयो ?

Can I transfer money from overseas?
pai·sah bi·*desh*·bah·ṭa *aun*·cha? — पैसा बिदेशबाट आउँछ ?

Can I use my credit card to withdraw money?
kre·ḍiṭ *kahrḍ*·le *pai*·sah *li*·nu·hun·cha? — क्रेडिट कार्डले पैसा लिनुहुन्छ ?

The ATM swallowed my card.
pai·sah·ko mi·*sin*·le *me*·ro kahrḍ khai *di*·yo — पैसाको मेसिनले मेरो कार्ड खाई दियो

at the post office

हुलाक अड्डा

Nepal's postal service is slow, but it's cheap and fairly reliable. There aren't many post offices and their hours are short, so be prepared to queue. In Kathmandu, try the small postal counters in Thamel, Chetrapati or Basantapur Square, instead of the GPO (unless you need poste restante). You can also buy stamps and post letters through some bookshops.

I want to send a/an ...	... pa·*ṭhau*·nu·par·yo	... पठाउनुपर्‍यो
aerogram	*ha*·wai·pa·tra	हवाईपत्र
fax	phyahks	फ्याक्स
letter	*ci*·ṭhi	चिठ्ठी
parcel	pu·*lin*·dah	पुलीन्दा
telegram	tahr	तार

I want to buy a/an ...	... *kin*·nu·par·yo	... किन्नुपर्‍यो
postcard	*posṭ*·kahrḍ	पोस्टकार्ड
stamp	*ṭi*·kaṭ	टिकट

How much is it to send this by ...?	yo ... *ka*·ti *pai*·sah *lahg*·cha?	यो ... कति पैसा लाग्छ ?
airmail	*ha*·wai·ḍahk *gar*·na	हवाई डाक गर्न
ship	ja·*hahj*·bah·ṭa pa·*ṭhau*·na	जहाजबाट पठाउन

Please give me some stamps.
ma·lai *ṭi*·kaṭ *di*·nu·hos — मलाई टिकट दिनुहोस

How much is it to send this to ...?
yo ...·mah pa·*ṭhau*·na *ka*·ti *lahg*·cha? — यो ...मा पठाउन कति लाग्छ ?

signed, sealed, delivered

Never post anything in letterboxes – even giving it to your hotel can be risky. Make sure you see the clerk postmark the stamps on your mail.

Please send it by air/surface.
yo ha·wai·ja·*hahj*·bah·ṭa/ *gah*·ḍi·bah·ṭa pa·*ṭhau*·nu·hos — यो हवाईजहाजबाट/ गाडीबाट पठाउनुहोस

Where's the poste restante section?
posṭ res·*ṭā̃ṭ* *ka*·hā̃h cha? — पोस्ट रेस्टन्ट कहाँ छ ?

Is there any mail for me?
me·ro *ci*·ṭhi·pa·tra cha? — मेरो चिठ्ठीपत्र छ ?

airmail	*ha*·wai·ḍahk	हवाईडाक
envelope	khahm	खाम
express mail	*chi*·ṭo posṭ	छिटो पोस्ट
mailbox	pa·tra·*many*·ju·sah	पत्रमञ्जुषा
pen	*ka*·lam	कलम
postcode	*posṭ*·koḍ	पोस्टकोड
registered mail	*dar*·tah·ko posṭ	पोष्ट दर्ता
surface mail	*gah*·ḍi·bah·ṭa posṭ	गाडीबाट पोष्ट

telecommunications

टेलेकोमहरू

In Nepalese towns there are now many small communications offices where you can make and receive phone calls and faxes and get on the Internet.

Where's the nearest phone?
na·ji·kai phon *ka*·hā̃h cha? — नजिकै फोन कहाँ छ ?

Could I please use the telephone?
ma phon *gar*·na *sak*·chu? — म फोन गर्न सक्छु ?

I want to call ...
ma·lai ...·mah phon *gar*·nu·par·yo — मलाई ...मा फोन गर्नुपर्यो

I want to make a reverse-charges/ collect call to ...
ma·lai *ya*·hā̃h·bah·ṭa ...·mah phon *gar*·nu·par·yo, *pai*·sah *tya*·hā̃h·bah·ṭa *tir*·cha — मलाई यहाँ ...मा फोन गर्नुपर्यो, पैसा त्यहाँबाट तिर्छ

The number is ...
nam·bar ... ho — नम्बर ... हो

How much is it per minute?
mi·naṭ·ko *ka*·ti ho? — मिनेटको कति हो ?

I will speak for (three) minutes.
(tin) *mi*·naṭ phon *gar*·chu — (तीन) मिनेट फोन गर्छु

How many minutes was that?
ka·ti *mi*·naṭ *bha*·yo? — कति मिनेट भयो ?

Please wait a moment.
ek·chin *par*·kha·nu·hos — एकछिन पर्खनुहोस

What's the area code for ...?
...·ko koḍ *nam*·bar *ka*·ti ho? — ...को कोड नम्बर कति हो ?

It's engaged.
phon *bi*·ji cha — फोन बीजी छ

We were cut off.
lain *kahṭ*·yo — लाइन काट्यो

I want to send a fax to ...
ma·lai phyahks ...·mah pa·*ṭhau*·nu·par·yo — मलाई फ्याक्स ...मा पठाउनु पर्यो

What's the fax charge per minute to ...?
...·mah phyahks pa·*ṭhau*·ne ek *mi*·naṭ·ko *ka*·ti *pai*·sah *lahg*·cha? — ...मा फ्याक्स पठाउने एक मिनेटको कति पैसा लाग्छ ?

fax	phyahks	फ्याक्स
operator	*a*·pre·ṭar	अप्रेटर
phone book	*phon*·ko ki·*tahb*	फोनको किताब
telephone	phon	फोन
urgent	ja·*ru*·ri	जरुरी

making a call — फोन गर्नु

Hello, do you speak English?
na·ma·*ste*, ang·*gre*·ji *bol*·nu·hun·cha? — नमस्ते, अङ्ग्रेजी बोल्नुहुन्छ ?

Hello? (answering a call)
ha·*jur?* — हजुर ?

Can I speak to ...?
...·sā̃·ga *bol*·na *sak*·chu? ...सँग बोल्न सक्छु ?

Is ... there?
... cha? ... छ ?

Yes, he's/she's here.
cha छ

One moment.
ek·chin एकिछन

Who's calling?
ya·hāh ko *hu*·nu·hun·cha? यहाँ को हुनुहुन्छ ?

It's ...
ma ... ho म ... हो

I'm sorry, (he's/she's) not here.
mahph *gar*·nu·hos, *(wa*·hāh) *chai*·na माफ गर्नुहोस, (वहाँ) छैन

What time will (he/she) be back?
(wa·hāh) *ka*·ti *ba*·je *phar*·kan·cha? (वहाँ) कति बजे फर्कन्छ ?

Can I leave a message?
san·desh *choḍ*·nu·hun·cha? सन्देश छोड्नुहुन्छ ?

Please tell ... I called.
...·lai *mai*·le phon *ga*·re·ko *bhan*·ni *di*·nu·hos ...लाई मैले मैले फोन गरेको भनि दिनुहोस

My number is ...
me·ro *nam*·bar ... ho मेरो नम्बर ... हो

I don't have a contact number.
me·ro *nam*·bar *chai*·na मेरो नम्बर छैन

I'll call back later.
ma *phe*·ri *pa*·chi phon *gar*·chu म फेरी पछि फोन गर्छु

What time should I call?
ka·ti *ba*·je *phe*·ri phon *gar*·ne? कति बजे फेरी फोन गर्ने ?

the internet इन्टरनेट

Is there a local Internet cafe?
ya·hāh ĩ·ṭar·neṭ *kyah*·phe cha? यहाँ इन्टरनेट क्याफे छ ?

I'd like to get Internet access.
ma·lai ĩ·ṭar·neṭ *ca*·hi·yo मलाई इन्टरनेट चाहियो

I'd like to check my email.
i·mel cek *gar*·nu·par·yo — ईमेल चेक गर्नुपर्यो

I'd like to send an email.
i·mel pa·*ṭhau*·nu·par·yo — इमेल पठाउनु पर्यो

sightseeing

घुमघाम

Nepal is full of fascinating historical and religious sights and local people will be happy to show you around and give background information.

When visiting temples, dress modestly and remove your shoes. At Hindu temples remove any leather items, such as belts, before entering the compound. Normally, only Hindus are permitted right inside a Hindu temple or shrine. You may wish to make a donation or pay a priest to perform a *pu*·jah (पूजा), 'puja ceremony', for you.

Where's the tourist information office?
par·*ya*·ṭan kahr·*yah*·la·ya *ka*·hãh cha? — पर्यटन कार्यालय कहाँ छ ?

Do you have a local map?
sthah·ni·ya *nak*·sah cha? — स्थानीय नक्सा छ ?

I'd like to see ...
ma·lai ... *her*·na man *lahg*·yo — मलाई ... हेर्न मन लाग्यो

Do you have a guidebook (in English)?
(ang·*gre*·ji) gaiḍ ki·*tahb* cha? — (अङ्ग्रेजी) गाईड किताब छ ?

happy snaps

Always ask people if it's okay to photograph them and be prepared to respect their wishes if they refuse. In particular, people involved in religious ceremonies or washing and bathing may not wish to be photographed. And do send photos if you promise to, as people can be very disappointed otherwise.

What are the main attractions?
pra·*mukh* shu·bha·*dar*·shan ke ho? — प्रमुख शुभदशर्न के हो ?

We only have one/two day(s).
hah·mi·sã·ga ek/*du*·i din *mah*·trai *bah*·ki cha — हामीसँग एक/दु इ दिन मात्रै बाकि छ

Is it OK to take photos?
tas·bir *khic*·nu·hun·cha? — तस्बीर खिच्नुहुन्छ ?

Please take my photo.
me·ro *tas*·bir *khic*·nu·hos — मेरो तस्बीर खिच्नुहोस

Can I take your photo?
ta·*paĩ*·ko *tas*·bir *khic*·nu·hun·cha? — तपाईको तस्बीर खिच्नुहुन्छ ?

I'll send you the photo.
tas·bir ta·*paĩ*·lai pa·*ṭhaun*·chu — तस्बीर तपाईलाई पठाउछु

Please write down your name and address.
ta·*paĩ*·ko nahm ra ṭhe·*gah*·nah *lekh*·nu·hos — तपाईको नाम र ठेगाना लेख्नुहोस

getting in — पस्नु

What time does it open/close?
ka·ti *ba*·je [*khol*·cha; *ban*·da *gar*·cha]? — कति बजे [खोल्छ; बन्द गर्छ] ?

How much is the entry fee?
pra·besh *shul*·ka *ka*·ti ho? — प्रबेश शुल्क कति हो ?

Is there a discount for ...?	...·lai gha·*ṭau*·nu·hun·cha?	...लाई घटाउनुहुन्छ ?
children	ke·ṭah·*ke*·ṭi	केटाकेटी
students	bi·*dyahr*·thi	बिद्यार्थी
pensioners	bu·ḍho·*bu*·ḍhi	बुढाबुढी

the sights — शुभदर्शन

What's that ...?	tyo ... ke ho?	त्यो ... के हो ?
building	*bha*·wan	भवन

monument	*smah*·rak	स्मारक
temple (Hindu)	*man*·dir	मन्दिर
temple (Buddhist)	*stu*·pah	स्टुपा

How old is it?
ka·ti pu·*rah*·no *bha*·yo? कति पुरानो भयो ?

Who built it?
kas·le ba·*nah*·ya·ko? कसले बनाएको ?

What's that?
tyo ke ho? त्यो के हो ?

ancient	*prah*·cin	प्राचीन
cremation	dah·ha·*sã*·skahr	दाहसंस्कार
cremation ghat	ghahṭ	घाट
cultural show	sãh·*skri*·tik pra·*dar*·shan	साँस्कृतिक प्रदर्शन
factory	kahr·*khah*·nah	कारखाना
gardens	ba·*gaĩ*·cah	बगैंचा
library	pus·ta·*kah*·la·ya	पुस्तकालय
market	ba·*jahr*	बजार
monastery	*gum*·bah	गुम्बा
monument	*smah*·rak	स्मारक
mosque	*mas*·jid	मस्जीद
old city	pu·*rah*·no *sha*·har	पुरानो शहर
pagoda	*ga*·jur	गजुर
palace	*dar*·bahr	दरबार
philosophy	*dhar*·ma	धर्म
religion	*dhar*·ma	धर्म
restaurant	bho·ja·*nah*·la·ya	भोजनालय
statue	*mur*·ti	मूर्ति
temple (Hindu)	*man*·dir	मन्दिर
temple (Buddhist)	*stu*·pah	स्तुपा
university	bi·shwa·bi·*dyah*·la·ya	विश्वबिद्यालय
zoo	*ci*·ḍi·yah·khah·nah	चिडियाखाना

tours भ्रमण

Are there regular tours we can join?
hah·mi ba·*rah*·bar *bhra*·maṇ *mil*·na *sak*·in·cha? हामी बराबर भ्रमण मिल्न सकिन्छ ?

Where can I hire a/an (English-speaking) guide?

ma·lai (ang·*gre*·ji *bol*·ne) *bah*·ṭo de·*khau*·ne *mahn*·che ka·hãh *pain*·cha?	मलाई (अंग्रेजी बोल्ने) बाटो देखाउने मान्छे कहाँ पाईन्छ ?

How much is the tour/a guide?

bhra·maṇ·le/ghu·*mau*·ne *mahn*·che·le *ka*·ti *pai*·sah *lin*·cha?	भ्रमणले/घुमाउने मान्छेले कति पैसा लिन्छ ?

How long is the tour?

bhra·maṇ *ka*·ti sa·*ma*·ya *lahg*·cha?	भ्रमण कति समय लाग्छ ?

Will we have free time?

hah·mi·lai *phur*·sat *hun*·cha?	हामीलाई फुर्सद हुन्छ ?

How long are we here for?

hah·mi *ya*·hãh *ka*·ti *bas*·chãu?	हामी यहाँ कति बस्छौ ?

What time should we be back?

hah·mi *ka*·ti *ba*·je *phar*·ka·nu·par·cha?	हामी कति बजे फर्कनुपर्छ ?

Our guide has paid/will pay.

hahm·ro ghu·*mau*·ne *mahn*·che·le *pai*·sah *ti*·re·ko/*tir*·cha	हामिलाई घुमाउने मान्छेलाई पैसा तिर्योर तिरौला

I'm with them.

ma *un*·i·ha·ru·sã·ga chu	म उनीहरुसँग छु

I've lost my group.

ma *me*·ro *dal*·bah·ṭa ha·*rah*·yo	म मेरो दलबाट हराएँ

Have you seen a group of (Australians)?

ta·*paĩ*·le (a·*sṭre*·li·yan) dal *dekh*·nu *bha*·yo?	तपाईले (अष्ट्रेलियन) दल देख्नु भयो ?

at the embassy

राजदूतावासमा

If you plan to extend your visa, be prepared for long waits at the immigration office. Although visa extensions are often available the following day, it's best to allow more time in case of delays.

Where can I extend my visa?
bhi·sah *ka*·hãh *thap*·ne? भिसा कहाँ थप्ने ?

I want to extend my visa for ... days.
ma·lai *ar*·ko ... *din*·ko *lah*·gi *bhi*·sah *li*·nu *par*·yo मलाई अर्को ... दिनको लागि भिसा लिनु पर्यो

When can I collect my passport?
me·ro rah·ha·*dah*·ni *ka*·hi·le *li*·na *au*·ne? मेरो राहदानी कहिले लिन आउने ?

going out

बाहिर जानु

There's much more nightlife in Kathmandu (and some other towns) than in the past, as many venues are now permitted to stay open past midnight. There are lots of pubs and bars and a flourishing local scene for live bands. There are also several nightclubs and a number of 24-hour casinos.

Local people tend to stay home after dark, but young Nepalese are beginning to go out more and the streets are still pretty safe at night, especially with the tourist police around.

where to go
कहाँ जानु

What's there to do in the evenings?
be·lu·kah ke *gar*·na *sa*·kin·cha? बेलुका के गर्न सकिन्छ ?

Where can I find out what's on?
ke *hun*·dai·cha *ka*·sa·ri *thah*·ha *pau*·nu? के हुन्दैछ कसरी थाहा पाउनु ?

What's on tonight?
ah·ja *be*·lu·kah ke *hun*·dai·cha? आज बेलुका के हुन्दैछ ?

I feel like going to a/the ...	*ma*·lai ...·mah *jah*·na man *lahg*·yo	मलाई ...मा जान मन लाग्यो
bar	pab	पब
cafe	*kyah*·phe	क्याफे
cinema	*si*·ne·mah	सिनेमा
concert	*kan*·sarṭ	कन्सट

nightclub	klab	क्लब
pub	pab	पब
restaurant	bho·ja·*nah*·la·ya	भोजनालय
theatre	*nahc*·ghar	नाचघर

I feel like ...	*ma*·lai ... man *lahg*·yo	मलाई ... मन लाग्यो
a stroll	*ghum*·na	घुम्न
dancing	*nahc*·na	नाच्न
having a coffee/drink	*ka*·phi/pi·*u*·ne *li*·na	कफी/पिउने लिन

nightclubs & bars क्लबहरू

Are there any good nightclubs?
rahm·ro *klab*·ha·ru chan? — राम्रो क्लबहरू छन ?

How do you get to this club?
yo *klab*·mah *ka*·sa·ri *jah*·ne? — यो क्लबमा कसरी जाने ?

Do you want to dance?
ta·*paĩ*·lai *nahc*·na man *lahg*·yo? — तपाईलाई नाच्न मन लाग्यो ?

I'm sorry, I'm a terrible dancer.
mahph *gar*·nu·hos, *ma*·lai *nahc*·na *aun*·di·na — माफ गर्नुहोस, मलाई नाच्न आउदैन

Come on!
au·nu·hos nah! — आउनुहोस न !

What type of music do you prefer?
ta·*paĩ*·lai *kas*·to *sang*·git man *par*·cha? — तपाईलाई कस्तो सङ्गीत मन पर्छ ?

I really like (reggae).
ma·lai (*re*·ge) *dhe*·rai man *par*·cha — मलाई (रेगे) धेरै मन पर्छ

Do you want to go to a karaoke bar?
ta·*paĩ*·lai kah·rah·*yo*·ke *bahr*·mah *jah*·na man *lahg*·yo? — तपाईलाई कारायोके बारमा जान मन लाग्यो ?

Do you have to pay to enter?
pra·besh *shul*·ka *di*·nu·par·cha? — प्रवेश शुल्क दिनुपर्छ ?

No, it's free.
di·nu·par·dai·na — दिनुपर्दैन

Yes, it's ...
di·nu·par·cha, ... ho | दिनुपर्छ, ... हो

This place is great!
yo ṭhaũ *rahm*·ro cha! | यो ठाउँ राम्रो छ !

I'm having a great time!
ma·lai *dhe*·rai *maj*·jah *lahg*·yo! | मलाई धेरै मज्जा लाग्यो !

I don't like the music here.
ma·lai *ya*·hãh·ko *sang*·git man *par*·dai·na | मलाई यहाँको सङ्गीत मन पर्दैन

Shall we go somewhere else?
hah·mi *ar*·ko *ṭhaũ*·mah jaũ? | हामी अर्को ठाउँमा जाउँ ?

invitations

निम्ताहरू

What are you doing this evening/weekend?
ta·*paĩ be*·lu·kah·mah/ wi·*kenḍ*·mah ke *gar*·nu·hun·cha? | तपाई बेलुकामा/ विकेन्डमा के गर्नुहुन्छ ?

Would you like to go out somewhere?
ta·*paĩ*·lai *bah*·hi·ra *jah*·na man *lahg*·yo? | तपाईलाई बाहिर जान मन लाग्यो ?

Do you know a good/cheap restaurant?
ta·*paĩ*·lai *rahm*·ro/*sas*·to bho·ja·*nah*·la·ya *thah*·ha cha? | तपाईलाई राम्रो/सस्तो भोजनालय थाह छ ?

Would you like to go for a drink/meal?
ta·*paĩ*·lai pi·*u*·na/*khah*·nah *jah*·na man *lahg*·yo? | तपाईलाई पिउन/खाना जान मन लाग्यो ?

My shout. (I'll buy)
me·ro *pah*·li | मेरो पालो

Do you want to come to the ... concert with me?
ta·*paĩ*·lai ...·ko *kan*·sarṭ·mah *ma*·sã·ga *au*·na man *lahg*·cha? | तपाईलाई ...को कन्सर्टमा म सँग आउन मन लाग्छ ?

signs	
बन्द	Closed
चिसो	Cold
खतरा	Danger
प्रबेश	Entrance
निकास	Exit
तातो	Hot
प्रवेश निषेध	No Entry
धूम्रपान मनाही छ	No Smoking
खुल्ला	Open
निषेध	Prohibited
बाटो बन्द	Road Closed
रोक्नुहोस	Stop
शौचालय	Toilets

We're having a party.
hahm·ro *pahr*·ṭi cha — हाम्रो पार्टी छ

Come along.
au·nu·hos — आउनुहोस

responding to invitations — निम्ताको जवाफ

Sure!
hun·cha! — हुन्छ !

Yes, I'd love to.
hun·cha, ma *aun*·chu — हुन्छ, म आउँछु

Yes, where shall we go?
hun·cha, *hah*·mi *ka*·hãh *jah*·ne? — हुन्छ, हामी कहाँ जाने ?

No, I'm afraid I can't.
mahph *gar*·nu·hos, ma *sak*·di·na — माफ गर्नुहोस, म सक्दिन

What about tomorrow?
a·ni *bho*·li? — अनि भोलि ?

arranging to meet

भेट् मिलाउनु

What time shall we meet?		
	hah·mi *ka*·ti *ba*·je *bheṭ*·ne?	हामी कति बजे भेट्ने ?
Where will we meet?		
	hah·mi *ka*·hãh *bheṭ*·ne?	हामी कहाँ भेट्ने ?
Let's meet at (eight o'clock) at the ...		
	(ahṭh *ba*·je·ti·ra) ...·mah *bhe*·ṭaũ	(आठ बजेतिर) ...मा भेटौं
OK, I'll see you then.		
	hun·cha, ma ta·*paĩ*·lai tyas *be*·lah *bheṭ*·chu	हुन्छ, म तपाईलाई त्यस बेला भेट्छु
Agreed!/OK!		
	hun·cha!	हुन्छ !
I'll come over at (six).		
	ma (cha *ba*·je·ti·ra) *aun*·chu	म (छ बजेतिर) आउँछु
I'll pick you up at (nine).		
	ma ta·*paĩ*·lai (nau *ba*·je·ti·ra) *li*·na *aun*·chu	म तपाईलाई (नौ बजेतिर) लिन आउँछु
I'll try to make it.		
	ma *au*·ne *ko*·sis *gar*·chu	म आउने कोसिस गर्छु
If I'm not there by (nine), don't wait for me.		
	ma (nau) *ba*·je·sam·ma na·*ah*·yẽ bhan·*ne*, *ma*·lai na·*kur*·nu·hos	म (नौ) बजेसम्म नआए भने, मलाई नकुर्नुहोस
I'll come later.		
	ma *pa*·chi *aun*·chu	म पछि आउँछु
Where will you be?		
	ta·*paĩ* *ka*·hãh *ho*·lah?	तपाई कहाँ होला ?
See you later/tomorrow.		
	pa·chi/*bho*·li *bhe*·ṭaũ·lah!	पछि/भोलि भेटौंला !
Sorry I'm late.		
	ma·lai mahph *gar*·nu·hos, *ḍhi*·lo *bha*·yo	मलाई माफ गर्नुहोस, ढिलो भयो

Shopping
किनमेल

In Kathmandu and other towns most shopkeepers speak some English, but outside the more populated areas this is not always the case. To address a shopkeeper, follow the suggestions in the Meeting People chapter (see page 112). He or she may respond with 'speak', *bhan*·nu·hos (भन्नुहोस). Remember that 'please' and 'thank you' are not necessary in Nepali. Just state what you want and add 'please give', *di*·nu·hos (दिनुहोस).

looking for ...

... खोज्नु

Where's the nearest ...?	*na*·ji·kai ... *ka*·hãh cha?	नजिकै ... कहाँ छ ?
bank	baĩk	बैंक
barber	ha·*jahm*	हजाम
book shop	ki·*tahb pa*·sal	किताब पसल
camera shop	*kyah*·me·rah *pa*·sal	क्यामेरा पसल
chemist	*au*·sa·dhi *pa*·sal	औषधि पसल
clothing store	*lu*·gah *pa*·sal	लुगा पसल
cobbler	*sahr*·ki	सार्की
fruit shop	*phal*·phul *pa*·sal	फलफूल पसल
handicraft shop	*has*·ta·ka·lah *pa*·sal	हस्तकला पसल
laundry	*lu*·gah·dhu·ne ṭhaũ	लुगाधुने ठाउँ
market	ba·*jahr*	बजार
music shop	*sang*·git *pa*·sal	सङ्गीत पसल
newsagency	*a*·kha·bahr *pa*·sal	अखबार पसल
optician	*cash*·mah *pa*·sal	चश्मा पसल
pharmacy	*au*·sa·dhi *pa*·sal	औषधि पसल
shoe shop	*jut*·tah *pa*·sal	जुत्ता पसल
souvenir shop	*ci*·no *pa*·sal	चिनो पसल
stationer	ci·ṭhi·*pa*·tra *pa*·sal	चिठ्ठीपत्र पसल
supermarket	su·par·*mahr*·keṭ	सुपरमार्केट

teashop	*ci*·yah *pa*·sal	चिया पसल
travel agency	*yah*·trah *li*·ne *pa*·sal	यात्रा लिने पसल
vegetable shop	tar·*kah*·ri *pa*·sal	तरकारी पसल

making a purchase

सामान किन्नु

I'm just looking.	*her*·dai·chu	हेर्दैछु
Where can I buy ...?	... *ka*·hãh *kin*·na *pain*·cha?	... कहाँ किन्न पाइन्छ ?
paper	*kah*·gaj	कागज
soap	*sah*·bun	साबुन
string	*ḍo*·ri	डोरी
Do you have a ...?	ta·*paĩ*·ka·hãh ... cha?	तपाई कहाँ ... छ ?
hat	*ṭo*·pi	टोपी
newspaper	*a*·kha·bahr	अखबार
pencil	*si*·sah·ka·lam	सिसाकलम

How much is this (pen)?
yo *(ka*·lam)·ko *ka*·ti *pai*·sah ho? — यो (कलम)को कति पैसा हो ?

How much do (eggs) cost?
(phul)·ko *ka*·ti ho? — (फुल)को कति हो ?

Four rupees each.
eu·ṭah·ko cahr ru·*pi*·yãh — एउटाको चार रुपैयाँ

Please write down the price.
mol lekh·*di*·nu·hos — मोल लेखिदिनुहोस

I'd like to buy ...
... *kin*·na man *lahg*·yo — ... किन्न मन लाग्यो

making rupee

The Nepalese currency is the rupee, ru·*pi*·yãh (रुपैयाँ), which is divided into 100 ***pai***·sah (पैसा), which is also the word for 'money'.

Do you have any others?
ar·ko *ku*·nai cha? अर्को कुनै छ ?

There is/are none.
chai·na छैन

Which one? This one?
kun *cah*·hĩ? yo *cah*·hĩ? कुन चाहिं ? यो चाहिं ?

Show it to me.
ma·lai de·*khau*·nu·hos मलाई देखाउनुहोस

Please show me the price.
mol de·*khau*·nu·hos मोल देखाउनुहोस

May I/we see it?
he·raũ? हेरौं ?

I like/don't like this.
ma·lai yo man *par*·cha/*par*·dai·na मलाई यो मन पर्छ/पर्दैन

What's it made of?
ke·le *ba*·ne·ko? केले बनेको ?

Where was it made?
ka·hãh *ba*·ne·ko? कहाँ बनेको ?

I'll take it.
lin·chu लिन्छु

What else do you need?
a·ru *ke*·hi *cah*·hin·cha? अरु केही चाहिन्छ ?

That's all. How much is it?
te·ti *mah*·trai, *ka*·ti *bha*·yo? त्यति मात्रै, कति भयो ?

Do you accept credit cards?
kre·ḍiṭ kahrḍ *hun*·cha? क्रेडिट कार्ड हुन्छ ?

Could I have a receipt please?
bil *di*·nu·hun·cha? बिल दिनुहुन्छ ?

Does it have a guarantee?
tyas·ko *bah*·cah cha? त्यसको ग्यारेन्टी छ ?

Can I have it sent abroad?
bi·*desh*·mah pa·*ṭhau*·nu·hun·cha? बिदेशमा पठाउनुहुन्छ ?

Please wrap it.
ber·nu·hos बेर्नुहोस

I'd like to return this.
yo phar·*kau*·nu·par·cha — यो फर्काउनु पर्छ

It's faulty.
yo kahm *gar*·dai·na — यो काम गर्दैन

It's broken.
yo *bi*·gre·ko cha — यो बिग्रेको छ

I'd like my money back.
me·ro *pai*·sah *phar*·kai *di*·nu·hos — मेरो पैसा फर्काइ दिनुहोस

bargaining

मोलतोल गर्नु

It's customary to bargain, *mol*·tol *gar*·nu (मोलतोल गर्नु), especially for tourist and luxury goods and transport. As in most Asian countries, friendly bargaining is a way of life and foreigners are presumed wealthier than locals. With a little patience and goodwill, you'll be able to reduce the price of most items to the satisfaction of both yourself and the shopkeeper. But there will generally be a going price for basic household goods and foodstuffs.

Really?
sãh·cai? — साँचै ?

That's expensive!
ma·*hã*·go cha! — महंगो छ !

It's cheap!
sas·to cha! — सस्तो छ !

The price is too high.
mol *dhe*·rai ma·*hã*·go cha — मोल धेरै महंगो छ

It's too much for us.
hahm·ro *lah*·gi *dhe*·rai *bha*·yo — हाम्रो लागि धेरै भयो

I don't have that much money.
ma·sã·ga *te*·ti *pai*·sah *chai*·na — मसँग त्यति पैसा छैन

Could you lower the price a little?
a·li·ka·ti gha·*ṭau*·nu·hun·cha? अलिकति घटाउनुहुन्छ ?

I'll give (200) rupees.
(du·i·say) ru·*pi*·yãh *din*·chu (दुइसय) रुपैयाँ दिन्छु

That's not possible, give me (250).
hun·dai·na, *(du*·i·say pa·*cahs)* *di*·nu·hos हुन्दैन, (दुइसय पचास) दिनुहोस

OK.
hun·cha हुन्छ

I don't want it.
cah·hin·dai·na चाहिन्दैन

Do you have something cheaper?
a·ru *ku*·nai *sas*·to cha? अरु कुनै सस्तो छ ?

No more than ...
...·*bhan*·dah kam ...भन्दा कम

souvenirs

चिनोहरू

anklet	*pau*·ju	पाउजु
bangle	*cu*·rah	चुरा
brassware	*pi*·tal·ko *sah*·mahn	पितलको सामान
carpet	ga·*laĩ*·cah	गलैंचा
chain	*si*·kri	सिक्री
doll	*pu*·ta·li	पुतली
(a pair of) earrings	(ek jor) ṭap	(एक जोर) टप
embroidery	*buṭ*·ṭah	बुट्टा
gem/jewel	ju·*hah*·raht	जुहारात
gold	sun	सुन
handicraft	*has*·ta·ka·lah	हस्तकला
incense burner	dhup *dah*·ni	धूप दानि
jewellery	*ga*·ha·nah	गहना
mask	ma·*kuṇ*·ḍo	मुकुण्डो
necklace	*mah*·lah	माला
Nepalese knife	*khu*·ku·ri	खुकुरी

Nepalese painting	*thahng*·kah	थाङ्का
ornament	*a*·lang·kahr	अलङ्कार
painting	*ci*·tra	चित्र
pottery	*mah*·ṭah·kah *bhãh*·ḍah	माटाका भाँडा
puppet	*kaṭh*·pu·ta·li	कठपुतली
ring	*aũ*·ṭhi	औंठी
rug	*sah*·no ga·*laĩ*·cah	सानो गलैंचा
silver	*cãh*·di	चाँदि
statue	*mur*·ti	मुर्ति
tapestry	*ci*·tra·paṭ	चित्रपट
wooden article	*kahṭh*·bah·ṭa ba·ne·ko *bas*·tu	काठबाट बनेको बस्तु

essential items

आबश्यक सामानहरू

Where can I find (a) ...?	... *ka*·hãh *kin*·na *pain*·cha?	... कहाँ किन्न पाइन्छ ?
I'd like (a) ...	*ma*·lai ... *cah*·hi·yo	मलाई ... चाहियो
batteries	*ma*·sa·lah	मसला
candles	*main*·bat·ti	मैनबत्ती
gas cylinder	gyãhs *si*·liṇ·ḍar	ग्याँस सिलीण्डर
matches	*sa*·lai	सलाइ
shampoo	*dhu*·lai	धुलाइ
soap	*sah*·bun	साबुन
toilet paper	*ṭwai*·leṭ *pe*·par	ट्वाईलेट पेपर
toothpaste	*many*·jan	मञ्जन
washing powder	*lu*·gah·dhu·ne *sah*·bun	लुगाधुने साबुन

clothing

लुगा

Nepalese national dress comprises a sari, *sah*·ḍi (साडी), and blouse, *co*·lo (चोलो), for women, and a cap, *ṭo*·pi (टोपी), tunic, *dau*·rah (दाउरा), and drawstring trousers, *su*·ru·wahl (सुरुवाल), for men.

belt	*pe*·ṭi	पेटी
boots	buṭ	बुट
button	ṭãhk	टाँख
cap	*ṭo*·pi	टोपी
clothing	*lu*·gah	लुगा
coat	koṭ	कोट
dress	*jah*·mah	जामा
gloves	*pan*·jah	पन्जा
hat	*ṭo*·pi	टोपी
jacket	*jyah*·keṭ	ज्याकेट
jeans	*jin*·painṭ	जीनपाइन्ट
jumper	*swi*·ṭar	स्विटर
muffler	gal·*ban*·di	गलबन्दी
pants (trousers)	painṭ	पाइन्ट
Nepalese trousers	*su*·ru·wahl	सुरुवाल
sandals	*cap*·pal	चप्पल
scarf	do·*paṭ*·ṭah	दोपट्टा
shirt	ka·*mij*	किमज
shoes	*jut*·tah	जुत्ता
shorts	*kaṭ*·ṭu	कट्ट
singlet	*gan*·ji	गन्जी
socks	*mo*·jah	मोजा
sweater	*swi*·ṭar	स्विटर
trousers	painṭ	पाइन्ट
T-shirt	*gan*·ji	गन्जी
underpants	*kaṭ*·ṭu	कट्ट
vest/waistcoat	*is*·ṭa·koṭ	इस्टकोट

Can I try it on?
la·gai *her*·nu·hun·cha? — लगाई हेर्नुहुन्छ ?

My size is ...
me·ro saij ... ho — मेरो सा इज ... हो

It fits well/doesn't fit.
ṭhik cha/*chai*·na — ठीक छ/छैन

Can you make this in my size?
ma·lai yo *lu*·gah *ba*·nai·di·na *sa*·kin·cha? — मलाई यो लुगा बनाईदिन सकिन्छ ?

It's too ...	*dhe*·rai ... cha	धेरै ... छ
big	*ṭhu*·lo	ठूलो
small	*sah*·no	सानो
short	*cho*·ṭo	छोटो
long	*lah*·mo	लामो
tight	*ka*·sin	कसिनु
loose	*khu*·ku·lo	खुकुलो

materials

भौतिकहरू

brass	*pi*·tal	पितल
cotton	*su*·ti	सुती
glass	kãhc	काँच
gold	sun	सुन
handmade	*haht*·le *ba*·ne·ko	हातले बनेको
leather	*chah*·lah	छाला
metal	*dhah*·tu	धातु
plastic	*plah*·sṭik	प्लास्टिक
pottery	*mah*·ṭah·kah *bhãh*·ḍah	माटाका भाँडा
silk	*re*·sham	रेशम
silver	*cãh*·di	चाँदि
wood	kahṭh	काठ
wool	un	ऊन
sheep wool	*bhe*·ḍah·ko un	भेडाको ऊन
yak wool	*caũ*·ri·ko un	चौंरीको ऊन

colours

रङ्गहरू

dark ...	*gah*·ḍhah ...	गाढा ...
light ...	*phi*·kah ...	फिका ...
bright ...	*ca*·ha·ki·lo ...	चहिकलो ...
pale ...	*phi*·kah ...	फिका ...
black	*kah*·lo	कालो

PRACTICAL

blue	*ni*·lo	निलो
brown	*khai*·ro	खैरो
green	*ha*·ri·yo	हरियो
grey	*kai*·lo	कैलो
multicoloured	*rang*·gin	रंगीन
orange	*sun*·ta·lah rang	सुन्तला रङ्ग
pink	gu·*lah*·phi	गुलाफी
purple	*pyah*·ji	प्याजी
red	*rah*·to	रातो
white	*se*·to	सेतो
yellow	pa·*hẽ*·lo	पहेंलो

toiletries

बाथरुमको सामान

comb	*kaĩ*·yo	काईंयो
condoms	ḍhahl	ढाल
hairbrush	*ka*·pahl *kor*·ne *bu*·rus	कपाल कोर्ने बुरुस
laxative	ju·*lahph*	जुलाफ
sanitary products	*ma*·hi·nah·bah·ri·ko *sah*·mahn	महीनाबारीको सामान
moisturiser (face cream)	*mukh*·mah la·*gau*·ne krim	मुखमा लगाउने क्रीम
razor	*chu*·rah	छुरा
razor blades	*pat*·ti	पत्ती

shopping nirvana

Nepalese clothing, handicraft and souvenir shops are full of wonderful things to buy. Look out for shawls, waistcoats and embroidered T-shirts, all kinds of bags, handmade paper items, woodcarvings, brassware and jewellery. Other popular items include handwoven carpets, *thahng*·kah (थाङ्का) paintings, traditional masks, pottery and Nepalese dolls and puppets. When you buy from handicraft cooperatives, you can be sure of paying a fair price and supporting local employment and training initiatives into the bargain!

shampoo	*dhu*·lai	धुलाइ
shaving cream	*khau*·ra·ne krim	खौरने क्रीम
soap	*sah*·bun	साबुन
tissues	*kah*·gaj·ko ru·*mahl*	कागजको रुमाल
toilet paper	*ṭwai*·leṭ *pe*·par	ट्वाईलेट पेपर
toothbrush	dãht *mahjh*·ne *bu*·rus	दाँत माझ्ने बुरुस
toothpaste	*many*·jan	मञ्जन

stationery & publications

चिठ्ठीपत्र र प्रकाशनहरू

Is there an English-language bookshop nearby?
ya·hãh *na*·ji·kai ang·*gre*·ji ki·*tahb pa*·sal cha? — यहाँ नजिकै अंग्रेजी किताब पसल छ ?

Do you have any books in English by ...?
ta·*paĩ*·ka·hãh ...·le *lekh*·yo ang·*gre*·ji ki·*tahb* cha? — तपाईकहाँ ...ले लेखेको अंग्रेजी किताब छ ?

Do you sell ...?	*ya*·hãh ... *bec*·cha?	यहाँ ... बे च्छ ?
magazines	*pa*·tri·kah	पत्रिका
newspapers	*a*·kha·bahr	अखबार
postcards	*posṭ*·kahrḍ	पोस्टकार्ड

aerogram	*ha*·wai·pa·tra	हवाईपत्र
book	ki·*tahb*	किताब
dictionary	*shab*·da·kosh	शब्दकोश
envelope	khahm	खाम
exercise book	*kah*·pi	कापी
ink	*ma*·si	मसी
letterpad	ci·thi·*lekh*·ne *kah*·pi	चिठीलेख्ने कापी
map	*nak*·sah	नक्सा
... map	...·ko *nak*·sah	...को नक्सा
city	*sha*·har	शहर
regional	*che*·tra	क्षेत्र
road	*bah*·ṭo	बाटो

notebook	*kah*·pi	कापि
novel	*u*·pan·yahs	उपन्यास
paper	*kah*·gaj	कागज
pen	*ka*·lam	कलम
pencil	*si*·sah·ka·lam	सिसाकलम
safety pin	huk	हुप
scissors	*kaĩ*·ci	कैंची
stamp	*ṭi*·kaṭ	टिकट
writing pad/paper	*lekh*·ne *kah*·pi	लेख्ने कापी

music

सङ्गीत

I'm looking for a ... CD.
ma ...·ko *si*·ḍi *khoj*·dai·chu — म ...को सीदी खोज्दैछु

Do you have any ...?
ta·*paĩ*·ka·hãh ... cha? — तपाईकहाँ ... छ ?

What's his/her best recording?
us·ko *sab*·bhan·dah *rahm*·ro git kun ho? — उस्को सबभन्दा राम्रो गीत कुन हो ?

I heard a band/singer called ...
mai·le ... *bhan*·ne bahṇḍ/ *gah*·yak *sun*·nẽ — मैले ... भन्ने बाण्ड/ गायक सुन्नें

Can I listen to this CD here?
yo *si*·ḍi *ya*·hãh *sun*·nu·hun·cha? — यो सीदी यहाँ सुन्नुहुन्छ ?

I need a blank tape.
ma·lai *khah*·li ṭep *cah*·hi·yo — मलाई खाली टेप चाहियो

photography

तिस्बर खिच्ने कला

How much is it to process this film?
eu·ṭah ril prinṭ *gar*·na, *ka*·ti *pai*·sah *lahg*·cha? — एउटा रील प्रिन्ट गर्न, कति पैसा लाग्छ ?

When will it be ready?
ka·hi·le *ta*·yahr *hun*·cha? कहिले तयार हुन्छ ?

Please give me a film for this camera.
yo *kyah*·me·rah·lai *eu*·ṭah ril *di*·nu·hos यो क्यामरालाई एउटा रील दिनुहोस

Do you fix cameras?
kyah·me·rah ba·*nau*·nu·hun·cha? क्यामरा बनाउनुहुन्छ ?

battery	*ma*·sa·lah	मसला
B&W film	*kah*·lo *se*·to ril	कालो सेतो रील
colour film	*rang*·gin ril	रंगीन रील
film	ril	रील
videotape	*bhi*·ḍi·yo	भिडीयो

smoking

धूम्रपान

Smoking is still very common in Nepal, particularly among men. Locally produced, often unfiltered, cigarettes (from government-owned factories) are the cheapest, while better quality, imported cigarettes and tobacco are quite expensive in local terms.

A packet of cigarettes, please.
ek *baṭ*·ṭah *cu*·roṭ *di*·nu·hos एक बट्टा चुरोट दिनुहोस

Are these cigarettes strong or mild?
yo *cu*·roṭ *ka*·ḍah ho ki ma·*dhu*·ro? यो चुरोट कडा हो कि मधुरो ?

through the haze

Smoking is technically banned on public transport and in public areas, but the ban is loosely enforced and smoking is still very common. Dubious advertising is everywhere. The government makes a good profit from the manufacture and sale of cigarettes, so public health messages about the risks of smoking are taking a while to be sent out.

Do you have a light?
sa·lai cha? सलाइ छ ?

Do you mind if I smoke?
mai·le *dhum*·ra·pahn *gar*·na *hun*·cha? मैले धूम्रपान गर्नुहुन्छ ?

Please don't smoke.
dhum·ra·pahn na·*gar*·nu·hos धूम्रपान नगर्नुहोस

I'm trying to give up.
choḍ·na *ko*·sis *gar*·dai·chu छोड्न कोसिस गर्दैछु

cigarettes	*cu*·roṭ	चुरोट
cigarette papers	*cu*·roṭ *kah*·gaj	चुरोट कागज
hookah	*huk*·kah	हुक्का
lighter	*lai*·ṭar	लाईटर
matches	*sa*·lai	सलाइ
pipe	*cu*·roṭ paip	चुरोट पाईप
tobacco	*sur*·ti	सुर्ती

sizes & comparisons

कत्रो र तुलनाहरू

a little	*a*·li *a*·li	अलिअलि
a little bit	a·li·*ka*·ti	अलिकति
also	*pa*·ni	पनि
any	*ke*·hi/*ku*·nai	केही/कुनै
big	*ṭhu*·lo	ठूलो
enough	pra·*shas*·ta	प्रशस्त
few	*tho*·rai	थोरै
heavy	*ga*·hraũ	गह्रौं
less	kam	कम
light	ha·*lu*·kah	हलुका
long	*lah*·mo	लामो
(too) many/much	*dhe*·rai	धेरै
more	*a*·jha *dhe*·rai	अझ धेरै
most	*dhe*·rai·ja·so	धेरैजसो
short	*cho*·ṭo	छोटो

small	*sah*·no	सानो
some	*ke*·hi/*ku*·nai	केही/कुनै
tall	*a*·glo	अ ग्लो
too	*sah*·hrai	सा है्

weights & measures

भार र नापहरू

The metric system is in common use, but there are some measures particular to Nepal, approximating the following:

50 grams	*mu*·thi	मुथी
100 grams	*cau*·thai	चौथाइ
200 grams	pau	पाउ
400 grams/0.5 litre	*mah*·nah	माना
800 grams	ser	सेर
2 kg (2.5 ser**)**	*dhahr*·ni	धार्नी
3.2 kg (4 ser**)**	*pah*·thi	पाथी
64 kg (20 *pah*·thi**)**	*mu*·ri	मुरी
180 grains	*to*·lah	तोला
span (0.25 m)	*bit*·to	बित्तो
metre	gaj	गज

Specific Needs
निश्चित आबश्यकता

travelling with the family

परिवारमा यात्रा गर्नुस

The Nepalese love children and they're welcome everywhere. Having them around is a great way to interact with the locals. You won't find many facilities specific to children, such as high chairs or kids' menus, and there are few playgrounds or swimming pools (except in five-star hotels). The staff in hotels, restaurants and other places, however, will often go to considerable lengths to ensure your children are well looked after.

Are there facilities for babies?
bac·cah·ko *su*·bi·dhah cha? — बच्चाको सुबिधा छ ?

Do you have a child-minding service?
bac·cah *her*·ne *se*·bah cha? — बच्चा हेर्ने सेवा छ ?

Could someone look after my child?
me·ro *bac*·cah·lai *her*·na *sa*·kin·cha? — मेरो बच्चालाई हेर्न सकिन्छ ?

Where can I find a/an (English-speaking) babysitter?
(ang·*gre*·ji *bol*·ne) *bac*·cah *her*·ne *mahn*·che *ka*·hãh *pain*·cha? — (अङ्ग्रेजी बोल्ने) बच्चा हेर्ने मान्छे कहाँ पाइन्छ ?

Can you put an (extra) bed/cot in the room?
(thap) khahṭ/*kha*·ṭi·yah *ko*·ṭhah·mah *rahkh*·nu·hun·cha? — (थप) खाट/खटिया कोठामा राख्नुहुन्छ ?

Is it suitable for children?
bac·cah·ko *lah*·gi su·*hau*·ne cha? — बच्चाको लागि सुहाउने छ ?

Is there a family discount?
pa·ri·bahr·ko chuṭ cha? — परिवारको छुट छ ?

Is there a discount for children?
bac·cah·ko *lah*·gi kam *hun*·cha? — बच्चाको लागि कम हुन्छ ?

Are children allowed?
bac·cah·lai *lyau*·nu·hun·cha? बच्चालाई ल्याउनुहुन्छ ?

Do you have a children's menu?
bac·cah·ko *men*·yu cha? बच्चाको मेन्यु छ ?

Are there any activities for children?
bac·cah·ha·ru·ko *lah*·gi *ke*·hi *kah*·rya·kram cha? बच्चाहरूको लागि केही कार्यक्रम छ ?

Is there a playground nearby?
khel·ne ṭhaũ *na*·ji·kai cha? खेल्ने ठाउँ नजिकै छ ?

disabled travellers

अपाङ्ग यात्रीहरू

I'm disabled.
ma a·*pahng*·ga hũ म अपाङ्ग हुँ

I need assistance.
ma·lai *mad*·dat *cah*·hi·yo मलाई मद्दत चाहियो

What services do you have for disabled people?
a·*pahng*·ga·ha·ru·lai ke *se*·bah·ha·ru chan? अपांगहरुलाई के सेवाहरु छन ?

Is there wheelchair access?
pahng·grah *bha*·ya·ko *mec*·ko *pa*·hũc cha? पाङ्ग्रा भएको मेचको पहुँच छ ?

I'm deaf.
ma *ba*·hi·ro hũ म बहिरो हुँ

Speak more loudly, please.
ṭhu·lo *swar*·le *bhan*·nu·hos ठूलो स्वरले भन्नुहोस

Are guide dogs permitted?
gaiḍ *ku*·kur·ko *a*·nu·ma·ti cha? गाइड कुकुरको अनुमति छ ?

braille	*an*·dhah·ha·ru·ko *paḍh*·ne *yan*·tra	अन्धाहरूको पढ्ने यन्त्र
disabled person	a·*pahng*·ga *mahn*·che	अपाङ्ग मान्छे
guide dog	gaiḍ *ku*·kur	गाइड कुकुर
wheelchair	*pahng*·grah *bha*·ya·ko mec	पाङ्ग्रा भएको मेच

pilgrimage & religion

तीर्थयात्रा र धर्म

Most Nepalese are Hindu or Buddhist or a mix of both; some are Muslims. Travellers from Western countries are generally assumed to be Christian. As there are few Christians in Nepal, the Nepalese do not differentiate between different types of Christians, such as Catholics and Protestants.

What's your religion?
ta·*paĩ* kun *dhar*·ma *mahn*·nu·hun·cha? तपाई कुन धर्म मान्नुहुन्छ ?

I'm ...	ma ... *mahn*·chu	म ... मान्छु
Buddhist	*bud*·dha *dhar*·ma	बुद्ध धर्म
Christian	*i*·sai *dhar*·ma	इसाई इर् धर्म
Hindu	*hin*·du *dhar*·ma	हिन्दु धर्म

I'm ...	ma ... hũ	म ... हुँ
Jewish	ya·*hu*·di	यहुदि
Muslim	*mu*·sal·mahn	मुसलमान

I'm not religious.
ma *ku*·nai *dhar*·ma *mahn*·di·na म कुनै धर्म मान्दिन

I'm (Christian), but not practising.
ma (*i*·sai *dhar*·ma) *mahn*·chu, *ta*·ra ma *prahr*·tha·nah *gar*·di·na म (इसाई इर् धर्म) मान्छु, तर म प्रार्थना गर्दिन

I think I believe in God.
me·ro bi·*cahr*·mah, *bha*·ga·bahn·lai bi·*shwahs gar*·chu मेरो बिचारमा, भगवानलाई बिश्वास गर्छु

I believe in destiny/fate.
ma *bhahg*·ya bi·*shwahs gar*·chu म भाग्यमा बिश्वास गर्छु

I'm interested in astrology/philosophy.
ma·lai *jyo*·tis·bi·dyah·mah/ dar·shan·*shah*·stra·mah cahkh *lahg*·cha मलाई ज्योतिष/ विद्यामार दर्शनशास्त्रमा चाख लाग्छ

I'm an atheist.
ma *nah*·stik hũ म नास्तिक हुँ

I'm agnostic.
ma jaḍ·*bah*·di hũ — म जडबादी हुँ

Can I attend this ceremony/ritual?
ma yo *ut*·sab·mah/*pu*·jah·mah u·*pas*·thit *hu*·na *sak*·chu? — म यो उत्सबमा/पूजामा उपस्थित हुन सक्छु ?

Can I pray here?
ma *ya*·hãh *prahr*·tha·nah *gar*·nu·hun·cha? — म यहाँ प्रार्थना गर्नुहुन्छ ?

Where can I pray/worship?
ma *ka*·hãh *prahr*·tha·nah/*pu*·jah *gar*·na *sak*·chu? — म कहाँ प्रार्थना/पूजा गर्न स क्छु ?

Brahmin	*bah*·hun	बाहुन
Buddhist monk	*bhi*·chu	भिक्षु
Buddhist priest	*lah*·mah	लामा
church	*gir*·jah·ghar	गिर्जाघर
funeral	ma·*lahm*	मलाम
funeral rites	*shrahd*·dha	श्राद्ध
god/goddess	*de*·va·tah	देवता
Hindu priest	bah·hun·*bah*·je	बाहुनबाजे
pilgrimage	tir·tha·*yah*·trah	तीर्थयात्रा
prayer	*prahr*·tha·nah	प्रार्थना
priest	pu·*jah*·ri	पूजारी
relic	*puṇ*·ya·sma·raṇ *bas*·tu	पुण्यस्मरण बस्तु
religious festival procession	*jah*·trah	जात्रा
ritual	*pu*·jah	पूजा
saint (Hindu)	ma·*haht*·mah	महात्मा
saint (Muslim)	pir	पीर
shrine	*de*·wal	देवल
temple (Buddhist)	*stu*·pah	स्तुपा
temple (Hindu)	*man*·dir	मन्दिर
worship	*pu*·jah	पूजा

It's easy to strike up a conversation in Nepal and it will not only add to your understanding and enjoyment of the country, but also ensure your share of warm Nepalese *bya*·ba·hahr (ब्यबहार), 'hospitality'!

you should know

थाहा हुनुपर्छ

Hello./Goodbye.	na·ma·*ste*	नमस्ते
Hello./Goodbye. (pol)	na·ma·*skahr*	नमस्कार
Pardon?	ha·*jur?*	हजुर ?
I'm sorry./Please forgive me.	mahph *gar*·nu·hos	माफ गनुर्होस

There are several ways of saying 'yes' or 'no'. Generally, the main verb in the question is repeated in the affirmative or negative. This will often involve some form of the verb 'to be'; cha, ho or *hun*·cha (see Grammar, page 27):

yes & no

Yes		No	
ho	हो	*hoi*·na	होइन
cha	छ	*chai*·na	छैन
hun·cha	हुन्छ	*hun*·dai·na	हुँदैन

A general word for 'yes' is ha·*jur* (हजुर) – see page 112.

In body language, nodding means 'yes' and a sideways shake of the head means 'no' as in a lot of countries. However, there's a kind of sideways tilt of the head, accompanied by a slight shrug of the shoulders, which the Nepalese often use to indicate agreement, during bargaining, for instance. Don't mistake this for a 'no'.

greetings & goodbyes

अभिवादनहरु

One key phrase to learn is the general Nepali greeting, na·ma·*ste* (नमस्ते). Literally meaning 'I bow to the god in you', this ex-pression covers all sorts of situations, from 'hello' to 'goodbye'. It can be used at any time of the day, and the Nepalese consider it appropriate between all people.

A more polite form of the same greeting is na·ma·*skahr* (नमस्कार), but it's less commonly used. Both na·ma·*ste* and na·ma·*skahr* should be accompanied by holding your palms together in front of your face, as if in prayer.

How are you?

ta·*paĩ*·lai *kas*·to cha?	तपाईलाई कस्तो छ ?
ah·rah·mai hu·nu·hun·*cha*? **(pol)**	आरामै हुनुहुन्छ ?

I'm fine. And you?

ma·lai *san*·cai cha	मलाई सन्चै छ
ani ta·*paĩ*·lai?	अनि तपाईलाई ?

Goodnight.

shu·bha·*rah*·tri	शुभरात्री

civilities

नम्रताहरू

The Nepali word for 'thank you', *dhan*·ya·bahd (धन्यबाद), is not used very often and is best kept to express thanks for particular favours – it would be inappropriate in shops and restaurants, for example. Similarly, the word for 'please', kri·*pa*·yah (कृपया), is very formal and reserved mainly for writing. Instead of 'please', the imperative verb suffix -hos (-होस) is used in spoken Nepali (see Grammar, page 32).

You're welcome.

swah·gat cha	स्वागत छ

Excuse me./Sorry. (pol)
mahph *gar*·nu·hos — माफ गर्नुहोस

May I?/Do you mind?
ga·re·hun·cha? — गरे हुन्छ ?

forms of address

नामहरू

In Nepal, people use kinship terms rather than first names. These kinship terms apply to non-relatives as well, and even strangers. For someone older than you (or someone you want to show respect to), use 'elder sister' for a woman or 'elder brother' for a man. If they're elderly, use 'grandmother' or 'grandfather'. For younger people and children, use 'younger sister' or 'younger brother'. Nepalese people will also use these terms towards you. Commonly used Nepali kinship terms include:

mother	*ah*·mah	आमा
father	*bu*·wah	बुवा
grandmother	*baj*·yai	बज्यै
grandfather	*bah*·je	बाजे
elder sister	*di*·di	दिदी
elder brother	dai	दाई
elder brother's wife	*bhau*·jyu	भाउजु
elder sister's husband	*bhi*·nah·jyu	भिनाजु
younger sister	*ba*·hi·ni	बिहनी
younger brother	bhai	भाई
little girl	*nah*·ni	नानी
little boy	*bah*·bu	बाबु

get shorty

Instead of kinship terms, friends often use nicknames for each other, such as *pud*·ke, 'Shorty'!

When they do address someone by name, the Nepalese usually add the suffix -ji (or sometimes -jyu) to the name as a sign of respect or affection. It's good manners for travellers to do the same.

Ram, where are you going?
rahm·ji, ta·*paĩ ka*·hãh *jah*·nu·hun·cha? — रामजी, तपाईकहाँ जानुहुन्छ ?

For other family terms, see Family (page 127).

attracting someone's attention

कोही बोलाउनु

To attract someone's attention, call yo, plus one of the kinship terms you'll find listed on page 111. Then say na·ma·*ste* and make your request. To beckon someone from a distance, wave your hand toward yourself, with the palm facing down and your fingers also pointing downwards.

Excuse me, sir/madam.
yo, dai/*di*·di — यो दाई/दिदी

Please come here.
ya·hãh *au*·nu·hos — यहाँ आउनुहोस

For the proprietor of a shop, restaurant, hotel or any business, use 'proprietor', *sah*·hu·ji/*sah*·hu·ni (m/f), (साहुजी/साहुनी).

please explain

A handy word that can be used in several different ways and for both men and women is ha·*jur* (हजुर). It literally means 'sir' but there's no exact equivalent in English. If someone calls out to you, respond with ha·*jur?* You can also use it to express agreement or confirm what someone has just said to you, or add it to the answer of a simple 'yes/no' question, for politeness. But for the learner its greatest usefulness lies in the fact that if you didn't hear or understand something said to you, and want it repeated, you simply need to say ha·*jur?*

body language

शरीरको सङ्केत

The Nepalese won't usually point out any mistakes to you directly (unless you ask) and are unlikely to be offended if you behave in a culturally inappropriate way. Just be sensitive to how the people around you are behaving.

Dressing conservatively, for example, means that Nepalese people will be much more at ease with you and so your contact with them will be even more friendly and effective. Ethnic Nepalese are very modest and will feel uncomfortable around travellers who are dressed revealingly. With the exception of some porters and labourers, the Nepalese don't wear shorts or short skirts, nor do men go without a shirt – not even in hot weather. It's still much more acceptable for women travellers to wear skirts than shorts or even long pants. If washing or bathing in public, be as discreet as possible and always keep at least some clothing on. Swimming costumes should be modest. Things are more relaxed for children, who can wear shorts and wash without clothing on.

Touching someone with your feet or legs is considered highly insulting in Nepal. If you accidentally do this, apologise by touching your hand to the person's arm or body and then touching your own head. It's also bad manners to step over someone's outstretched legs, and when you're sitting be sure to withdraw your own legs while someone is walking past you.

Open displays of affection between couples are distasteful to the Nepalese. Apart from the new custom of shaking hands, only close friends physically touch each other in public. But don't be surprised to see men and boys walking with arms around each other's shoulders or even holding hands, and women walking arm-in-arm. This kind of behaviour has no homosexual connotations as Nepal is generally not a gay-friendly society. If you're travelling with your children, it's accepted that you're affectionate with them.

first encounters

पहिलो भेट्हरू

In Nepal, civilities are a bit more formal than in Western countries and, as in many Asian cultures, the Nepalese way of going about things, including conversation, is often rather subtle and indirect. Get used to lots of small talk (and cups of *ci*·yah, चिया, 'tea') before the main reason for the contact can be stated openly. It's common to start chatting by asking where someone is going, or whether they have eaten (rather than how they are).

How are you?
ke cha? **(inf)** — के छ ?

Fine.
ṭhik cha — ठीक छ

What's your name?
ta·*paĩ*·ko nahm ke ho? — तपाईको नाम के हो ?

My name is ...
me·ro nahm ... ho — मेरो नाम ... हो

Please introduce yourself.
ta·*paĩ*·ko *pa*·ri·ca·ya *gar*·nu·hos — तपाईको परिचय गर्नुहोस

How are things?
hahl·kha·bar ke cha? — हालखबर के छ ?

OK./Not bad.
ṭhi·kai cha — ठीकै छ

Where are you going?
ta·*paĩ ka*·hãh *jahn*·dai·hu·nu·hun·cha? — तपाईकहाँ जाँदै हुनुहुन्छ ?

Have you eaten?
khah·nah *khah*·nu *bha*·yo? — खाना खानु भयो ?

I hope we meet again!
phe·ri *bhe*·ṭaũ·lah! — फेरी भेटौंला !

making conversation

गफ गर्नु

It's very easy to strike up conversation with the Nepalese – you'll be asked all sorts of questions about how you like Nepal, where you come from, your family, marital status, job and so on. If things get too personal, steer the conversation away by asking the other person about themselves or about Nepal and their region.

Do you live here?
ta·*paĩ ya*·hãh *bas*·nu·hun·cha? — तपाई यहाँ बस्नुहुन्छ ?

What are you doing?
ta·*paĩ* ke *gar*·dai·hu·nu·hun·cha? — तपाई के गर्दै हुनुहुन्छ ?

This is my friend.
yo *me*·ro *sah*·thi ho — यो मेरो साथी हो

This is my partner/spouse.
yo *me*·ro *ji*·ban *sah*·thi ho — यो मेरो जीबन साथी हो

What do you think (about ...)?
(...·*bah*·re) ta·*paĩ*·ko bi·*cahr* ke ho? — (...बारे) तपाईको बिचार के हो ?

May I take a photo (of you)?
(ta·*paĩ*·ko) *tas*·bir *khic*·nu·hun·cha? — (तपाईको) तस्बीर खिच्नुहुन्छ ?

What's this called?
yas·lai ke bhan·*cha*? — तपाईलाई के भन्छ ?

How do you like Nepal?
ta·*paĩ*·lai ne·*pahl kas*·to *lahg*·yo? — तपाईलाई नेपाल कस्तो लाग्यो ?

casual talk

When constructing sentences in Nepali, remember information that's either clear from context or less important, such as 'I' or the plural ending -ha·ru, is often omitted in casual speech.

We love it here.
hah·mi·lai *ya*·hãh *ek*·dam man *par*·cha — हामीलाई यहाँ एकदम मन पर्छ

It's great here.
ya·hãh *ek*·dam *rahm*·ro cha — यहाँ एकदम राम्रो छ

I like Nepal.
ma·lai ne·*pahl* man *par*·cha — मलाई नेपाल मन पर्छ

I like Nepal a lot.
ma·lai ne·*pahl ek*·dam *rahm*·ro *lahg*·cha — मलाई नेपाल एकदम राम्रो लाग्छ

What a cute baby!
kas·to *rahm*·ro *bac*·cah! — कस्तो राम्रो बच्चा !

Are you waiting too?
ta·*paĩ pa*·ni *par*·kha·nu·hun·cha? — तपाई पनि पर्खनु हुन्छ ?

That's strange!
kas·to a·*nau*·ṭho! — कस्तो अनौठो !

That's funny! (amusing)
kas·to *hãh*·so·lahg·do! — कस्तो हाँसो लाग्दो !

How beautiful!
kas·to *rahm*·ro! — कस्तो राम्रो !

Are you here on holiday?
ta·*paĩ ya*·hãh *bi*·dah·mah *ghum*·na *au*·nu *bha*·ya·ko? — तपाई यहाँ बिदामा घुम्न आउनु भएको ?

I'm here ...	ma *ya*·hãh ... *ah*·ya·ko	म यहाँ ... आएको
for a holiday	*bi*·dah·mah *ghum*·na	बिदामा घुम्न
on business	*be*·pahr *gar*·na	व्यापार गर्न
to study	*paḍh*·na	पढ्न

How long are you here for?
ta·*paĩ ya*·hãh *ka*·ti *bas*·nu·hun·cha? — तपाई यहाँ कति बस्नुहुन्छ ?

I'm here for ... weeks/days.
ma *ya*·hãh ... *hap*·tah/din *bas*·chu — म यहाँ ... हप्ता/दिन बस्छु

We're here with our family.
hah·mi *ya*·hãh *pa*·ri·bahr·sã·ga *ah*·yaũ — हामी यहाँ परिवारसँग आयौं

I'm here with my partner.
ma *ya*·hãh *ji*·ban *sah*·thi·sã·ga *ah*·ya·ko — म यहाँ जीबन साथीसँग आएको

No worries.
bhai·hahl cha, ni — भैहाल छ, नि

Get lost!
bhahg! — भाग !

Really?
sãh·cai? — साँचै ?

Have a good rest.
rahm·ro·sã·ga *bas*·nu·hos — राम्रोसँग बस्नुहोस

Have a good/safe trip home.
rahm·ro·sã·ga *jah*·nu·hos — राम्रोसँग जानुहोस

What's to be done?
ke *gar*·ne? — के गर्ने ?

It's OK.
ṭhik cha — ठीक छ

It's important.
ma·*hat*·twa·pur·ṇa cha — महत्वपूर्ण छ

It's not important.
ma·*hat*·twa·pur·ṇa *chai*·na — महत्वपूर्ण छैन

It's possible.
sam·bhab cha — सम्भब छ

It's not possible.
sam·bhab *chai*·na — सम्भब छैन

Look!
her·nu·hos! — हेर्नुहोस !

Listen (to this)!
(yo) *sun*·nu·hos! — (यो) सुन्नुहोस !

Are you ready?
ta·*paĩ ta*·yahr *hu*·nu·hun·cha? — तपाई तयार हुनुहुन्छ ?

I'm ready.
ma *ta*·yahr chũ — म तयार छुँ

It's nothing./It doesn't matter.
ke·hi *hoi*·na — केही होइन

How much is it (this)?
(yo) *ka*·ti ho? — (यो) कति हो ?

What's this/that?
yo/tyo ke ho? — यो/ त्यो के हो ?

What's the matter?
ke *bha*·yo? — के भयो ?

You're right.
ta·*paĩ*·le ṭhik *bhan*·nu *bha*·yo — तपाईले ठीक भन्नुभयो

It is/was enough.
pug·cha/*pug*·yo — पुग्छ/पुग्यो

... isn't it/aren't they?
... ho ki *hoi*·na? — ... हो कि होइन ?

OK.	ṭhik cha	ठीक छ
	hun·cha **(pol)**	हुन्छ
	has **(very pol)**	हस

nationalities

राष्ट्रियताहरु

You'll find that many country names in Nepali are similar to English, with all 't's and 'd's pronounced as retroflex (see Pronunciation, page 14).

Where are you from?
ta·*paĩ* kun *desh*·bah·ṭa *au*·nu *bha*·ya·ko? — तपाई कुन देशबाट आउनु भएको ?

I'm/We're from ...	*me*·ro/*hahm*·ro desh ... ho	मेरो/हाम्रो देश ... हो
Africa	*a*·phri·kah	अफ्रिका
Australia	a·*sṭre*·li·yah	अष्ट्रेलिया
Belgium	*bel*·ji·yam	बेल्जीयम

Britain	be·*lah*·yat	बेलायत
Canada	*kyah*·nah·ḍah	क्यानाडा
China	cin	चीन
Egypt	*mis*·ra	मिस्र
England	*ĩg*·laĩḍ	ईग्लैन्ड
Europe	*yu*·rop	युरोप
France	phrahns	फ्रान्स
Germany	*jar*·ma·ni	जर्मनी
Greece	yu·*nahn*	यूनान
Holland	*ha*·laĩḍ	हलैंड
India	*bhah*·rat	भारत
Iran	i·*rahn*	ईरान
Ireland	*ah*·yar·laĩḍ	आयरलैंड
Israel	*i*·ja·rail	इजराइल
Italy	*i*·ṭa·li	इटली
Japan	jah·*pahn*	जापान
Malaysia	mah·*le*·shi·yah	मालेशिया
Myanmar (Burma)	*bar*·mah	बर्मा
Nepal	ne·*pahl*	नेपाल
New Zealand	nyu *ji*·laĩḍ	न्यूजील्याण्ड
Pakistan	*pah*·ki·stahn	पाकिस्तान
Russia	rus	रूस
Scotland	is·*kaṭ*·laĩḍ	इस्कट्लैंड
Spain	spen	स्पेन
Sri Lanka	sri *lang*·kah	श्रीलंका
Taiwan	cin ja·na·*bah*·di ga·na·*tan*·tra	चीन जनबादी गनतन्त्र
Thailand	*thai*·laĩḍ	थाइलैंड
Tibet	*ti*·bet	तिब्बत
Turkey	*ṭar*·ki	टर्की
the USA	a·*me*·ri·kah	अमेरिका
Vietnam	*bhi*·yat·nahm	भियतनाम
Wales	welj	वेल्ज

fire hazard

Fire is sacred in Nepal, to both Hindus and Buddhists. Never throw rubbish or anything else into one!

I live in/at the/a ...	ma ...·mah *bas*·chu	म ...मा बस्छु
city	*sha*·har	शहर
countryside	*sha*·har *bah*·hi·ra·ko bheg	शहर बाहिरको भेग
mountains	pa·*hahḍ*	पहाड
seaside	sa·*mu*·dra·ko ki·*nahr*	समुद्रको किनार
suburbs of ...	...·ko kãhṭh	...को काँठ
village	gaũ	गाउँ

cultural differences

साँस्कृतिक अनेकताहरू

How do you do this in your country?
ta·*paĩ*·ko *desh*·mah, yo *ka*·sa·ri *gar*·ne?
तपाईको देशमा, यो कसरी गर्ने ?

Is this a local or national custom?
yo *ca*·lan *sthah*·ni·ya ho ki *rah*·sṭri·ya ho?
यो चलन स्थानीय हो कि राष्ट्रिय हो ?

local	*sthah*·ni·ya	स्थानीय
national	*rah*·sṭri·ya	राष्ट्रिय

I don't want to offend you.
ma ta·*paĩ*·lai *cit*·ta du·*khau*·na man *par*·dai·na
म तपाईलाई चित्त दुखाउन मन पर्दैन

I'm sorry, it's not the custom in my country.
mahph *gar*·nu·hos, *me*·ro *desh*·mah yo *hahm*·ro *ca*·lan *hoi*·na
माफ गनुर्होस, मेरो देशमा यो हाम्रो चलन होइन

I'm not accustomed to this.
yo *me*·ro *ca*·lan *hoi*·na
यो मेरो चलन होइन

I don't mind watching, but I'd prefer not to participate.
ma *her*·chu, *ta*·ra bhahg *li*·na man *par*·dai·na
म हेर्छु, तर भाग लिन मन पर्दैन

I'll give it a go.
ma *ko*·sis *gar*·chu — म कोसिस गर्छु

I'm sorry, it's against my ...	mahph *gar*·nu·hos, yo *me*·ro ... *hoi*·na	माफ गनुर्होस, यो मेरो ... होइन
beliefs	bi·*shwahs*	बिश्वास
culture	sã·*skri*·ti	संस्कृति
religion/philosophy	*dhar*·ma	धर्म

age

उमेर

In Nepal, it's not impolite to ask someone's age, particularly a child, an elderly person or someone younger than you. But many Nepalese do not know their exact age!

Remember to use the informal *ti*·mi for 'you' when talking to children.

How old are you?	ta·*paĩ*/*ti*·mi *ka*·ti *bar*·sa *bha*·yo? **(pol/inf)**	तपाई/तिमी कति वर्ष भयो ?
I'm ... years old.	ma ... *bar*·sa *bha*·yo	म ... वर्ष भयो
18	a·*ṭhah*·ra	अठार
35	*paĩ*·tis	पैंतीस

(See Numbers & Amounts, page 35, for your age.)

occupations

कामहरू

The list below includes some typical Nepali occupations, as well as a few common Western occupations.

What's your occupation?
ta·*paĩ*·ko kahm ke ho? — तपाईको काम के हो ?

Where do you work?
ta·*paĩ ka*·hãh kahm *gar*·nu·hun·cha? — तपाई कहाँ काम गर्नुहुन्छ ?

How do you enjoy your work?
ta·*paĩ*·ko kahm *kas*·to *lahg*·cha? — तपाईको काम कस्तो लाग्छ ?

I enjoy/don't enjoy my work.
me·ro kahm ra·*mai*·lo cha/*chai*·na — मेरो काम रमाईलो छ/छैन

I'm a/an ...	ma ... hũ	म ... हुँ
actor	a·bhi·*ne*·tah/ a·bhi·*ne*·tri (m/f)	अभिनेता/ अभिनेत्री
architect	*vahs*·tu·kahr	वास्तुकार
artist	*ka*·lah·kahr	कलाकार
boatman/-woman	nau	नाउ
businessperson	*be*·pah·ri	व्यापारी
chef/cook	*bhahn*·se	भान्से
cleaner	*sa*·phah *gar*·ne *mahn*·che	सफा गर्ने मान्छे
clerk	*ba*·hi·dahr	बहिदार
dancer	*nar*·ta·ki	नर्तकी
doctor	*ḍahk*·ṭar	डाक्टर
elephant driver	*mah*·hu·te	माहुते
engineer	in·ji·*ni*·yar	ईन्जिनियर
factory worker	kah·ra·*khah*·nah·ko *maj*·dur	कारखानाको मजदूर
farmer	ki·*sahn*	किसान
fisherman/-woman	*mah*·jhi	माझी
gardener	*mah*·li	माली
gold-/silversmith	su·*nahr*	सुनार
guide	*bah*·ṭo de·*khau*·ne *mahn*·che	बाटो देखाउने मान्छे
housewife	*ghar*·bu·ḍhi	घरबूढी
journalist	*pa*·tra·kahr	पत्रकार
labourer	*maj*·dur	मजदूर
laundryman/-woman	*dho*·bi	धोबी
lawyer	*wa*·kil	वकील

manager	*hah*·kim	हाकिम
mechanic	*mi*·stri	मिस्त्री
musician	*sang*·git·kahr	सङ्गीतकार
nurse	nars	नर्स
office worker	kar·ma·*cah*·ri	कर्मचारी
painter	*ci*·tra·kahr	चित्रकार
police officer	pra·*ha*·ri	प्रहरी
porter	*bha*·ri·yah	भरिया
priest	pu·*jah*·ri	पूजारी
scientist	bai·*gyah*·nik	बैज्ञानिक
secretary	*sa*·cib	सचिव
soldier	si·*pah*·hi	सिपाही
student	bi·*dyahr*·thi	विधार्थी
tailor	*su*·ci·kahr	सूचिकार
teacher	*shi*·chak	शिक्षक
tracker/hunter	shi·*kah*·ri	शिकारी
university lecturer	a·*dhyah*·pak	अध्यापक
waiter	*be*·rah	बेरा
writer	*le*·khak	लेखक

I'm retired.	ma a·wa·*kahsh li*·ẽ	म अवकाश लियें
I'm unemployed.	ma be·*kah*·ri chũ	म बेकारी छुँ
What are you studying?	ta·*paĩ* ke *paḍh*·nu·hun·cha?	तपाई के पढ्नुहुन्छ ?

I'm studying ...	ma ... *paḍh*·dai·chu	म ... पढ्दैछु
arts/humanities	ka·*lah*	कला
business	*be*·pahr	व्यापार
economics	ar·tha·*shahs*·tra	अर्थशास्त्र
engineering	in·ji·*ni*·yar	इन्जिनियर
English	ang·*gre*·ji	अङ्ग्रेजी
languages	*bhah*·sah·ha·ru	भाषाहरु
law	*kah*·nun	कानुन
medicine	*ḍahk*·ṭa·ri	डाक्टरी
Nepali	ne·*pah*·li *bhah*·sah	नेपाली भाषा
painting	*ci*·tra	चित्र
science	bi·*gyahn*	बिज्ञान
teaching	*shi*·chaṇ	शिक्षण

feelings

भावनाहरु

How do you feel?
ta·*paĩ*·lai *kas*·to cha? — तपाईलाई कस्तो छ ?

Are you happy/sad?
ta·*paĩ khu*·si/*du*·khi *hu*·nu·hun·cha? — तपाई खुसी/दु:खी हुनुहुन्छ ?

Do you feel ...?	ta·*paĩ*·lai ... *lahg*·yo?	तपाईलाई ... लाग्यो ?
I feel/don't feel ...	*ma*·lai ... *lahg*·yo/ *lah*·ge·na	मलाई ... लाग्यो/ लागेन
afraid	ḍar	डर
angry	ris	रिस
cold	*jah*·ḍo	जाडो
depressed	u·*dahs*	उदास
drunk	*rak*·si	रक्सी
grateful	gun	गुण
happy	*khu*·si	खुसी
hot	*gar*·mi	गर्मी
hungry	bhok	भोक
lost	ha·*rau*·na	हराउन
OK/fine	ṭhik	ठीक
sad	*du*·khi	दु:खी
sick	bi·*rah*·mi	बिरामी
sleepy	*ni*·drah	निन्द्रा
sorry (condolence)	*da*·yah	दया
sorry (regret)	*du*·khit	दु:खित
thirsty	*tir*·khah	तिर्खा
tired	*tha*·kai	थकाइ
well	*san*·cai	सन्चै

breaking the language barrier

भाषाको अवरोध गर्नु

Do you speak English?
ta·*paĩ* ang·*gre*·ji *bhah*·sah *bol*·nu·hun·cha? — तपाई अङ्ग्रेजी भाषा बोल्नुहुन्छ ?

Yes, I speak English.
ha·*jur*, ma ang·*gre*·ji *bhah*·sah *bol*·chu — हजुर, म अङ्ग्रेजी भाषा बोल्छु

No, I don't speak English.
ma ang·*gre*·ji *bhah*·sah *bol*·di·na — म अङ्ग्रेजी भाषा बोल्दिन

Does anyone here speak English?
ya·hãh *ko*·hi ang·*gre*·ji *bhah*·sah *bol*·na *sak*·nu·hun·cha? — यहाँ कोही अङ्ग्रेजी भाषा बोल्न सक्नुहुन्छ ?

I only speak a little (Nepali).
ma *a*·li *a*·li (ne·*pah*·li *bhah*·sah) *bol*·chu — म अलिअलि (नेपाली भाषा) बोल्छु

Do you understand?
ta·*paĩ* *bujh*·nu·hun·cha? — तपाई बुझ्नुहुन्छ ?

I understand/understood.
ma *bujh*·chu/*mai*·le *bu*·jhẽ — म बुझ्छु/मैले बुझिन

I don't understand.
mai·le bu·*jhi*·na — मैले बु झीन

Please speak more slowly.
bi·*stah*·rai *bol*·nu·hos — बिस्तारै बोल्नुहोस

Please say it again.
phe·ri *bhan*·nu·hos — फेरी भन्नुहोस

Please write that down.
tyo *ku*·rah lekh·*di*·nu·hos — त्यो कुरा लेखिदिनुहोस

How do you say ...?
...·lai ke *bhan*·cha? — ...लाई के भन्छ ?

What does ... mean (in English)?
(ang·*gre*·ji *bhah*·sah·mah) ...·lai ke *mah*·ne cha? — (अङ्ग्रेजी भाषामा) ...लाई के भन्छ ?

I'm looking for it in this book.
ma yo ki·*tahb*·mah *her*·dai·chu — म यो किताबमा हेर्दैछु

Please wait a minute.
ek·chin *par*·kha·nu·hos — एकछिन पर्खनुहोस

I know/don't know.
ma·lai *thah*·hah cha/*chai*·na — मलाई थाहा छ/छैन

Do you speak ...?	ta·*paĩ* ... *bhah*·sah *bol*·nu·hun·cha?	तपाई ... भाषा बोल्नुहुन्छ ?
I speak ...	ma ... *bhah*·sah *bol*·chu	म ... भाषा बोल्छु
Bengali	bã·*gah*·li	बंगाली
Chinese	cai·*nij*	चाइनीज
Dutch	ḍac	डच
English	ang·*gre*·ji	अङ्ग्रेजी
French	phrenc	फ्रेन्च
German	*jar*·man	जर्मन
Hindi	*hin*·di	हिन्दी
Indonesian	iṇ·ḍo·*ne*·si·yah·ko	इन्डोनेसियाको
Japanese	ja·pa·*nij*	जापानिज
Nepali	ne·*pah*·li	नेपाली
Tibetan	ti·*be*·tan	तिबेतन

Family
प्रिवार

In Nepal, family life is paramount. In all ethnic groups, the domestic circle is the heart of social and cultural life and a person is identified primarily by their familial associations – and for women, their marital status.

Large families are the norm, and boys are favoured over girls, not only for cultural reasons but because in the absence of any social security system, the elderly need their children (especially sons) to look after them. Another factor is the appallingly high rates of infant (and maternal) mortality: the more likely your children are to die before adulthood, the more children you need to have as a safeguard.

Most Nepalese (especially those who work in tourism) are aware of behavioural norms in different cultures and are generally not offended by the idea that couples may be living together without being married. However, in remote areas of the country it may be easier for everyone if you simply say you're married. For all couples, open displays of affection are not acceptable in Nepalese society: in films, even the romantic leads never kiss!

questions

प्रश्नहरु

Are you married?
ta·*paĩ*·ko bi·*hah bha*·yo? — तपाईको बिहा भयो ?

Do you have a boyfriend/girlfriend?
ta·*paĩ*·ko *pre*·mi/*pre*·mi·kah cha? — तपाईको प्रेमि/प्रेमिका छ ?

Do you have any children?
ta·*paĩ*·ko cho·rah·*cho*·ri chan? — तपाईको छोराछोरी छन ?

How many children do you have?
ta·*paĩ*·ko cho·rah·*cho*·ri *ka*·ti *ja*·nah chan? — तपाईको छोराछोरी कति जना छन ?

Who looks after the children?

cho·rah·*cho*·ri·lai *kas*·le *rekh*·dekh *gar*·nu·hun·cha? — छोराछोरीलाई कसले रेखदेख गर्नुहुन्छ ?

Do you have grandchildren?

ta·*paĩ*·ko nah·ti·*nah*·ti·ni chan? — तपाईको नातिनातिनी छन ?

How many brothers/sisters do you have?

ta·*paĩ*·ko dah·ju·*bhai*/ di·di·*ba*·hi·ni *ka*·ti *ja*·nah chan? — तपाईको दाजुभाइ/ दिदीबिहनी कति जना छन ?

How old are they?

u·ni·ha·ru *ka*·ti *bar*·sa *bha*·yo? — उनीहरू कति वर्ष भयो ?

How many in your family?

ta·*paĩ*·ko *pa*·ri·bahr·mah *ka*·ti *ja*·nah chan? — तपाईको परिवारमा कति जना छन ?

Do you live with your family?

ta·*paĩ pa*·ri·bahr·mah *bas*·nu·hun·cha? — तपाईको परिवारमा बस्नुहुन्छ ?

Is your husband/wife here?

ta·*paĩ*·ko *sri*·mahn/sri·*ma*·ti *ya*·hãh *hu*·nu·hun·cha? — तपाईको श्रीमान/श्रीमती यहाँ हुनुहुन्छ ?

Are your parents alive?

ta·*paĩ*·ko *ah*·mah, *bu*·wah *a*·hi·le·sam·ma ji·*un*·dai *hu*·nu·hun·cha? — तपाईको आमा, बुवा अहिलेसम्म जिउदैं हुनुहुन्छ ?

replies

जवाफहरू

I'm married/not married.

me·ro bi·*hah bha*·yo/*bha*·ya·ko *chai*·na — मेरो बिवाह भयो/भएको छैन

I'm ...	ma ... hũ	म ... हुँ
divorced	*cho*·ḍe·ko	छोडेको
single	*ek*·lai	एक्लै
separated	*chuṭ*·ṭai	छुट्टै
widowed	*bi*·dha·wah	बिधवा

homosexuality in nepal

While Nepali culture can be fairly conservative, homosexual activity was decriminalised in 2007 and anti-discrimination laws were established in 2015. Nepal has become something of a leader in gay rights in the region. Even so, the local gay community tends to keep a low profile, and harassment can occur, so it's best to be discreet.

I have a partner.
me·ro *ji*·ban *sah*·thi cha — मेरो जीबन साथी छ

We live together but we're not married.
hah·mi *sã*·gai *bas*·chaũ *ta*·ra *hahm*·ro bi·*hah bha*·ya·ko *chai*·na — हामी सँगै बस्छौं तर हाम्रो बिवाह भएको छैन

I don't have any children.
me·ro cho·rah·*cho*·ri *chai*·na — मेरो छोराछोरी छैन

I have (two) children.
me·ro *(du*·i) *ja*·nah cho·rah·*cho*·ri chan — मेरो (दुइ) जना छोराछोरी छन

I have a daughter/son.
me·ro ek *ja*·nah *cho*·ri/ *cho*·rah cha — मेरो एक जना छोरी/ छोरा छ

I live with my family.
me·ro *pa*·ri·bahr·mah *bas*·chu — मेरो परिवारमा बस्छु

family

परिवार

baby	*bac*·cah	बच्चा
boy	*ke*·ṭah	केटा
brothers	dah·ju·*bhai*	दाजुभाइ
children (general)	ke·ṭah·*ke*·ṭi	केटाकेटी
children (own)	cho·rah·*cho*·ri	छोराछोरी
dad	bah	बा
daughter	*cho*·ri	छोरी
elder brother's wife	*bhau*·jyu	भाउज्यू

extended family	san·*tahn*	सन्तान
family	*pa*·ri·bahr	परिवार
family name	thar	थर
father	*bu*·wah	बुवा
father-in-law	*sa*·su·rah	ससुरा
girl	*ke*·ṭi	केटी
given name	*shu*·bha·nahm	शुभनाम
grandfather	*bah*·je	बाजे
grandmother	*ba*·jyai	बज्यै
grandparents	*bah*·je *ba*·jyai	बाजे बज्यै
husband (general)	*sri*·mahn	श्रीमान
husband (own)	*log*·ne	लोग्ने
mother	*ah*·mah	आमा
mother-in-law	*sah*·su	सासू
mum	*ah*·mai	आमा
nickname	*u*·pa·nahm	उपनाम
parents	*ah*·mah *bu*·wah	आमा बुवा
sisters	di·di·*ba*·hi·ni	दिदीबिहनी
son	*cho*·rah	छोरा
wife (general)	sri·*ma*·ti	श्रीमती
wife (own)	*swahs*·ni	स्वास्नी
wife's in-laws	ja·*hahn*	जहान

talking with parents

बा आमासँग गफ गर्नु

When is your baby due?
ta·*paĩ*·ko *bac*·cah *ka*·hi·le *aun*·cha? — तपाईको बच्चा कहिले आउछ ?

What are you going to call your baby?
ta·*paĩ*·ko *bac*·cah·lai ke nahm *di*·nu·hun·cha? — तपाईको बच्चालाई के नाम दिनुहुन्छ ?

Is this your first child?
yo ta·*paĩ*·ko *pa*·hi·lo *bac*·cah ho? — यो तपाईको पहिलो बच्चा हो ?

How old are your children?
ta·*paĩ*·ko cho·rah·*cho*·ri *ka*·ti *bar*·sa *bha*·yo? — तपाईको छोराछोरी कति वर्ष भयो ?

Does he/she attend school?
u·ni bi·*dyah*·la·ya·mah *jahn*·cha? — ऊनी बिद्यालयमा जान्छ ?

Is it a private or government school?
bi·*dyah*·la·ya ah·*pas*·ko ho ki sar·*kahr*·ko ho? — बिद्यालय आपसको हो कि सरकारको हो ?

What's the baby's name?
bac·cah·ko nahm ke ho? — बच्चाको नाम के हो ?

Is it a boy or a girl?
cho·rah ho, ki *cho*·ri? — छोरा हो, कि छोरी ?

Does he/she let you sleep at night?
u·ni·le ta·*paĩ*·lai *sut*·na *din*·cha? — ऊनीले तपाईलाई सुत्न दिन्छ ?

He's/She's very big for his/her age!
u·ni·ko *u*·mer·mah *ṭhu*·lo cha! — ऊनीको उमेरमा ठूलो छ !

What a beautiful child!
kas·to *rahm*·ro *bac*·cah! — कस्तो राम्रो बच्चा !

He/She looks like you.
u·ni ta·*paĩ jas*·tai cha — ऊनी तपाई जस्तै छ

Who does he/she look like, Mum or Dad?
u·ni *ah*·mah *jas*·tai cha, ki *bu*·wah? — ऊनी आमा जस्तै छ, कि बुवा ?

talking with children

केटाकटीसँग गफ गर्नुस

What's your name?
tim·ro nahm ke ho? — तिम्रो नाम के हो ?

How old are you?
ti·mi *ka*·ti *bar*·sa *bha*·yo? — तिमी कति वर्ष भयो ?

little adults

Nepal is an extremely poor country and many families can't afford to send all or any of their children to school, even where schooling is free, because they can't manage without the children's input into the family household or business. Many children, especially girls, work instead of going to school (or leave school very early), although only a minority work in commercial employment. In fact, some children work to pay for the education of their younger siblings.

When's your birthday?
tim·ro *jan*·ma·din *ka*·hi·le ho? — तिम्रो जन्मदिन कहिले हो ?

Do you have brothers and sisters?
tim·ro dah·ju·*bhai* di·di·*ba*·hi·ni chan? — तिम्रो दाजुभाइ दिदीबिहनी छन ?

Do you have a pet at home?
tim·ro *ghar*·mah *pahl*·tu ja·*nah*·war cha? — तिम्रो घरमा पाल्तु जनावर छ ?

Do you go to school or kindergarten?
ti·mi is·*kul jahn*·cha ki *nar*·sa·ri? — तिमी स्कुल जान्छ कि नर्सरी ?

Is your teacher nice?
tim·ro *shi*·chak *rahm*·ro cha? — तिम्रो शिक्षक राम्रो छ ?

Do you like school?
ti·mi·lai is·*kul* man *par*·cha? — तिमीलाई स्कुल मनपर्छ ?

Do you play sport?
ti·mi *khel*·kud *khel*·cha? — तिमी खेलकुद खेल्छ ?

What sport do you play?
ti·mi kun *khel*·kud *khel*·cha? — तिमी कुन खेलकुद खेल्छ ?

What do you do after school?
is·*kul*·pa·chi *ti*·mi ke *gar*·cha? — स्कुल पछि तिमी के गर्छ ?

Do you learn English?
ti·mi ang·*gre*·ji *bhah*·sah *paḍh*·cha? — तिमी अङ्ग्रेजी भाषा पढ्छ ?

Many travellers visit Nepal for trekking, but there are plenty of other activities to suit all tastes. These include rafting, kayaking and mountain biking and there's a fascinating array of cultural activities to observe and participate in for anthropology, history and architecture buffs. Religion and spirituality may also be of interest, especially Buddhism or yoga and meditation.

talking about travelling

यात्राको गफ

Have you travelled much?
ta·*paĩ*·le *dhe*·rai *yah*·trah *gar*·nu *bha*·yo? — तपाईले धेरै यात्रा गर्नु भयो ?

How long have you been travelling?
ta·*paĩ*·ko *yah*·trah *ka*·ti *bha*·yo? — तपाईको यात्रा कति भयो ?

I've been travelling for (two) months.
me·ro *yah*·trah (*du*·i) *ma*·hi·nah *bha*·yo — मेरो यात्रा (दुईइ) महीना भयो

When did you come to Nepal?
ta·*paĩ* ne·*pahl*·mah *ka*·hi·le *au*·nu *bha*·ya·ko? — तपाई नेपालमा कहिले आउनु भएको ?

(Two weeks) ago.
(*du*·i *hap*·tah) *bha*·yo — (दुई हप्ता) भयो

How long will you stay?
ka·ti *bas*·nu·hun·cha? — कति बस्नुहुन्छ ?

I'll stay in Nepal for (one year).
ma ne·*pahl*·mah (ek *bar*·sa) *bas*·chu — म नेपालमा (एक वर्ष) बस्छु

Where have you been?
ta·*paĩ* *ka*·hãh *jah*·nu *bha*·yo? — तपाई कहाँ जानुभयो ?

I've been to ...
ma ...·mah *ga*·yẽ — म ...मा गए

Did you go alone?
ta·paĩ ek·lai *jah*·nu *bha*·yo? तपाई ए क्लै जानुभयो ?

What did you think of (Pokhara)?
ta·paĩ·lai *(po*·kha·rah) *kas*·to *lahg*·yo? तपाईलाई (पोखरा) कस्तो लाग्यो ?

I thought it was ...	*ma*·lai ... *lahg*·yo	मलाई ... लाग्यो
boring	*wahk*·ka	वाक्क
great	*ek*·dam *rahm*·ro	एकदम राम्रो
horrible	*na*·rahm·ro	नराम्रो
OK	*ṭhi*·kai	ठीकै
too expensive	*dhe*·rai ma·*hã*·go	धेरै महंगो

There are too many tourists there.
tya·hãh par·*ya*·ṭak *dhe*·rai chan त्यहाँ पयर्टक धेरै छन

Not many people speak (English).
tho·rai *ja*·na·tah (ang·*gre*·ji) *bol*·chan थोरै जनता (अङ्ग्रेजी) बो ल्छन

I was ripped off in ...
...·mah *ma*·lai *ṭhag*·yo ...मा मलाई ठग्यो

People are really friendly there.
tya·hãh *ja*·na·tah *dhe*·rai ra·*mai*·lo chan त्यहाँ जनता धेरै रमाइलो छन

What's there to do in (Chitwan)?
(chit·wan)·mah ke *gar*·na *paun*·cha? (चितवन)मा के गर्न पाउँछ ?

The best time to go is in (Dasain).
tya·hãh *jah*·na *sab*·bhan·dah *rahm*·ro *be*·lah *(da*·saĩ) ho त्यहाँ जान सबभन्दा राम्रो बेला (दसैं) हो

I'm going to Pokhara for (three weeks).
ma (tin *hap*·tah)·ko *lah*·gi *po*·kha·rah·mah *jan*·chu म (तीन हप्ता)को लागि पोखरामा जान्छु

Is it expensive?
ma·*hã*·go cha? महंगो छ ?

Is it safe for women travellers on their own?
ek·lai *nah*·ri *yah*·tri·ko *lah*·gi su·*ra*·chit cha? — एक्लै नारी यात्रीको लागि सुरक्षित छ ?

Is it safe to hitch?
lipht *li*·nu su·*ra*·chit cha? — लिफ्ट लिनु सुरक्षित छ ?

common interests

संयुक्त चाखहरू

What do you do in your spare time?
ta·*paĩ*·ko *phur*·sat·mah ke *gar*·nu·hun·cha? — तपाईको फुर्सदमा के गर्नुहुन्छ ?

Do you have any hobbies?
ta·*paĩ*·ko *ke*·hi sokh cha? — तपाईको केही सोख छ ?

Do you like ...?	ta·*paĩ*·lai ... man *par*·cha?	तपाईलाई ... मन पर्छ ?
I like/don't like ...	*ma*·lai ... man *par*·cha/*par*·dai·na	मलाई ... मन पर्छ/पर्दैन
basketball	*bahs*·keṭ·bal	बास्केट्‌बल
football	*laht*·te *bha*·kun·ḍo	लात्ते भकुन्डो
trekking	*pai*·dal *hĩḍ*·na	पैदल हिड्न
music	*sang*·git	सङ्गीत
photography	*tas*·bir *khic*·na	तिस्बर खिच्न
playing cards	tahs *khel*·na	तास खेल्न
playing games	khel *khel*·na	खेल खेल्न
playing sport	*khel*·kud *khel*·na	खेलकुद खेल्न
reading	*paḍh*·na	पढ्न
seeing films	cal·*ci*·tra *her*·na	चलिचत्र हेर्न
shopping	*kin*·mel *gar*·na	किनमेल गर्न
skiing	is·*ki* *khel*·na	इस्की खेल्न
swimming	*pau*·ḍi *khel*·na	पौडी खेल्न
talking	*ku*·rah *gar*·na	कुरा गर्न
travelling	*yah*·trah *gar*·na	यात्रा गर्न
watching sport	*khel*·kud *her*·na	खेलकुद हेर्न

I make ...	ma ... ba·*naun*·chu	म ... बनाउँछु
pottery	*mah*·ṭah·kah *bhā̃h*·ḍah	माटाका भाँडा
jewellery	*ga*·ha·nah	गहना
I collect ...	ma ... ja·*maun*·chu	म ... जमाउँछु
books	ki·*tahb*	किताब
coins	*mu*·drah	मुद्रा
dolls	*pu*·ta·li	पुतली
stamps	*ṭi*·kaṭ	टिकट
It's fun.	*maj*·jah *lahg*·cha	मज्जा लाग्छ

music

सङ्गीत

Do you like ...?	ta·*paĩ*·lai ... man *par*·cha?	तपाईलाई ... मन पर्छ ?
to dance	*nahc*·na	नाच्न
listening to music	*sang*·git *sun*·na	सङ्गीत सुन्न

traditional music

Music and song are fundamental to all the cultures of Nepal. Traditional Nepalese music is generally either classical/religious or folk music. Classical ragas originated in India but have acquired a Nepalese character. Hinduism and Buddhism each have distinctive styles of religious song, including the blast of Tibetan horns.

Folk music themes include love, nature and heroic sagas, performed by traditional singers called *gaine* who play the *sarangi*, a small stringed instrument. *Damai* or members of the musical caste traditionally play instruments such as the *sahnai* (a stringed instrument), *narsingha* (large trumpets) and various kinds of drums, but these days their profession mainly involves playing Hindi film music on brass instruments for wedding processions.

they may say

mahph *gar*·nu·hos, *ṭi*·kaṭ *sa*·bai *be*·ci·yo
Sorry, we're sold out.

Do you ...?	ta·*paĩ*·lai ... *aun*·cha?	तपाईलाई ... आउँछ?
play an instrument	*bah*·jah ba·*jau*·na	बाजा बजाउन
sing	git *gau*·na	गीत गाउन

What sort of music do you like?
ta·*paĩ*·lai ke *sang*·git man *par*·cha? — तपाईलाई के सङ्गीत मन पर्छ ?

Which bands do you like?
ta·*paĩ*·lai ke bahṇḍ man *par*·cha? — तपाईलाई के ब्याण्ड मन पर्छ ?

I like (the) ...
ma·lai ... man *par*·cha — मलाई ... मनपर्छ

Have you heard the latest release by ...?
ta·*paĩ*·le ...·ko ah·*dhu*·nik git *sun*·nu *bha*·yo? — तपाईले ...को आधुनिक गीत सुन्नुभयो ?

Which radio station plays good music?
kun *re*·ḍi·yo is·*ṭe*·san·mah *rahm*·ro *sang*·git su·*naun*·cha? — कुन रेडियो इस्टेसनमा राम्रो सङ्गीत सुनाउँछ ?

What frequency is it on?
kun *re*·ḍi·yo *beṇḍ*·mah cha? — कुन रेडियो बेण्डमा छ ?

This radio station, is it FM or AM?
yo *re*·ḍi·yo is·*ṭe*·san *eph*·em ho ki *ai*·em? — यो रेडियो इस्टेसन एफ एम हो कि ऐ एम ?

Where can you hear traditional music around here?
ya·hãh sãh·*skri*·tik *sang*·git *ka*·hãh *sun*·ne? — यहाँ सास्कृतिक सङ्गीत कहाँ सुन्ने ?

cinema & theatre

सिनेमा र अभिनय

Most of the cinemas are hugely crowded and show only Hindi (Indian) and occasionally Nepali films – without subtitles – but you can find some European films and live theatre, and there are plenty of Nepalese cultural performances. Some restaurants also show English-language videos, although they're often poor quality pirated versions.

I feel like going to a ...	*ma*·lai ... *her*·na man *lahg*·yo	मलाई ... हेर्न मन लाग्यो
film	philm	फिल्म
play	*li*·lah	लीला

What's on at the cinema tonight?
be·lu·kah *si*·ne·mah *hal*·mah ke cha? बेलुका सिनेमा हलमा के छ ?

Where can I find a cinema guide?
si·ne·mah *a*·kha·bahr *ka*·hãh *paun*·cha? सिनेमा अखबार कहाँ पाउँछ ?

Are there any tickets for ...?
...·ko *ṭi*·kaṭ *paun*·cha? ...को टिकट पाउँछ ?

Is the performance in English?
nah·ṭak ang·*gre*·ji·mah cha? नाटक अङ्ग्रेजीमा छ ?

nepalese dance

Traditional Nepalese dance is either classical/religious/festival dance or folk dance, and there are many varieties of each. Classical dances include the Hindu *Bhairav-Kali* and the Buddhist *Bajra-Yogini*, while mask dances, such as the *Newar Lakhe* dance, are performed during religious festivals. Popular folk dances include the *Tharu* Stick dance, the women's *Sakhi* dance, the *Maruni* dance (sung and danced by a group of men and a group of women), and the *Panche* dance (performed during wedding processions).

Does it have English subtitles?
ang·*gre*·ji *le*·khe·ko cha? — अङ्ग्रेजी लेखेको छ ?

Shall we sit or stand?
bas·ãu ki *u*·ṭhi·bas·ne? — बसौं कि उठीबसौं ?

Where shall we sit?
ka·hãh *bas*·ne? — कहाँ बस्ने ?

Are those seats taken?
ti *ṭhãu*·ha·ru·mah *ko*·hi *ba*·se·cha? — ती ठाउँहरुमा कोही बसेछ ?

opinions

भनाइहरू

Do you agree?
ta·*paĩ* *mahn*·nu·hun·cha? — तपाई मान्नुहुन्छ ?

I agree/disagree.
ma *mahn*·chu/*mahn*·di·na — म मान्छु/मान्दिन

What do you think?
ta·*paĩ*·ko bi·*cahr* ke ho? — तपाईको बिचार के हो ?

I think that ...
me·ro bi·*cahr*·mah ... — मेरो बिचारमा ...

That's my opinion.
tya·hi *me*·ro bi·*cahr* ho — त्यही मेरो बिचार हो

Do you like it?
ta·*paĩ*·lai yo man *par*·cha? — तपाईलाई यो मन पर्छ ?

I like/don't like it.
ma·lai yo man *par*·cha/*par*·dai·na — मलाई यो मन पर्छ/पर्दैन

That's true/not true.
tyo *sa*·tya ho/*hoi*·na — त्यो सत्य हो/हो इन

This is good/bad.
yo *rahm*·ro/kha·*rahb* cha — यो राम्रो/खराब छ

politics

राजनीति

Democracy only came to Nepal after the 1990 people's uprising and as yet it's failed to meet the people's high expectations. The Maoist People's War (1996–2006) and rampant corruption have also contributed to an atmosphere of insecurity and repression. However, the Nepalese do love to debate politics, so it's not a taboo subject – just be sensitive to the current, somewhat difficult, political climate.

What do you think of the current government?
a·hi·le·ko *sar*·kahr ke bi·*cahr* *gar*·nu·hun·cha? — अहिलेको सरकार के बिचार गर्नुहुन्छ ?

I agree/don't agree with their policy on ...	...·ko sar·*kah*·ri *ni*·ti ma *mahn*·chu/ *mahn*·di·na	...को सरकारी नीति म मान्छु/ मान्दिन
drugs	*o*·kha·ti	औषधि
the economy	*ar*·tha	अर्थ
education	*shi*·chah	शिक्षा
the environment	bah·tah·*ba*·raṇ	वातावरण
social welfare	sah·*mah*·jik *bha*·lai	सामाजिक भलाइ

I'm against ...
ma ...·ko bi·*rodh* hũ — म ...को बिरोध हुँ

I'm in favour of ...
ma ...·ko *pa*·cha *lin*·chu — म ...को पक्ष लिन्छु

Who do you vote for?
ta·*paĩ kas*·lai mat kha·*sahl*·nu·hun·cha? — तपाई कसलाई मत खसाल्नुहुन्छ ?

I support the ... party.	ma ... *dal*·lai sa·*mar*·than *gar*·chu	म ... दललाई समर्थन गर्छु
I'm a member of the ... party.	ma ...·ko *dal*·ko sa·*das*·ya hũ	म ...को दलको सदस्य हुँ

communist	*sahm*·ya·bah·di	साम्यबादी
conservative	pu·rah·tan·*bah*·di	पुरातनबादी
green	*ha*·ri·yo	हरियो
social democratic	sah·*mah*·jik pra·*jah*·tan·tra	सामाजिक प्रजातन्त्र
socialist	sa·*mahj*·bah·di	समाजबादी

I don't vote.
ma mat kha·*sahl*·di·na — म मत खसाल्दिन

In my country we have a (socialist) government.
me·ro *desh*·mah (sa·*mahj*·bah·di) *sar*·kahr cha — मेरो देशमा (समाजबादी) सरकार छ

Politicians are all the same.
rahj·*ni*·ti·gyã *sa*·bai *e*·kai ho — राजनीतिज्ञ सबै एकै हो

candidate's speech	u·*me*·da·bahr·ko *bhah*·saṇ	उमेदबारको भाषण
corrupt	*bhras*·ṭa	भ्रष्ट
counting of votes	mat *gan*·nu	मत गन्नु
democracy	pra·*jah*·tan·tra	प्रजातन्त्र
demonstration	ju·*lus*	जुलूस
... election	... cu·*nahb*	... चुनाब
local council	na·gar·*pah*·li·kah	नगरपालिका
regional	prah·*de*·shik	प्रादेशिक
national	*rah*·sṭri·ya	राष्ट्रिय
electorate	*mat*·dah·tah sa·*mu*·ha	मतदाता समूह
exploitation	*sho*·saṇ	शोषण
to legalise	*kah*·nu·ni *ah*·dhahr *di*·nu	कानुनी आधार दिनु
to legislate	*ni*·yam *nir*·mahṇ *gar*·nu	नियम निर्माण गर्नु
misogyny	ai·mai·*pra*·ti·ko *ghri*·ṇah	आईमाई प्रतिको घृणा
parliament	*sã*·sad	संसद
policy	*ni*·ti	नीति
political speech	*rahj*·nai·tik *bhah*·saṇ	राजनैतिक भाषण

polling	*mat*·dahn	मतदान
president	*rah*·sṭra·pa·ti	राष्ट्रपति
prime minister	pra·*dhahn man*·tri	प्रधानमन्त्री
racism	*jah*·ti·bahd	जातिबाद
rally	ja·*maht*	जमात
sexism	ai·mai·*pra*·ti·ko *ghri*·ṇah	आईमाई प्रतिको घृणा
strike	*haḍ*·tahl	हडताल
trade union	*kahm*·ko sa·*mi*·ti	कामको सिमित
unemployment	be·*kah*·ri	बेकारी
vote	mat	मत
to vote	mat kha·*sahl*·nu	मत खसाल्नु

environment

वातावरण

Does Nepal have a pollution problem?
ne·*pahl*·ko *du*·sit sa·*ma*·syah cha? नेपालको दुषित समस्या छ ?

Does Kathmandu have a recycling programme?
kahṭh·mah·*ḍãu*·ko ri·*sai*·kal *yo*·ja·nah cha? काठ्माडौंको रीसाईकल योजना छ ?

Is this recyclable?
yo ri·*sai*·kal *gar*·na *sa*·ki·ne *bas*·tu ho? यो रीसाईकल गर्न सकिने बस्तु हो ?

Are there any protected ... in Nepal?
ne·*pahl*·mah *ke*·hi ba·*cah*·ya·ko ... cha? नेपालमा केही बचाएको ... छ ?

Is this a protected ...?	yo ba·*cah*·ya·ko ... ho?	यो बचाएको ... हो ?
forest	ban	बन
park	u·*dyahn*	उद्यान
species	*bar*·ga	बर्ग

Where do you stand on ...?
...·bah·re ta·*paĩ*·ko bi·*cahr* ke ho? ...बारे तपाईको बिचार के हो ?

conservation	*sã*·ra·chaṇ	संरक्षण
deforestation	ban·bi·*nahs*	वन विनास
to dispose of	*phyãhk*·nu	फ्याक्नु
drought	*suk*·khah	सुक्खा
endangered species	*kha*·ta·rah·mah *par*·ne *bar*·ga	खतरामा पर्ने वर्ग
hunting	*shi*·kahr	शिकार
industrial pollution	au·*dyo*·gik *du*·sit	औद्योगिक दुषित
irrigation	*sĩ*·cai	सिंचाइ
pollution	*du*·sit	दुषित
recycling	ri·*sai*·kal	रीसाईकल
reservoir	*pah*·ni *po*·kha·ri	पानी पोखरी

staying in touch

नबिर्सनु

(Tomorrow) is my last day here.
(bho·li) *ya*·hãh *me*·ro *an*·tim din ho — (भोलि) यहाँ मेरो अन्तिम दिन हो

Let's swap addresses.
hahm·ro ṭhe·*gah*·nah *sah*·ṭaũ — हाम्रो ठेगाना साटौं

Do you have a pen and paper?
ta·*paĩ*·sã·ga *ka*·lam ra *kah*·gaj cha? — तपाईसंग कलम र कागज छ ?

Do you have an email address?
ta·*paĩ*·ko *i*·mel ṭhe·*gah*·nah cha? — तपाईको ईमेल ठेगाना छ ?

What's your (email) address?
ta·*paĩ*·ko (*i*·mel) ṭhe·*gah*·nah ke ho? — तपाईको (ईमेल) ठेगाना के हो ?

Here's my (email) address.
yo *me*·ro (*i*·mel) ṭhe·*gah*·nah ho — यो मेरो (ईमेल) ठेगाना हो

Do you have access to a fax machine?
ta·*paĩ* phyahks *gar*·na *sa*·kin·cha? — तपाईकहाँ फ्याक्स गर्न सकिन्छ ?

If you ever visit (Scotland), please come and visit us.

ta·*paĩ* (is·*kaṭ*·laĩḍ)·mah *ah*·yo *bha*·ne, *hah*·mi·lai *bheṭ*·na *au*·nu·hos — तपाई (इस्कट्लैंड)मा आयो भने, हामीलाई भेट्न आउनुहोस

If you come to (Birmingham), you have a place to stay.

ta·*paĩ (bahr*·ming·ham)·mah *ah*·yo *bha*·ne, ta·*paĩ*·lai bahs *hun*·cha — तपाई (बर्मिंगहाम)मा आयो भने, तपाईलाई बास हुन्छ

I'll send you copies of the photos.

ma ta·*paĩ*·lai *tas*·bir pa·*ṭhaun*·chu — म तपाईलाई तस्बीर पठाउँछु

Don't forget to write!

ma·lai *ci*·thi pa·*ṭhau*·na na·*bir*·sa·nu·hos! — मलाई चिठ्ठी पठाउन नबिर्सनुहोस !

It's been great meeting you.

ma·lai ta·*paĩ*·sã·ga *bhe*·ṭe·ko·mah *rahm*·ro *lahg*·yo — मलाई तपाईसँग भेटेकोमा राम्रो लाग्यो

Keep in touch!

ma·lai na·*bir*·sa·nu·hos! — मलाई निबसर्नुहोस !

Trekking & Mountaineering
ट्रेकिंग गर्नु र पहाड चढ्नु

Nepal is well known for having some of the best trekking in the world. Naturally, most trekking areas are remote, and the Nepalese who live in the mountains and high valleys are still more traditional than those in Kathmandu and other towns. Most people you meet while trekking will speak Nepali, even if it's not their first language.

The hillpeople are generally devout and observant of local customs, which are deeply rooted in their religion, a harmonious mixture of Hinduism, Buddhism and ancient Tantrism. As you walk along you'll come across holy buildings, stupas (white domes with prayer flags) and walls of prayer stones. Always walk around these clockwise, keeping them on your right as you pass.

requesting information
जानकारी सोध्नु

Where can I find out about trekking trails in the region?

yo *che*·tra·mah, *ṭre*·king *bah*·ṭo·ko *jahn*·kah·ri *ka*·hãh *pain*·cha? — यो क्षेत्रमा, ट्रेकिंग बाटोको जानकारी कहाँ पाइन्छ ?

I'd like to talk to someone who knows this area.

ma·lai yo *che*·tra·ko·bah·re *thah*·ha *hu*·ne *mahn*·che·sã·ga *ku*·rah *gar*·na man *lahg*·yo — मलाई यो क्षेत्रकोबारे थाह हुने मान्छेसँग कुरा गर्न मन लाग्यो

did you know ...

Eight of the world's 14 highest mountains are found in Nepal and its northern frontier is the mighty Himalaya (which is pronounced with the stress on the second, not third, syllable: hi·mah·la·ya).

bed & breakfast

If you order an evening meal on less popular trekking routes, the price quoted to you traditionally includes accommodation for the night.

Where can I hire mountain gear?
pa·*hahḍ caḍh*·ne *sah*·mahn *ka*·hãh *bhah*·ḍah·mah *li*·ne? — पहाड चढ्ने सामान कहाँ भाडामा लिने ?

Where can we buy supplies?
cah·hi·ne *sah*·mahn *ka*·hãh *kin*·ne? — चाहिने सामान कहाँ किन्ने ?

Is it safe to climb this mountain?
yo pa·*hahḍ caḍh*·na su·*ra*·chit cha? — यो पहाड चढ्न सुरक्षित छ ?

Do I need a guide?
bah·ṭo de·*khau*·nu·par·cha? — बाटो देखाउनु पर्छ ?

Are you going by yourself?
ta·*paĩ ek*·lai *jah*·ne? — तपाई एक्लै जाने ?

How long is the trail?
bah·ṭo *ka*·ti *lah*·mo cha? — बाटो कति लामो छ ?

Is the track (well-)marked?
bah·ṭo·mah *(rahm*·ro·sã·ga) *ci*·no la·*gah*·ya·ko cha? — बाटोमा (राम्रोसँग) चिनो लगाएको छ ?

How high is the climb?
ka·ti *u*·co *caḍh*·nu·par·cha? — कति उचाइ चढ्नुपर्छ ?

Is there a lodge up there?
u *mah*·thi laj cha? — माथि लज छ ?

Can I get there on foot?
tya·hãh hĩ·*ḍe*·ra *jah*·na *sa*·kin·cha? — त्यहाँ हिंडेर जान सकिन्छ ?

Which is the shortest/easiest route?
sab·bhan·dah *cho*·ṭo/*sa*·ji·lo *bah*·ṭo kun ho? — सबभन्दा छोटो/सजिलो बाटो कुन हो ?

Is the path open?
bah·ṭo *kho*·le·ko cha? — बाटो खोलेको छ ?

When does it get dark?
ka·ti *be*·lah ã·*dhyah*·ro *hun*·cha? कति बेला अँध्यारो हुन्छ ?

Is it very scenic?
dri·shya *rahm*·ro cha? दृश्य राम्रो छ ?

hiring porters

भरिया लिनु

It's well worth the relatively small expense of hiring a guide or porter, *bha*·ri·yah (भरिया), as you learn much more about the area and you could practise your new-found language skills with your companions. You'll also get cheaper rates.

Excuse me, will you go with me to ...?
e, ta·*paĩ ma*·sã·ga ...·sam·ma *jah*·nu·hun·cha? ए, तपाई मसँग ...सम्म जानुहुन्छ ?

How long will it take, to get there and back?
jah·na, *au*·na, *ka*·ti sa·*ma*·ya *lahg*·cha? जान, आउन, कति समय लाग्छ ?

How much are you asking?
ta·*paĩ ka*·ti *li*·nu·hun·cha? तपाई कति लिनुहुन्छ ?

With/Without food?
khah·nah *sa*·met/*bah*·hek? खाना समेत/बाहेक ?

With/Without a load?
bhah·ri *sa*·met/*bah*·hek? भारी समेत/बाहेक ?

guides v. porters

Trekking guides and porters carry out different roles. A guide will know the trails, speak English, arrange accommodation and supervise porters, but will not carry a load or cook. In addition to carrying a load, versatile porters sometimes act as guides and cook too.

I'll give you ... rupees per day.
ma ta·*paĩ*·lai *din*·ko ... ru·*pi*·yãh *din*·chu — म तपाईलाई दिनको ... रुपियाँ दिन्छु

We'll leave on (Monday at 10 am).
hah·mi (*som*·bahr, das *ba*·je) *jahn*·chaũ — हामी (सोमबार, दस बजे) जान्छौं

We'll meet at (Tatopani).
(tah·to·*pah*·ni)·mah *bheṭ*·ne — (तातोपानी)मा भेट्ने

asking directions

बाटो सोध्नु

To get your bearings along the way, you'll probably need to ask directions, the names of villages and distances. It's better to ask 'Which is the way to ...?' rather than 'Is this the way to ...?' as people would hate you to feel lost and so will usually answer 'yes' to the second question, whether it's true or not!

Distances are often measured in kos (कोस): one *kos* is about three kilometres. If the answer is *du*·i kos (दुइ कोस), two *kos*, this is not literally true but a common expression meaning 'not far'.

Which is the way to (Lukla)?
(luk·lah) *jah*·ne *bah*·ṭo kun ho? — (लुक्ला) जाने बाटो कुन हो ?

Does this path go to ...?
yo *bah*·ṭo ...·mah *jahn*·cha? — यो बाटो ...मा जान्छ ?

What's the next village?
au·ne *gaũ*·ko nahm ke ho? — आउने गाउँको नाम के हो ?

How far is it to ...?
... *ka*·ti *ṭah*·ḍhah cha? — ... कति टाढा छ ?

Which direction?
kun *di*·shah? — कुन दिशा ?

I'm lost.
ma ha·*rah*·yẽ — म हराएँ

Are there any tourist attractions near here?
ya·hãh *ka*·tai par·*ya*·ṭak shu·bha·*dar*·shan cha? — यहाँ कतै पर्यटक शुभदर्शन छ ?

parks & plains

Nepal has a good number of national parks, plus wildlife reserves, conservation areas and hunting reserves. The best-known for tourism are the Sagarmatha National Park and Annapurna Conservation Area Project (ACAP) in the mountains, and the Royal Chitwan National Park in the Terai plains bordering India. All parks and reserves maintain a careful balance between the conservation of animals and environment and people's needs.

May I cross your property?
ma ta·*paĩ*·ko *jag*·gah·bah·ṭa *jah*·na *hun*·cha? — म तपाईको जग्गाबाट जान हुन्छ ?

Can we go through here?
hah·mi *ya*·hãh·bah·ṭa *jah*·na *hun*·cha? — हामी यहाँबाट जान हुन्छ ?

Can I swim here?
ya·hãh *pau*·ḍi *khel*·na *sa*·kin·cha? — यहाँ पौडी खेल्न सकिन्छ ?

Where have you come from?
ka·hãh·bah·ṭa *au*·nu *bha*·ya·ko? — कहाँबाट आउनु भएको ?

From (Pokhara).
(*po*·kha·rah)·bah·ṭa — (पोखरा)बाट

How long did it take you?
ta·*paĩ*·lai *ka*·ti sa·*ma*·ya *lahg*·yo? — तपाईलाई कति समय लाग्यो ?

How many hours/days?
ka·ti *ghaṇ*·ṭah/din? — कति घण्टा/दिन ?

It takes us (three) hours.
hah·mi·lai (tin) *ghaṇ*·ṭah *lahg*·cha — हामीलाइ (तिन) घण्टा लाग्छ

For you, it'll take (four to five) hours.
ta·*paĩ*·lai (cahr·*pãhc*) *ghaṇ*·ṭah *lahg*·cha — तपाईलाई (चार पाँच) घण्टा लाग्छ

downward	*ta*·la·ti·ra	तलतिर
downhill	o·*rah*·lo	ओरालो
steep downhill	bhi·*rah*·lo	भिरालो
level	*ter*·so	तेस्रो
straight ahead	*si*·dhah	सिधा
this side	*wah*·ri	वारी
that side	*pah*·ri	पारी
upward	*mahs*·ti·ra	मास्तिर
uphill	u·*kah*·lo	उकालो
steep uphill	*ṭhah*·ḍo	ठाडो

on the path

बाटोमा

Where can I spend the night?
bahs *bas*·na *ka*·hãh *pain*·cha? बास बस्न कहाँ पाइन्छ ?

Can I leave some things here for a while?
me·ro *sah*·mahn *ya*·hãh *choḍ*·na *sak*·chu? मेरो सामान यहाँ छोड्न सक्छु ?

There are (three) of us.
hah·mi (tin) *ja*·nah chaũ हामी (तीन) जना छौं

Do you provide meals?
khah·nah *paun*·cha? खाना पाउँछ ?

What kind of food?
ke *khah*·nah *paun*·cha? के खाना पाउँछ ?

Is this water OK to drink?
yo *pah*·ni *khah*·nu·hun·cha? यो पानी खानुहुन्छ ?

I have to rest.
ma·lai *ah*·rahm *li*·nu·par·cha मलाई आराम लिनुपर्छ

Let's sit in the shade.
shi·tal *ṭhaũ*·mah *ba*·saũ शीतल ठाउँमा बसौं

I need to go to the toilet. (urinate/defecate)
ma·lai *pi*·sahb/*di*·sah *lahg*·yo मलाई पिसाब/दिसा लाग्यो

Please ask about ...	...·bah·re *sodh*·nu·hos	...बारे सोध्नुहोस
boiled water	u·*mah*·le·ko *pah*·ni	उमालेको पानी
bread	*ro*·ṭi	रोटी
food	*khah*·nah	खाना
tea	*ci*·yah	चिया
Please give me ...	*ma*·lai ... *di*·nu·hos	मलाई ... दिनुहोस
cooked rice	bhaht	भात
lentils	dahl	दाल
liquor	*rak*·si	रक्सी
rice beer	chyahng	छयाङ्ग
shelter	bahs	बास
tobacco	*sur*·ti	सुर्ती
vegetables	tar·*kah*·ri	तरकारी
Where's the ...?	... *ka*·hāh cha?	... कहाँ छ ?
bridge	pul	पुल
inn	*bhaṭ*·ṭi	बत्ती
resting place tree	cau·*tah*·rah	चौतारा
statue	*mur*·ti	मुर्ति
teashop	*ci*·yah *pa*·sal	चिया पसल
village	gaũ	गाउँ
Do you have (a) ...?	ta·*paĩ*·sā·ga ... cha?	तपाईसँग ... छ ?
bag	*jho*·lah	झोला
carry basket	*ḍo*·ko	डोको
firewood	*dau*·rah	दाउरा
knife	*cak*·ku	चक्कु
Nepalese knife	*khu*·ku·ri	खुकुरी
stove	sṭobh	स्टोभ
What time are you ...?	*ka*·ti *ba*·je ...?	कति बजे ... ?
getting up	*uṭh*·ne	उठ्ने
going to sleep	*sut*·na *jah*·ne	सुत्न जाने
altitude	*uc*·cai	उचाई
binoculars	*dur*·bin	दूरबीन
camping	*shi*·bir	शिविर
candles	*main*·bat·ti	मैनबत्ती
compass	di·shah·*su*·cak *yan*·tra	दिशासूचक यन्त्र

flashlight	ṭarc	टर्च
gloves	*pan*·jah	पन्जा
guide	*bah*·ṭo de·*khau*·ne *mahn*·che	बाटो देखाउने मान्छे
hunting	*shi*·kahr	शिकार
ledge	cheu	छेउ
lookout	dau	दाउ
map	*nak*·sah	नक्सा
mountain climbing	pa·*hahḍ caḍh*·ne	पहाड चढ्ने
pickaxe	*gaĩ*·ti	गैंती
provisions	*khah*·dya *sah*·ma·gri	खाद्य सामाग्री
rope	*ḍo*·ri	डोरी
signpost	sang·ket·*cin*·ha	संकेत चिन्ह
trekking	*pai*·dal *yah*·trah	पैदल यात्रा

camping

शिविर गर्नु

Independent camping is uncommon and there are few public camping grounds. However, people may allow you to set up a tent on their property. Many trekking companies have their own sites, which aren't generally available to independent travellers.

Is there a camp site nearby?
ya·hãh *ke*·hi *shi*·bir *na*·jik cha? यहाँ केही शिविर नजिक छ ?

Am I allowed to camp here?
ya·hãh *shi*·bir *gar*·nu·hun·cha? यहाँ शिविर गर्नुहुन्छ ?

Who owns this land?
yo *jag*·gah *kas*·ko ho? यो जग्गा कस्को हो ?

Can I talk to him/her?
ma·lai *wa*·hãh·sã·ga *ku*·rah *gar*·na *sak*·chu? मलाई वहाँसँग कुरा गर्न सक्छु ?

Are there shower facilities?
snahn *kak*·sha cha? स्नान कक्ष छ ?

toilet training

All villages have a communal pit toilet, a *car*·pi (चर्पी), which trekkers are welcome to use. If you do need to go outside, keep well away from water sources and out of sight. Dig a hole, and burn your toilet paper, as nothing looks worse than piles of paper littering the landscape! The Nepalese don't use toilet paper, they use a waterjug, lo·tah (लोता), and their left hand, which is not used for anything else (giving or receiving, shaking hands or eating!)

Where can I hire a tent?
pahl *ka*·hãh *bhah*·ḍah·mah *pain*·cha? — पाल कहाँ भाडामा पाइन्छ ?

I want to hire a ...	*ma*·lai ... *bhah*·ḍah·mah *cah*·hi·yo	मलाई ... भाडामा चाहियो
backpack	*jho*·lah	झोला
sleeping bag	*sut*·ne *jho*·lah	सुत्ने झोला
stove	sṭobh	स्टोभ
tent	pahl	पाल

weather

मौसम

What's the weather like?
mau·sam *kas*·to cha? — मौसम कस्तो छ ?

The weather is ... today.
ah·ja *mau*·sam ... cha — आज मौसम ... छ

Will it be ... (tomorrow)?	(*bho*·li) *mau*·sam ... *ho*·lah?	(भोलि) मौसम ... होला ?
bad	kha·*rahb*	खराब
cloudy	*bad*·li	बदली
cold	*jah*·ḍo	जाडो
foggy	ku·*i*·ro	कुहिरो
frosty	tu·*sah*·ro	तुसारो

good	*rahm*·ro	राम्रो
hot	*gar*·mi	गर्मी
humid	*bahs*·pi·ya	वाष्पिय
rainy	*pah*·ni *par*·cha	पानी पर्छ
sunny	gha·*mai*·lo	घमाईलो
windy	*hah*·wah *lahg*·ne	हावा लाग्ने

It's raining heavily.	*pah*·ni *ek*·dam *par*·dai·cha	पानी एकदम पर्दैछ
It's raining lightly.	*pah*·ni *a*·li *a*·li *par*·dai·cha	पानी अलिअलि पर्दैछ
It's flooding.	*bah*·ḍhi *aun*·cha	बाढी आउँछ

blizzard	*hiũ*·ko *ãh*·dhi	हिउँको आँधी
climate	hah·wah·*pah*·ni	हावापानी
cloud	*bah*·dal	बादल
ice	*ba*·raph	बरफ
lightning	*bi*·ju·li *cam*·kai	बिजुली चम्काई
mud	*hi*·lo	हिलो
rainbow	in·*dre*·ni	इन्द्रेनी
sky	*ah*·kahsh	आकाश
snow	hiũ	हिउँ
storm	*hu*·ri	हुरी
sun	*sur*·ya	सुर्य
thunder	*gar*·jan	गर्जन

banyan reunion

Along trails and in villages, you'll come across a kind of community resting or meeting place, made by building rocks and stones into a comfortable seating area at the base of a large, shady banyan or peepal tree. This is called a cau•*tah*•rah (चौतारा) and the locals will be more than happy for you to join them there. The resting areas are easy to recognise and are commonly referred to when giving directions. One of the most well-known cau•*tah*•rahs is in New Road, Kathmandu (where newspaper sellers, shoe-shiners and camera shops are found).

seasons

ऋतुहरू

summer	*gar*·mi *mau*·sam	गर्मी मौसम
autumn	*sha*·rad *ri*·tu	शरद ऋतु
winter	*jah*·ḍo *ma*·hi·nah	जाडो महीना
spring	*ba*·san·ta *ri*·tu	बसन्त ऋतु
monsoon	*bar*·khah	वर्षायुक्त
rainy season	*bar*·saht	वर्षात

geographical terms

भौगोलिक शब्द

beach	ba·*lau*·ṭe ki·*nahr*	बलौटे किनार
bridge	pul	पुल
cave	*gu*·phah	गुफा
cliff	bhir	भीर
creek	*kho*·lah	खोला
earthquake	bhuĩ·*cah*·lo	भूईंचालो
farm	*khet*·bah·ri	खेतबारी
footpath	*go*·re·ṭo	गोरेटो
forest	ban	बन
gap	*khah*·li ṭhaũ	खालि ठाउँ
hanging bridge	*jho*·lung·ge pul	झुलुङ्गे पुल
hill	*ḍãh*·ḍah	डाँडा
hot spring	*tah*·to *pah*·ni mul	तातो पानी मूल
island	*ṭah*·pu/dwip	टापु/द्वीप
jungle	ban	बन
lake	tahl	ताल
landslide	*pa*·hi·ro	पहिरो
mountain	pa·*hahḍ*	पहाड
mountain path	pa·*hah*·ḍi *bah*·ṭo	पहाडी बाटो
high mountain path	hi·*mahl*·ko *bah*·ṭo	हिमालको बाटो
pass	*bhan*·jyahng	भन्ज्याङ
narrow pass	*sãh*·ghu·ro *bhan*·jyahng	साँघुरो भन्ज्याङ

trekking & mountaineering

peak	*cu*·*cu*·ro	चुचुरो
plains	*ma*·desh/ta·*rai*	मदेश/तराई
pond	*po*·kha·ri	पोखरी
river	*na*·di	नदी
scenery	*dri*·shya	दृश्य
sea	sa·*mu*·dra	समुद्र
snow peak	hi·*mahl*	हिमाल
trail	*sah*·no *bah*·ṭo	सानो बाटो
valley	u·*pa*·tya·kah	उपत्यका
waterfall	*jhar*·nah	झरना

fauna

जनावरहरू

Nepal's national animal is the cow, which is sacred in Hinduism.

What's that animal called?
tyo ja·*nah*·war·lai ke *bhan*·cha? त्यो जनावरहरु के भन्छ ?

bat	*ca*·me·ro	चमेरो
bear	*bhah*·lu	भालु
buffalo	*rãh*·gah/ *bhaĩ*·si **(m/f)**	राँगा/ भैंसी
camel	ũṭ	ऊँट
cat	bi·*rah*·lo	बिरालो
cobra	*go*·man	गौमन
cow	gai	गाई
crocodile	*go*·hi	गोही
deer	*mri*·ga/*ha*·riṇ	मृग/हरिण
black buck	*nil*·gai	निलगाई
musk	*kas*·tu·ri *mri*·ga	कस्तूरी मृग
sambar	*sahm*·bahr	सामबार
spotted	*ci*·tal	चितल
dog	*ku*·kur	कुकुर
donkey	*ga*·dhah	गधा
eel	bahm	बाम
elephant	*haht*·ti	हात्ती
fish	*mah*·chah	माछा

fox	*phyau*·ro	फ्याउरो
frog	*bhyah*·gu·to	भ्यागुतो
goat	*bahkh*·ro	बाख्रा
castrated goat	*kha*·si	खसी
horse	*gho*·ḍah	घोडा
jackal	syahl	स्याल
leopard	*ci*·tu·wah	चितुवा
snow leopard	*se*·to *ci*·tu·wah	सेतो चितुवा
lion	*sĩ*·ha	सिंह
lizard	che·*pah*·ro	छेपारो
mole	chu·*cun*·dro	छुचुन्द्रो
mongoose	*nyau*·ri *mu*·sah	न्याउरी मूसा
monkey	*bãh*·dar	बाँदर
mouse	*mu*·sah	मूसा
mouse hare	*pi*·kah	पीका
otter	õt	ओंत
ox	*go*·ru	गोरु
pig	*sũ*·gur	सुँगुर
porcupine	*dum*·si	दुम्सी
rabbit	kha·*rah*·yo	खरायो
rat	*mu*·sah	मूसा
red panda	*rah*·to *pahṇ*·ḍah	रातो पाण्डा
rhinoceros	*gaĩ*·ḍah	गैंडा
sheep	*bhẽ*·ḍah	भेंडा
snake	*sar*·pa	सर्प
squirrel	*lo*·khar·ke	लोखर्के
tiger	bahgh	बाघ
tortoise/turtle	*ka*·chu·wah	कछुवा
wolf	*bwãh*·so	ब्वाँसो
yak	*caũ*·ri·gai	चौरीगाई
yeti	*ye*·ti	यती

insects

कीराहरू

ant	ka·*mi*·lah	कमिला
bee	*mau*·ri	मौरी
butterfly	*pu*·ta·li	पुतली

cockroach	*sãhng*·glo	साङ्लो
flea	u·*pi*·yãh	उपियाँ
fly	*jhĩ*·gah	झिंगा
leech	*ju*·kah	जुका
louse	*jum*·rah	जुम्रा
mosquito	*lahm*·khuṭ·ṭe	लामखुट्टे
scorpion	*bic*·chi	बिच्छी
snail	*shã*·kha·ki·rah	शंखकिरा
spider	*mah*·ku·rah	माकुरा
tick	*kir*·no	किर्नो
worm	*ki*·rah	कीरा

birds

चराहरू

chicken	*ku*·khu·rah	कुखुरा
crane	*sah*·ras	सारस
crow	kahg	काग
cuckoo	*koi*·li	कोइली
dove	*dhu*·kur	ढुकुर
duck	hãhs	हाँस
eagle	cil	चील
falcon	bahj	बाज
hen	*ku*·khu·ri	कुखुरी
heron	ba·*kul*·lah	बकुल्ला
kite	cil	चील
mynah	*mai*·nah	मैना
owl	*ul*·lu	उल्लु
parrot	*su*·gah	सुगा

did you know ...

Nepal is home to over 800 bird species, which is close to 10% of the global total. The Royal Chitwan National Park is one of the top ten places for bird-watching in the world. Nepal's national bird is the *dãh*·phe (डाँफे), 'Impeyan pheasant', a rare bird found in the high Himalaya.

peacock	ma·*yur*	मयुर
pheasant	*kah*·lij	कालिज
pigeon	*pa*·re·wah	परेवा
stork	*dha*·nesh/*nil*·ca·rah	धनेश/नीलचरा
vulture	*gid*·dha	गिद्ध

flora & agriculture

फूल र खेतीपाती

What tree/flower is that?
tyo rukh/phul ke ho? त्यो रूख/फूल के हो ?

What's it used for?
tyo *ke*·ko *lah*·gi u·pa·*yuk*·ta cha? त्यो केको लागि उपयुक्तछ ?

Can you eat the fruit?
tyas·ko phul *khah*·nu·hun·cha? त्यस्को फूल खानुहुन्छ ?

banyan	*bar*·ko rukh	बरको रूख
cedar	*de*·wa·dahr	देवदार
chestnut	*ka*·ṭus rukh	कटुस रूख
deodar	*de*·wa·dahr	देवदार
elephant grass	*haht*·ti ghãhs	हात्तीघाँस
grassland	*phahn*·tah	फान्ता
juniper	dhu·pi·*sal*·lah	धुपीसल्ला
peepal	*pi*·pal	पीपल
pine	*sal*·lah·ko rukh	सल्लाको रूख
rosewood	*gu*·lahph·ko rukh	गुलाफको रूख
sal	sahl	साल

herbs, flowers & crops

जडीबुटी, फूल र बाली

Nepal's national flower is the red rhododendron lah·li·*gu*·rãhs (लालीगुँरास), which grows in the Himalaya.

agriculture	*khe*·ti·pah·ti	खेतीपाती
bamboo	bãhs	बाँस

barley	jau	जौ
branch	*hãh*·gah	हाँगा
bush (bushland)	*jhah*·di	झाडी
bush (shrub)	boṭ	बोट
corn	*ma*·kai	मकै
crops	*bah*·li	बाली
fern	*un*·yu	उन्यू
flower	phul	फूल
harvest (n)	*bah*·li·nah·li	बालीनाली
irrigation	*sĩ*·cai	सिूचाइ
jasmine	*ca*·me·li	चमेली
leaf	paht	पात
marigold	*sa*·ya·pa·tri phul	सयपत्री फूल
millet	*ko*·do	कोदो
orchard	*vah*·ṭi·kah	वाटिका
orchid	*ar*·kiḍ	अर्किट
poinsettia	lah·li·*pah*·te	लालीपाते
rhododendron	*gu*·rãhs	गुँरास
red rhododendron	lah·li·*gu*·rãhs	लालीगुँरास
rice field/paddy	*dhahn*·bah·ri	धानबारी
stick	*laṭh*·ṭhi	लठ्ठी
sugar cane	*u*·khu	उखु
terraced land	*ga*·rah	गरा
tobacco	*sur*·ti	सुतीर्
tree	rukh	रूख
wheat	*ga*·hũ	गहुँ
wood	kahṭh	काठ

SOCIAL

In larger towns, especially Kathmandu, restaurants serve all kinds of dishes, including a wide range of Western-style food. In the countryside and on trekking routes, however, only a few different food items will be available at any time of year.

The most typical Nepali meal is dahl bhaht tar·*kahri* (दाल भात तरकारी) – lentils, boiled rice and vegetable curry. Curries are usually mild, but often served with a fresh pickle or relish, a·*cahr* (अचार), which may be spicy, *pi*·ro (पिरो). If you don't want spicy food, request *pi*·ro na·*hahl*·nu·hos (पिरो नहाल्नुहोस). Potatoes, corn, millet and other carbohydrates are also staple foods up in the hills.

through the day

दिनभरि

In Nepal, eating two meals a day is the norm: one late in the morning around 10 or 11 am and the second at 7 or 8 pm, with just a glass of tea (and perhaps a sweet snack) first thing. In less touristy

one essential word

The verb *khah*·nu (खानु), 'to eat', is also commonly used for drinking and smoking:

I eat rice/food.
ma bhaht *khahn*·chu — म भात खान्छु

I drink tea.
ma *ci*·yah *khahn*·chu — म चिया खान्छु

I don't smoke cigarettes.
ma *cu*·roṭ *khahn*·di·na — म चुरोट खाँदिन

areas, you may find it difficult to get a Western-style breakfast or much food before 10 am, or lunch after midday or so.

breakfast	bi·*hah*·na·ko *khah*·nah	बिहानको खाना
lunch	*ca*·me·nah	चमेना
dinner/food/meal	bhaht	भात
snack	*khah*·jah	खाजा

vegetarian & special meals

साकाहारी र विशेष खाना

Vegetarian meals are widely available, due to the fact that high-caste Hindus are traditionally vegetarian and meat is relatively scarce – although Newar cuisine is renowned for its many meat dishes. Dairy products are also uncommon, except for yogurt (which is a luxury food), so vegans will have few difficulties. Soy products apart from tofu are not often available.

I'm vegetarian.
ma sah·kah·*hah*·ri hũ — म साकाहारी हुँ

Do you have any vegetarian dishes?
ta·*paĩ*·ka·hãh sah·kah·*hah*·ri *khah*·nah cha? — तपाईकहाँ साकाहारी खाना छ ?

table manners

In Hindu Nepal, there are strict rules about keeping food and drink ritually pure and unpolluted. Food becomes 'contaminated', *jhu·ṭo* (जुठो), if touched by someone else's hand or mouth, or by a serving plate or utensil. So take care when handling food (only use your right hand), and remember sharing food from your plate (or someone else's) is a big no-no. You should also be careful not to contaminate a buffet table of food by placing your used plate on it. Nepalese people share a common drinking vessel (jug or cup) by tipping the water straight into their upturned mouths without touching. This is quite a skill!

Does this dish have (meat)?
yo *khah*·nah·mah *(mah*·su) cha? — यो खानामा (मासु) छ ?

Can I get this without (meat)?
yo *(mah*·su) na·*hah*·le·ko *paun*·cha? — यो (मासु) नहालेको पाउँछ ?

Does it contain (eggs)?
yo *khah*·nah·mah (phul) cha? — यो खानामा (फुल) छ ?

I'm allergic to (peanuts).
ma *(ba*·dahm) *khah*·nu *hun*·dai·na — म (बदाम) खानु हुन्दैन

I don't eat ...	ma ... *khahn*·di·na	मा ... खाँदिन
chicken	*ku*·khu·rah·ko *mah*·su	कुखुराको मासु
dairy products	*dudh*·ko *khah*·nah	दूधको खाना
fish	*mah*·chah	माछा
meat	*mah*·su	मासु
pork	*sũ*·gur·ko *mah*·su	सुगुरको मासु
spicy food	*pi*·ro	पिरो

snacks

खाजाहरू

Various snacks can be bought on Nepalese streets, mainly from mobile stalls. Most of these are cold snack-type food, except for the occasional evening stall selling fresh hot *mo*·mo (म:म:), which are like dim sims, wontons or dumplings. Fruit is mostly available at stalls and you can bargain. Street ice cream is not hygienically prepared and best avoided (although ice cream shops are OK). One favourite snack is a mix of dried peas, chickpeas and puffed rice, made up for you with onion, lemon and chilli to your taste, *bhu*·jah (भुजा). Another great street snack is corn on the cob, cooked over hot coals.

corn	*ma*·kai	मकै
ice cream	*khu*·wah *ba*·raph	खुवा बरफ
mixed dried peas	*bhu*·jah	भुजा
momo	*mo*·mo	म:म:
pappadam	*pah*·paḍ	पापड

a matter of taste		
bitter	*ti*·to	तीतो
hot (spicy)	*pi*·ro	पिरो
salty	nu·*ni*·lo	नुनीलो
sour	*a*·mi·lo	अमीलो
spicy	*pi*·ro	पिरो
stale	*bah*·si	बासी
sweet	*gu*·li·yo	गुलियो

peanuts	*ba*·dahm	बदाम
popcorn	*bhu*·ṭe·ko *ma*·kai	भुटेको मकै

eating out

बाहिर खानु

Restaurants in tourist areas have wildly ambitious menus offering all kinds of cuisine from Tibetan, Chinese and Thai to American, Italian, German and Mexican! However, the dish that actually arrives may not bear an exact resemblance to what you were expecting. These restaurants have little on offer when it comes to Nepalese food, although some do a set meal of curry, rice, dahl and pickle. In Kathmandu there are several high-priced restaurants that specialise in Nepalese and Newar food in traditional surroundings, some with entertainment as well. If it's within your budget, this experience is well worth it.

Waiter!
dah·jyu! **(man)**/bhai! **(boy)** — दाज्यू !/भाई !
di·di! **(woman)**/*ba*·hi·ni! **(girl)** — दिदी !/बिहनी !

A table for (five), please.
(pãhc) *ja*·nah·ko *lah*·gi *ṭe*·bul *di*·nu·hos — (पाँच) जनाको लागि टेबुल दिनुहोस

Please give me/us the menu.
men·yu *di*·nu·hos — मेन्यु दिनुहोस

Could you recommend something?
su·jhahb *di*·nu·hun·cha? सुझाब दिनुहुन्छ ?

I'll have what they're having.
u·ni·ha·ru·le ke *lin*·chan *ma*·lai *pa*·ni *te*·hi *di*·nu·hos उनीहरूले के लिन्छन मलाई पनि तेही दिनुहोस

What's in that dish?
tyo *pa*·ri·kahr·mah ke cha? त्यो परिकारमा के छ ?

Please give me (a little) ...	*(a*·li·ka·ti) ... *di*·nu·hos	(अलिकति) ... दिनुहोस
drinking water	*khah*·ne *pah*·ni	खाने पानी
rice	bhaht	भात
soup	*su*·ru·wah	सुरुवा

Please give me (a) ...	*ma*·lai ... *di*·nu·hos	मलाई ... दिनुहोस
cold beer	*ci*·so *bi*·yar	चिसो बियर
meal/food	*khah*·nah	खाना

Please bring me a/an/the ...	*ma*·lai ... *lyau*·nu·hos	मलाई ... ल्याउनुहोस
ashtray	*ahsh*·ṭre	आस्ट्रे
bill	bil	बिल
fork	*kãh*·ṭah	काँटा
glass of water	ek gi·*lahs pah*·ni	एक गिलास पानी
with ice	*ba*·raph·sã·ga	बरफसँग
without ice	*ba*·raph na·*hah*·le·ko	बरफ नहालेको
knife	*cak*·ku	चक्कु
plate	thahl	थाल

taxes & tips

As with accommodation, middle-priced and expensive restaurants charge government tax on top of the bill, while cheaper places usually don't bother. Tipping is not mandatory but will be greatly appreciated as wages are very low. Leave around 5% in budget restaurants and a bit more in others.

home truths

When invited into a private home always remove your shoes, leaving them outside the door or where everyone else leaves theirs.

Hindus, particularly those of high caste, don't usually eat in company and it's a great honour to be asked to share a meal. However, the Newars of Kathmandu and most hill people are mainly Buddhists and don't place so much emphasis on privacy. All Nepalese are generally very sociable and love a good feast. But don't be too surprised if you're the only person eating or if the women don't participate in the meal except to serve it.

Remember that there are strict rules about food in Nepal (more on page 162). It's important to wash or rinse your right hand and your mouth before sitting down – and again after eating – for both etiquette and hygiene. Don't touch your mouth to a common drinking vessel and wait to be served food rather than serving yourself. You'll often be treated as an honoured guest and your plate refilled (several times) without your asking!

When sharing a meal, you usually sit on a mat on the floor with your legs crossed. You eat from a dish placed on the floor, using your right hand only. You can use your left hand to hold a glass.

Do I get it myself or do they bring it to me?
ah·phai *li*·ne ki *be*·rah·le *lyaun*·cha? — आफै लिने कि बेराले ल्याउँछ ?

What's this/that?
yo/tyo ke ho? — यो/ त्यो के हो ?

I'm hungry/thirsty.
ma·lai bhok/*tir*·khah *lahg*·yo — मलाई भोक/तिर्खा लाग्यो

No ice in my drink, please.
me·ro *pahn*·mah *ba*·raph na·*hahl*·nu·hos — मेरो पानी बरफ नहाल्नुहोस

typical dishes पक्का परिकारहरु

a·cahr अचार
freshly made pickle or relish, served with curry and made from vegetables such as tomato, potato or radish; often spicy

ah·lu *kau*·li आलु काउली
potato and cauliflower curry

ah·lu *tah*·mah आलु तामा
popular soup-like dish made from potatoes, bamboo shoots and beans

bhu·ṭu·wah भुटुवा
fried meat curry, usually goat or water buffalo (all meat in Nepal comes from castrated male animals)

cau·cau चाउचाउ
fried noodles with meat and/or vegetables

cyu·rah च्यूरा
flat, crunchy dried rice often eaten with snacks or at feasts instead of boiled rice

dahl bhaht tar·*kahri* दाल भात तरकारी
Nepal's national dish – lentils, rice and vegetable curry

gun·druk गुन्द्रुक
dried bitter mustard, radish or cauliflower leaves, served as a side dish or soup

mo·mo म:म:
very popular snack of meat or vegetable dumplings, steamed or fried, often served with tomato pickle; usually round but sometimes crescent-shaped and then called *ko*·the (कोथे) (Tibetan)

rah·yo·ko sahg रायोको साग
mustard greens

shel *ro*·ṭi शेल रोटी
fried rice-flour bread shaped like thin doughnuts

su·ku·ti सुकुति
fried air-dried meat (usually water buffalo)

newar dishes नेवारी खाना

bhu·tan भुतन
fried chopped intestines

ca·*tãh*·ma·ri चटामरी
rice-flour pancakes served with meat/egg filling or with a curry

chwe·lah छोएला
dish of boiled (sometimes grilled) spicy water buffalo

gwah·rah·ma·ri ग्वारामरी
deep-fried sweet dough balls (like doughnuts)

ka·ci·lah कचिला
raw, spiced minced water buffalo (like steak tartare)

kwah·ti क्वाति
soup of mixed beans (usually nine kinds)

mus·yah मुस्या
soybeans; served fresh as a side dish or roasted as a snack

se·ku·wah सेकुवा
roasted or grilled water buffalo

swã·pu·kah स्वँः पुका
stuffed fried goat lung

ta·khah त :खा
jellied meat (usually water buffalo)

wo/*bah*·ḍah व/बाडा
savoury patties made from mung or other beans ground into a wet paste, pan-fried (wo) or deep-fried (*bah*·ḍah)

How do you like the food?
khah·nah *kas*·to *lahg*·yo? खाना कस्तो लाग्यो ?

The meal was delicious.
khah·nah *mi*·ṭho *lahg*·yo खाना मीठो लाग्यो

The food isn't hot. (temperature)
khah·nah *tah*·to *chai*·na खाना तातो छैन

sweets	मिठाई
bar·phi soft, fudge-like sweet made from milk	बर्फी
je·ri/ju·*le*·bi large (*je*·ri) or small (ju·*le*·bi) orange flower-shaped sweets, deep-fried then soaked in sugar syrup	जेरी/जुलेबी
khir rice pudding	खिर
lad·du sweet yellow chickpea-flour balls, often used as an offering to the gods, especially Ganesh	लड्डु
lahl *mo*·han sweet, milky dough balls, deep-fried and then soaked in sugar syrup	लाल मोहन
si·*kar*·ni sweet yogurt pudding	सीकर्नी

I love this dish.
ma·lai yo *pa*·ri·kahr *ek*·dam man *par*·cha — मलाई यो परिकार एकदम मनपर्छ

We love the local cuisine.
hah·mi·lai swa·*de*·shi *khah*·nah *ek*·dam man *par*·cha — हामीलाई स्वदेशी खाना एकदम मन पर्छ

Our compliments to the chef.
bhahn·se·lai *hahm*·ro *tah*·riph *di*·nu·hos — भान्छेलाई हाम्रो तारीफ दिनुहोस

Is service included in the bill?
se·bah *bil*·sa·met ho? — सेबा बिलसमेत हो ?

at the market

बजारमा

Where's the weekly market?
haht ba·*jahr ka*·hãh cha? — हात बजार कहाँ छ ?

tibetan food	तिबेतको खाना

thuk·pah — थुक्पा
noodle soup with meat and/or vegetables

ti·*be*·tan *ci*·yah — तिबेतन चिया
Tibetan tea made in a churn with butter and salt

tsam·pah — त्सम्पा
barley or other flour, eaten mixed with milk, water or tea

tum·bah — तूम्बा
mildly alcoholic drink of fermented millet topped with hot water and served in a large wooden receptacle

When's the weekly market?
haht ba·*jahr ka*·hi·le *hun*·cha? — हात बजार कहिले हुन्छ ?

How much per kilo?
ek *ki*·lo·ko *ka*·ti ho? — एक किलोको कति हो ?

Do you have anything cheaper?
tyo·bhan·dah *sas*·to ke cha? — त्योभन्दा सस्तो के छ ?

What's the local speciality?
swa·de·shi bi·*shes*·tah ke ho? — स्वदेशी बिशेषता के हो ?

Give me (half a/one) kilo please.
ma·lai (*ah*·dhah/ek) *ki*·lo *di*·nu·hos — मलाई (आधा/एक) किलो दिनुहोस

I'd like (six slices of cheese).
ma·lai (cha *ṭuk*·rah cij) *cah*·hi·yo — मलाई (छ टुक्रा चीज) चाहियो

May I taste it?
ma·lai *cahkh*·na *paun*·cha? — मलाई चाख्न पाउँछ ?

That's all. How much is it?
te·ti *mah*·trai, *ka*·ti *bha*·yo? — त्यती मात्रै, कति भयो ?

Where can I find ...?	... *ka*·hãh *paun*·cha?	... कहाँ पाउँछ ?
I'd like some ...	*ma*·lai ... *cah*·hi·yo	मलाई ... चाहियो
bread (loaf)	*pau*·ro·ṭi	पाउरोटी
butter	*ma*·khan	मखन

cauliflower	*kau*·li	काउली
cheese	cij	चीज
chilli	khur·*sah*·ni	खुर्सानी
chocolate/candy	*cak*·leṭ	चक्लेट
eggs	phul	फुल
flour	*pi*·ṭho	पीठो
garlic	*la*·sun	लसुन
ginger	*a*·du·wah	अदुवा
ghee	ghi·*u*	घिउ
honey	*ma*·ha	मह
leafy greens	*sahg*·paht	सागपात
milk	dudh	दूध
oil	tel	तेल
pepper	*ma*·ric	मरिच
potato	*ah*·lu	आलु
rice (uncooked)	*cah*·mal	चामल
salt	nun	नुन
sugar	*ci*·ni	चिनी
tea leaves	*ci*·yah *pat*·ti	चिया पत्ती
yogurt	*da*·hi	दही

meat

मासु

Meat is scarce and expensive, and tends to be served mainly on festival days and other special occasions. Remember that in Hindu Nepal, cows are sacred and beef is not eaten (it's illegal). Popular meat includes buff (water buffalo), goat, chicken and yak.

beef	*gai*·ko *mah*·su	गाईको मासु
buff (water buffalo)	*rãh*·gah·ko *mah*·su	राँगाको मासु
chicken	*ku*·khu·rah·ko *mah*·su	कुखुराको मासु
dried meat	*su*·ku·ti	सुकुति
duck meat	*hãhs*·ko *mah*·su	हाँसको मासु
eel	bahm	बाम
(dried) fish	*(su*·ke·ko) *mah*·chah	(सुकेको) माछा
goat meat	*kha*·si·ko *mah*·su	खसीको मासु

lamb	*bhẽ*·ḍah·ko *mah*·su	भेंडाको मासु
liver	*ka*·le·jo·ko *mah*·su	कलेजोको मासु
mutton	*bhẽ*·ḍah·ko *mah*·su	भेंडाको मासु
pork	*sũ*·gur·ko *mah*·su	सुँगुरको मासु
prawn	*jhing*·ge *mah*·chah	झिङ्गे माछा
tongue	*ji*·bro	जिब्रो
venison	*mri*·ga·ko *mah*·su	मृगको मासु
yak meat	*caũ*·ri·gai·ko *mah*·su	चौरीगाईको मासु

vegetables

तरकारी

asparagus	*ku*·ri·lo	कुरिलो
bamboo shoot	*tah*·mah	तामा
beans	*si*·mi	सिमी
beetroot	cu·*kan*·dar	चुकन्दर
broad beans	*ba*·ku·lah	बकुला
cabbage	ban·dah·*ko*·bi	बन्दाकोबि
carrot	*gah*·jar	गाजर
cauliflower	*kau*·li	काउली
chilli	khur·*sah*·ni	खुर्सानी
choko squash	is·*kus*	स्कुस
corn	*ma*·kai	मकै
cucumber	*kãh*·kro	काँक्रो
eggplant (long)	*bhahṇ*·ṭah	भाण्टा
eggplant (ovoid)	*brin*·jal	ब्रीन्जल
garlic	*la*·sun	लसुन
green beans	*ha*·ri·yo *si*·mi	हरियो सिमी
green garlic	*ha*·ri·yo *la*·sun	हरियो लसुन
green/spring onion	*ha*·ri·yo pyahj	हरियो प्याज
green pepper	*bhẽ*·ḍah khur·*sah*·ni	भेंडा खुर्सानी
leafy greens	*sahg*·paht	सागपात
lettuce	*ji*·ri·ko sahg	जिरीको साग
mushroom	cyau	च्याउ
mustard greens	*rah*·yo·ko sahg	रायोको साग
nettles	*sis*·nu	सिस्नु
okra	rahm·*to*·ri·yah	रामतोरिया

table articles		
cup	kap	कप
dish/utensil	*bhãh*·ḍah	भाँडा
dishes/utensils	bhãh·ḍah·*kũ*·ḍah	भाँडाकुडा
glass	gi·*lahs*	गिलास
jug	su·*rah*·hi	सुराही
napkin/towel	ru·*mahl*	रुमाल
spoon	*cam*·cah	चम्चा
toothpick	*sin*·ko	सिन्को

onion	pyahj	प्याज
peas	*ke*·rau	केराउ
potato	*ah*·lu	आलु
pumpkin	*phar*·si	फर्सी
radish	*mu*·lah	मुला
spinach	pah·*lung*·go	पालुङ्गो
squash (bitter gourd)	ka·*re*·lo	करेलो
squash (long green)	*lau*·kah	लौका
squash (zucchini)	ghi·*raũ*·lo	घिरौंलो
sweet potato	*sa*·khar *khaṇ*·ḍa	सखर खण्ड
tomato	gol·*bhẽ*·ḍah	गोलभेंडा
turnip	*sal*·gam	सल्गम
yam	*ta*·rul	तरुल
zucchini	ghi·*raũ*·lo	घिरौंलो

cereal & legumes

दाल खालको अन्नहरू

barley	jau	जौ
buckwheat	*phah*·par	फापर
chickpea	*ca*·nah	चना
lentils (black)	*kah*·lo dahl	कालो दाल
lentils (brown)	*khai*·ro dahl	खैरो दाल
lentils (red)	*mu*·sur dahl	मुसुर दाल
lima beans	*ba*·ku·lah	बकुला
millet	*ko*·do	कोदो

oats	jai	जौ
red kidney beans	*rah*·to *su*·ke·ko *si*·mi	रातो सुकेको सिमी
rice (beaten)	*cyu*·rah	च्यूरा
rice (cooked)	bhaht	भात
rice (uncooked)	*cah*·mal	चामल
rice (unhusked)	dhahn	धान
semolina	*su*·ji	सुजि
soybeans	*bhaṭ*·mahs	भटमास
wheat	*ga*·hũ	गहुँ
white dried beans	*se*·to *su*·ke·ko *bo*·di	सेतो सुकेको बोदि

fruit & nuts

फलफूल र बदामहरू

almond	*ma*·di·se *ba*·dahm	मदिसे बदाम
apple	syau	स्याउ
apricot	khur·*pah*·ni	खुरपानी
banana	*ke*·rah	केरा
berry	*ba*·yar	बयर
betel nut	su·*pah*·ri	सुपारी
blueberry	*cu*·tro	चुत्रो
cashew	*kah*·ju	काजु
cherry	pai·*yũ*·khahl·ko phal	पैयुँखालको फल
coconut	*na*·ri·wal	नरिवल
custard apple	*sa*·riph	सरिफा
date (hard)	*kha*·jur	खजुर
date (soft)	cho·*ha*·rah	छोहरा
fig	*an*·jir	अंजीर
grape	*ã*·gur	अंगुर
grapefruit	*bho*·ga·ṭe	भोगटे
guava	*am*·bah	अम्बा
jackfruit	*rukh*·ka·ṭa·har	रूखकटहर
lapsi	*a*·mi·li	लप्सी
lemon	*kah*·ga·ti	कागती
lime	*jya*·mir	ज्यामीर
lychee	*li*·ci	लीची
mandarin	*sun*·ta·lah	सुन्तला

mango	ãhp	आँप
melon	*tar*·bu·jah	तरबुजा
orange	*sun*·ta·lah	सुन्तला
papaya	*me*·wah	मेवा
peach	*ah*·ru	आरु
peanut	*ba*·dahm	बदाम
pear	*nahs*·pah·ti	नास्पाती
persimmon	*ha*·lu·wah·bed	हलुवाबेद
pineapple	*bhuĩ*·ka·ṭa·har	भुईंकटहर
pistachio	*pis*·tah	पिस्ता
plum	ah·ru·*ba*·kha·ḍah	आरुबखडा
pomegranate	a·*nahr*	अनार
pomelo	*bho*·ga·ṭe	भोगटे
raisin	dahkh	दाख
raspberry	*ai*·sa·lu	ऐंसेलु
strawberry	kau·wah·*kah*·phal	कौवाकाफल
sweet lime	*mu*·sam	मौसम
walnut	*o*·khar	ओखर
watermelon	*khar*·bu·jah	खरबुजा

bread

रोटी

bread	*ro*·ṭi	रोटी
flat bread	ca·*pah*·ti	चपाती
deep fried bread	*pu*·ri	पुरी
loaf of bread	*pau*·ro·ṭi	पाउरोटी
flour	*pi*·ṭho	पीठो
chickpea flour	*be*·san	बेसन
fine wheat flour	*mai*·dah	मैदा
wholemeal flour	*aht*·tah	आत्ता

spices & condiments

मसलाहरू

aniseed	soph	सोंफ
asafoetida	hing	हिङ्ग

basil	*tul*·si	तुलसी
bay leaf	*tej*·paht	तेजपात
cardamom (black)	a·*laĩ*·ci	अलैंची
cardamom (green)	*su*·ku·mel	सुकुमेल
chilli	khur·*sah*·ni	खुर्सानी
chives	*chyah*·pi	छ्यापी
cinnamon	*dahl*·ci·ni	दाल्चिनी
cloves	lwahng	ल्वाङ्ग
coriander (dried)	*dha*·ni·yãh	धनीया
coriander (fresh)	*ha*·ri·yo *dha*·ni·yãh	हरियो धनिया
cumin	*ji*·rah	जीरा
fennel	soph	सोफ
fenugreek	*me*·ṭhi	मेथी
ginger (dried)	*su*·ṭho	सूठो
ginger (fresh)	*a*·du·wah	अदुवा
honey	*ma*·ha	मह
horseradish	*sar*·syu	सरस्युँ
jam	jahm	जाम
lapsi	*a*·mi·li	लप्सी
mango powder	*am*·cur	अम्चुर
mint	*bah*·ba·ri	बाबरी
mixed spice	*ga*·ram *ma*·sa·lah	गरम मसला
molasses	*cah*·ku/*khu*·do	चाक/खुदो
mustard oil	*to*·ri·ko tel	तोरीको तेल
mustard seed	*to*·ri·ko bi·*u*	तोरीको बिउ
nutmeg	*jai*·phal	जाईफल
oil	tel	तेल
parsley	*jwah*·nu	ज्वानो
peanut butter	*ba*·dahm·ko *ma*·khan	बदामको मखन
pepper(corn)	*ma*·ric	मरिच
pickle	a·*cahr*	अचार
... powder	...·ko *dhu*·lo	...को धूलो
saffron	*ke*·shar	केशर
salt	nun	नुन
sesame seeds	*til*·ko bi·*u*	तिलको बिउ
sugar (brown)	*sak*·kar	सख्खर
sugar (white)	*ci*·ni	चिनी
sugar cane	*u*·khu	उखु

tamarind	*a*·mi·li	अमिलो
turmeric	*be*·sahr	बेसार
vinegar	*sir*·khah	सीर्खा
yeast	*kham*·bir	खम्बीर

dairy products

दूधको खाना

butter	*ma*·khan	मखन
cheese	cij	चीज
cream	tar	तर
egg	phul/*aṇ*·ḍah	फुल/अण्डा
ghee	ghi·*u*	घिउ
ice cream	*khu*·wah *ba*·raph	खुवा बरफ
milk	dudh	दूध
yogurt (curd)	*da*·hi	दही

drinks

पिउने पदार्थहरु

There's a great variety of drinks available. Most water, however, is undrinkable unless boiled or treated with iodine (filtering alone is not sufficient). Local licensed bottlers produce the usual softdrinks, but the Nepalese speciality, lemon juice with (club) soda (and sugar or even salt), is much more refreshing!

hot drinks

तातो पिउने पदार्थहरु

As far as hot drinks go, Nepalese tea is always safe and available everywhere, while coffee is usually instant although coffee beans are grown locally and some places do serve real coffee. Hot chocolate is available and another local favourite is lemon juice with hot water, 'hot lemon', *tah*·to *pah*·ni·mah *kah*·ga·ti (तातो पानीमा कागती).

ci·yah चिया
Nepalese tea – hot, sweet and milky (cai in India)

ti·be·tan ci·yah तिबेतन चिया
Tibetan tea – made in a churn with butter and salt

black tea	*kah*·lo *ci*·yah	कालो चिया
lemon tea	*kah*·ga·ti *ci*·yah	कागती चिया
black coffee	*kah*·lo *ka*·phi	कालो कफी
milk coffee	dudh *ka*·phi	दूध कफी
hot chocolate	*tah*·to *cak*·leṭ	तातो चक्लेट

cold drinks चिसो पिउने पदार्थहरु

boiled water	u·*mah*·le·ko *pah*·ni	उमालेको पानी
fresh lemon juice	*kah*·ga·ti·ko ras	कागतीको रस
lemon soda	*so*·ḍah·mah *kah*·ga·ti	सोडामा कागती
water	*pah*·ni	पानी
yogurt drink (sweet or salty)	*la*·si	लस्सी

alcoholic drinks मादक पदार्थहरु

All kinds of alcohol are widely available, both locally-made and imported versions (which can be more expensive than at home). Except for some high castes, the Nepalese like a drink and their traditional drinks, including *rak*·si (रक्सी), the local firewater, are extremely cheap. Western-style bars serve beer and all kinds of cocktails.

chyahng छ्याङ
mildly alcoholic rice beer made at home (sometimes also from corn, barley or millet); also called jãhḍ (जाँड) in Nepali and thõ (थों) in Newari

rak·si रक्सी
local distilled liquor; can be very rough

bi·yar बियर
Western-style beer (many brands brewed locally)

tum·bah तून्बा
mildly alcoholic Tibetan drink of fermented millet topped with hot water, served in a large wooden receptacle

Nepal is still a relatively safe place to travel, although petty theft from rooms or bags (especially when they're on top of buses) is not uncommon. In main centres, there are special tourist police to help out or, in cases of serious difficulty, you can go to Police Headquarters in Kathmandu. Also take the time to register with your embassy or consulate.

Help!	gu·*hahr*!	गुहार !
Stop!	rok!	रोक !
Go away!	jau!	जाउ !
Thief!	cor!	चोर !
Fire!	*ah*·go!	आगो !
Watch out!	*he*·ra!	हेर !

It's an emergency.
ah·pat *bha*·yo — आपत्त भयो

There's been an accident.
dur·*gha*·ṭa·nah bha·yo — दुर्घटना भयो

Could you help me please?
ma·lai *mad*·dat *gar*·na *sak*·nu·hun·cha? — मलाई मद्दत गर्न सक्नुहुन्छ ?

Could I please use the telephone?
ma phon *gar*·na *sa*·kin·cha? — म फोन गर्न सकिन्छ ?

I'm lost.
ma ha·*rah*·yẽ — म हराएँ

Where's the toilet?
shau·*cah*·la·ya *ka*·hãh cha? — शौचालय कहाँ छ ?

police

प्रहरी

It's a good idea to get the name and position of the person you're speaking with, asking politely at the beginning. Give your own name first, and show some identification. Nepal has plenty of lawyers, but if you need extra help, it's probably best to contact your embassy or consulate first.

Call the police!
pra·*ha*·ri·lai bo·*lau*·nu·hos! — प्रहरीलाई बोलाउनुहोस !

Where's the police station?
ṭhah·nah *ka*·hāh cha? — थाना कहाँ छ ?

We want to report an offence.
hah·mi·lai dos ni·*be*·dan *rahkh*·nu·par·yo — हामीलाई दोष निबेदन राख्नुपर्यो

I've been raped.
ma·lai ba·*laht*·kahr *gar*·yo — मलाई बलत्कार गर्यो

I've been robbed.
cor·le *ma*·lai *luṭ*·yo — चोरले मलाई लुट्यो

They stole my ...	*us*·le *me*·ro ... *cor*·yo	उसले मेरो ... चोर्यो
I've lost my ...	*me*·ro ... ha·*rah*·yo	मेरो ... हरायो
bag/backpack	*jho*·lah	झोला
bags	*jho*·lah·ha·ru	झोलाहरु
camera	*kyah*·me·rah	क्यामरा
handbag	byahg	ब्याग
money	*pai*·sah	पैसा
papers	*kah*·gaj·pa·tra	कागजपत्र
passport	rah·ha·*dah*·ni	राहदानी
travellers cheques	*ṭrah*·bhlar cek	ट्राभलर चेक
wallet	*thai*·li	थैली

My possessions are insured.
me·ro *sah*·mahn·ko *bi*·mah cha — मेरो सामानको बिमा छ

SAFE TRAVEL

I'm sorry./I apologise.
ma·lai maph *gar*·nu·hos — मलाई माफ गर्नुहोस

I didn't realise I was doing something wrong.
ma·lai *thah*·hah *bha*·ya·na — मलाई थाहा भएन
me·ro *gal*·ti *bha*·yo — मेरो गल्ती भयो

I didn't do it.
mai·le *ga*·ri·nã — मैले गरिन

We're innocent.
hah·mi nir·pa·*rahdh* chaũ — हामी निरपराध छौं

We're foreigners.
hah·mi bi·*de*·shi chaũ — हामी बिदेशी छौं

I want to contact my embassy/consulate.
ma *rahj*·du·tah·vahs·mah — मलाई राजदूतावासमा
sam·par·ka *gar*·nu·par·yo — सम्पर्क गर्नुपर्यो

Can I call someone?
ma·lai *ko*·hi bo·*lai* — मलाई कोही बोलाइ
di·nu·hun·cha? — दिनुहुन्छ ?

Can I have a lawyer who speaks English?
ma·lai ang·*gre*·ji *bol*·ne — मलाई अङ्ग्रेजी बोल्ने
wa·kil *pain*·cha? — वकील पाइन्छ ?

Is there a fine we can pay to clear this?
yo *bin*·ti ca·*ḍhau*·na·lai, — यो बिन्ती चढाउनलाई,
hah·mi·lai ja·ri·*mah*·nah — हामीलाई जरिवाना
tir·nu·hun·cha? — तिर्नुहुन्छ ?

Can we pay an on-the-spot fine?
hah·mi·le ja·ri·*mah*·nah — हामीले जरिवाना
tu·*run*·ta *tir*·nu·par·cha? — तुरून्त तिर्नुपर्छ ?

I understand.
ma *bujh*·chu — म बुझ्छु

I don't understand.
mai·le bu·*jhi*·na — मैले बुझिन

I know my rights.

me·ro *a*·dhi·kahr·ko *bah*·re *ma*·lai *thah*·hah cha — मेरो अधिकारको बारे मलाई थाहा छ

What am I accused of?

ma·lai *ke*·ko dos la·*gah*·yo? — मलाई केको दोष लगायो ?

You'll be charged with ...	ta·*paĩ*·lai ...·ko dos la·*gaun*·cha ho·*lah*	तपाईलाई ...को दोषा् लगाउँछ होला
He'll/She'll be charged with ...	wa·*hãh*·lai ...·ko dos la·*gaun*·cha ho·*lah*	वहाँलाई ...को दोषा् लगाउँछ होला
anti-government activity	sar·*kahr*·ko bi·*rodh* *ta*·ra·khar	सरकारको बिरोध तरखर
assault	ba·*laht*·kahr	बलात्कार
disturbing the peace	a·*shahn*·ti *gar*·ne	अशान्ति गर्ने
illegal entry	*ni*·yam·bi·rodh pra·*besh*	नियम विरोध प्रबेश
murder	*hat*·yah	ह त्या
not having a visa	*bhi*·sah·bi·nah	भिसाबिना
overstaying your visa	*bhi*·sah·bhan·dah *dhe*·rai *bas*·ne	भिसाभन्दा धेरै बस्ने
possession (of illegal substances)	(*ni*·yam·bi·rodh *sahr*·ko) *a*·dhi·kahr *pau*·ne	(नियम विरोध सारको) अधिकार पाउने
rape	ba·*laht*·kahr	बलात्कार
robbery/theft	*cor*·ne	चोर्ने
shoplifting	*mahl*·cor·ne	माल चोर्ने
a traffic violation	ah·wat·*jah*·wat·ko *ul*·lang·ghan	आवतजावतको उल्लङ्घन
working without a permit	*a*·nu·ma·ti·pa·tra·bi·nah kahm *gar*·ne	अनुमति पत्र विना काम गर्ने

arrested	hi·*rah*·sat·mah *rahkh*·yo	हिरासतमा राख्यो
cell	khor	खोर
consulate	*rahj*·du·tah·vahs	राजदूतावास
embassy	*rahj*·du·tah·vahs	राजदूतावास
fine (payment)	ja·ri·*mah*·nah	जरिवाना
guilty	a·pa·*rah*·dhi	अपराधी
lawyer	*wa*·kil	वकील
not guilty	a·pa·*rah*·dhi *hoi*·na	अपराधी होइन
police officer	pra·*ha*·ri/pu·*lis*	प्रहरी/पुलिस
police station	*ṭhah*·nah	थाना
prison	*jhyahl*·khah·nah	झ्यालखाना
trial	*mud*·dah	मुद्दा

health

स्वास्थ्य

On the trekking circuits, there are small hospitals in Jiri, Phaplu and Khunde (near Namche Bazaar), while the Himalayan Rescue Association (HRA) has a medical facility in Pheriche, on the Everest Trek, and the Edmund Hilary Hospital is at Khumjung. On the Annapurna Circuit, go to the HRA aid post at Manang.

Please call a doctor!
ḍahk·ṭar·lai bo·*lau*·nu·hos! — डाक्टरलाई बोलाउनुहोस !

Please call an ambulance!
em·bu·lens bo·*lau*·nu·hos! — एम्बुलेन्स बोलाउनुहोस !

Please call a helicopter!
he·li·kep·ṭar bo·*lau*·nu·hos! — हेलिकेप्टर बोलाउनुहोस !

I'm ill.
ma bi·*rah*·mi chu — म बिरामी छु

My friend is ill.
me·ro *sah*·thi bi·*rah*·mi cha — मेरो साथी बिरामी छ

I have altitude sickness.
ma·lai uc·*cai*·le bi·*rah*·mi *lahg*·yo — मलाई उचाईले बिरामी लाग्यो

emergencies

He/She has altitude sickness.

wa·hãh·lai uc·*cai*·le bi·*rah*·mi *lahg*·yo — वहाँलाई उचाईले बिरामी लाग्यो

I have medical insurance.

me·ro *ḍahk*·ṭa·ri *bi*·mah cha — मेरो डाक्टरी बिमा छ

We need transport.

hah·mi·lai *yah*·tah·yaht *cah*·hi·yo — हामीलाई यातायात चाहियो

Health
स्वास्थ्य

Western-style clinics are more expensive than local ones, however, communication will be easier and service may be quicker. Kathmandu has good medical facilities, as do some other towns. But if you have an accident or fall ill while trekking, you may need some help from the locals to reach a doctor.

at the doctor

डाक्टरमा

I'm sick.
ma bi·*rah*·mi chu — म बिरामी छु

My friend is sick.
me·ro *sah*·thi bi·*rah*·mi cha — मेरो साथी बिरामी छ

I need a doctor (who speaks English).
ma·lai (ang·*gre*·ji *bol*·ne) *ḍahk*·ṭar *cah*·hi·yo — मलाई (अङ्ग्रेजी बोल्ने) डाक्टर चाहियो

Where can I find a good doctor?
rahm·ro *ḍahk*·ṭar *ka*·hāh *paun*·chu? — राम्रो डाक्टर कहाँ पाउन्छु ?

Please call a doctor.
ḍahk·ṭar·lai bo·*lau*·nu·hos — डाक्टरलाई बोलाउनुहोस

Where's the/a ...?	... *ka*·hāh cha?	... कहाँ छ ?
chemist/pharmacy	*au*·sa·dhi *pa*·sal	औषधि पसल
dentist	*dāht*·ko *ḍahk*·ṭar	दाँतको डाक्टर
doctor	*ḍahk*·ṭar	डाक्टर
health post/clinic	ci·kit·*sah*·la·ya	चिकित्सालय
hospital	*as*·pa·tahl	अस्पताल

Where's the nearest hospital?
na·ji·kai *as*·pa·tahl *ka*·hāh cha? — नजिकै अस्पताल कहाँ छ ?

the doctor may ask ...

ke *bha*·yo? **What's the matter?**	के भयो ?
khah·nah *khah*·nu *bha*·yo? **Have you eaten?**	खाना खानु भयो ?
au·sa·dhi *khah*·nu *bha*·yo? **Have you taken any medicine?**	औषधि खानु भयो ?
ka·tai *du*·khe·ko cha? **Do you feel any pain?**	कतै दुखेको छ ?
ka·hãh *dukh*·cha? **Where does it hurt?**	कहाँ दुख्छ ?
ta·*paĩ*·ko *ma*·hi·nah·bah·ri *bha*·ya·ko cha? **Are you menstruating?**	तपाईको महीनाबारी भएको छ ?
ta·*paĩ*·ko *ja*·ro cha? **Do you have a temperature?**	तपाईको जरो छ ?
ka·hi·le *de*·khi *bha*·yo? **How long have you been like this?**	कहिलेदेखि भयो ?
ta·*paĩ*·lai *yas*·to *pa*·hi·lah *ka*·hi·le *bha*·ya·ko cha? **Have you had this before?**	तपाईलाई यस्तो पहिला कहिले भएको छ ?
ta·*paĩ* *dhum*·ra·pahn *gar*·nu·hun·cha? **Do you smoke?**	तपाई धूम्रपान गर्नुहुन्छ ?
ta·*paĩ* jãhḍ·*rak*·si pi·*u*·nu·hun·cha? **Do you drink?**	तपाई जाँड–रक्सी पिउनुहुन्छ ?
ta·*paĩ* *o*·kha·ti ki na·*sah*·lu *au*·sa·dhi *li*·nu·hun·cha? **Do you take medication or illegal drugs?**	तपाई औषधी कि नसालु औषधी लिनुहुन्छ ?
ta·*paĩ*·ko *ke*·hi *a*·lahr·ji cha? **Are you allergic to anything?**	तपाईको केही एलर्जी छ ?
ta·*paĩ* *gar*·bha·va·ti *hu*·nu·hun·cha? **Are you pregnant?**	तपाई गर्भवती हुनुहुन्छ ?

I need a porter.
ma·lai *bha*·ri·yah *cah*·hi·yo — मलाई भरिया चाहियो

Please carry me to ...
...·sam·ma *ma*·lai *bok*·nu·hos — ...सम्म मलाई बोक्नुहोस

Please send a message.
kha·bar pa·*ṭhau*·nu·hos — खबर पठाउनुहोस

ailments

दुःखहरू

I don't feel well.
ma·lai *san*·co *chai*·na — मलाई सन्चो छैन

I feel nauseous.
ma·lai *wahk*·wahk *lahg*·yo — मलाई वाकवाक लाग्यो

I've been vomiting.
mai·le *bahn*·tah *ga*·rẽ — मैले बान्ता गरें

I can't sleep.
ma *sut*·na *sa*·ki·na — म सुत्न सकिन

I feel dizzy/weak.
ma·lai ring·*ga*·ṭah/ *kam*·jor *lahg*·yo — मलाई रिङ्गटा/ कमजोर लाग्यो

I've been bitten.
ma·lai *ṭok*·yo — मलाई टोक्यो

I'm having trouble breathing.
ma·lai sahs *pher*·na *gah*·hro *lahg*·yo — मलाई सास फेर्न गाह्रो लाग्यो

I have (a/an) ...	*ma*·lai ... *lahg*·yo	मलाई ... लाग्यो
I've had (a/an) ...	*ma*·lai ... *lah*·ge·ko *thi*·yo	मलाई ... लागेको थियो
addiction	lat	लत
anaemia	rak·ta·*chiṇ*·tah	रक्तक्षीणता
arthritis	bahth	बाथ

bite	*ṭo*·kai	टोकाइ
blister	*pho*·kah	फोका
bronchitis	swahs *na*·li·ko rog	स्वास नलीको रोग
cancer	*kyahn*·sar	क्यान्सर
chicken pox	*ṭheu*·lah	ठेउला
cholera	*hai*·jah	हैजा
cold	*ru*·ghah	रुघा
constipation	*di*·sah *ka*·se·ko	दिसा कसेको
cough	*kho*·ki	खोकी
cramp	*baũ*·ḍyai	बौंडया इ
cut/wound	ghau	घाउ
diarrhoea	*jhah*·ḍah/*pa*·khah·lah	झाडा/पखाला
disease	rog	रोग
dysentery	ra·gat·*mah*·si	रगतमासी
fever	*ja*·ro	जरो
food poisoning	*khah*·nah kha·*rahb*	खाना खराब
frostbite	tu·*sah*·ro·le *khah*·ya·ko	तुसारोले खाएको
gastroenteritis	*gyah*·sṭrik	ग्याँसट्रिक
glandular fever	*gãh*·ṭho·ko *ja*·ro	गाँठोको ज्वरो
headache	*ṭau*·ko *dukh*·yo	टाउको दुख्यो
heart condition	*mu*·ṭu·ko bi·*rah*·mi	मुटुको बिरामी
hepatitis	*ka*·le·jo·ko rog	कलेजोको रोग
illness	rog	रोग
indigestion	*a*·pac	अपच
inflammation	*sun*·ni·ya·ko *a*·bas·thah	सुन्नीयको अबस्था
influenza	ru·ghah·*kho*·ki·ko *ja*·ro	रुघाखोकीको ज्वरो
itch	ci·*lau*·na	चिलाउन
jaundice	*ka*·mal·pit·ta	कमलपित्त

altitude sickness

Acute mountain sickness (AMS) or altitude sickness is the most dangerous environmental hazard trekkers may face. Know the symptoms (breathlessness, dizziness, fatigue, insomnia, mental confusion, a pounding heart) and be alert for their appearance. Other potential health hazards for all travellers include heatstroke, prickly heat rash, sunburn and hypothermia.

kidney disease	mir·*gau*·lah·ko rog	मृगौलाको रोग
leprosy	*kus*·ṭa·rog	कुष्टरोग
lice	*jum*·rah	जुम्रा
lump	*ḍal*·lo	डल्लो
malaria	*au*·lo	औलो
measles	dah·*du*·rah	दादुरा
meningitis	me·nĩ·*jai*·ṭis	मेनिंजाइटीस
nausea	*wahk*·wah·ki	वाकवाकि
pain	du·*khai*	दुखाई
paralysis	*pa*·cha·baht	पक्षबाथ
poliomyelitis	*po*·li·yo	पोलियो
rash	sujh	सुझ
rheumatism	bahth	बाथ
sore throat	*ghãh*·ṭi *du*·khe·ko	घाँटी दुखेको
sprain	*mar*·kai	मर्काइ
stomachache	peṭ *du*·khe·ko	पेट दुखेको
sunburn	ḍa·*ḍhau*·na	डढाउन
sunstroke	lu	लु
swelling	*su*·jan	सुजन
tetanus	*dha*·nu·rog	धनुरोग
toothache	dãht *du*·khe·ko	दाँत दुखेको
travel sickness	*gah*·di·mah *lahg*·ne *wahk*·wahk	गाडीमा लाग्ने वाकवाक
tuberculosis	*cha*·ya·rog	क्षयरोग
typhoid	*ṭai*·phaiḍ	टाइफाइड
urinary infection	*pi*·sahb·ko rog	पिसाबको रोग
venereal disease	*bhi*·rĩ·gi	भिरिंगी
worms	*ju*·kah	जुका

It hurts here.
ya·hãh *dukh*·yo — यहाँ दुख्यो

I feel better/worse.
ma·lai ṭhik/jhan *na*·rahm·ro *lahg*·yo — मलाई ठीक/ झन नराम्रो लाग्यो

This is my usual medicine.
ma yo *au*·sa·dhi *li*·ne *gar*·thẽ — म यो औषधि लिने गर्थे

I've been vaccinated.
mai·le khop *li*·sa·kẽ — मैले खोप लिइसकें

Can I have a receipt for my insurance?
me·ro *bi*·mah·ko *lah*·gi bil *di*·nu·hun·cha? — मेरो बिमाको लागि बिल दिनुहुन्छ ?

I'm feeling fine now.
a·hi·le ṭhik *bha*·yo — अहिले ठीक भयो

blood pressure	*rak*·ta·cahp	रक्तचाप
blood test	*ra*·gat·ko jãhc	रगतको जाँच
examination	jãhc	जाँच
injection	*su*·i	सूई
health	*swahs*·thya	स्वास्थ्य
patient (n)	*ro*·gi	रोगी
test	jãhc	जाँच

women's health

महिलाको स्वास्थ्य

Could I see a female doctor?
ma *ai*·mai *ḍahk*·ṭar *her*·na *sak*·chu? — म आईमाई डाक्टर हेर्न सक्छु ?

I haven't menstruated for ...
me·ro *ma*·hi·nah·bah·ri na·*bha*·ya·ko ... *bha*·yo — मेरो महीनाबारी नभएको ... भयो

I think I'm pregnant.
ma *gar*·bha·va·ti chu ma bi·*cahr gar*·chu — म गर्भवती छु म बिचार गर्छु

I'd like to have a pregnancy test.
ma·lai *gar*·bha·va·ti·ko jãhc *cah*·hi·yo — मलाई गर्भवतीको जाँच चाहियो

I'm (... weeks) pregnant.
ma *gar*·bha·va·ti chu (... *hap*·tah *bha*·yo) — म गर्भवती छु (... हप्ता भयो)

hit the bottle

Never drink tap or river water unless it has been boiled and preferably also filtered. You may need to insist on properly sterilised water. Water that's only been filtered (in a basic Nepalese sandstone filter) is still unsafe to drink, but not all Nepalese people are aware of this.

Water purification tablets are useless against Nepal's waterborne amoebae, and only iodine (or chlorine) is effective. Bottled water is widely available and quite cheap, but does lead to litter. Remember also to avoid ice and street ice cream.

I'm taking the contraceptive pill.
ma *pa*·ri·bahr ni·*yo*·jan·ko *au*·sa·dhi *lin*·dai·chu — म परिवार नियोजनको औषधि लिदैछु

I'd like to use contraception.
ma·lai *pa*·ri·bahr ni·*yo*·jan·ko *au*·sa·dhi *li*·na man *lahg*·yo — मलाई परिवार नियोजनको औषधि लिन मनलाग्यो

I'd like to get the morning-after pill.
ma·lai mar·ning·*ahph*·ṭar·pil *cah*·hi·yo — मलाई मर्निङ आफ्टर पील चाहियो

abortion	*gar*·bha·paht	गर्भपात
contraceptive device	*pa*·ri·bahr ni·*yo*·jan·ko *sah*·dhan	परिवार नियोजनको साधन
cystitis	*pi*·sahb·ko rog	पिसाबको रोग
family planning	*pa*·ri·bahr ni·*yo*·jan	परिवार नियोजन
menstruation	*ma*·hi·nah·bah·ri	महीनाबारी
miscarriage	*rak*·ta·paht	रक्तपात
period pain	*ma*·hi·nah·bah·ri·ko du·*khai*	महीनाबारीको दुखाई
the Pill	*pa*·ri·bahr ni·*yo*·jan·ko *au*·sa·dhi	परिवार नियोजनको औषधि
pregnancy test kit	*gar*·bha·va·ti *jãhc*·ne *sah*·mahn	गर्भवती जाँच्ने सामान

special health needs

विशेष स्वास्थ्य आबश्यकता

I have ...	*ma*·lai ... *lahg*·yo	मलाई ... लाग्यो
asthma	*dam*·ko *bya*·thah	दमको ब्यथा
diabetes	ma·dhu·*me*·ha	मधुमेह
epilepsy	*chah*·re rog	छारे रोग

I'm allergic to ...	*ma*·lai ... *li*·nu *hun*·dai·na	मलाई ... लिनु हुदैन
antibiotics	ahṇ·ṭi·bi·*yo*·ṭik	आन्टीबायोटिक
aspirin	*ais*·pi·rin	आईसपिरिन
bees	*mau*·ri	मौरी
dairy products	*dudh*·ko *khah*·nah	दूधको खाना
penicillin	pe·ni·*si*·lin	पेनिसिलिन
pollen	pa·*rahg*	पराग
that medicine	tyo *au*·sa·dhi	त्यो औषधि

I have a skin problem.
me·ro *chah*·lah·ko sa·*mas*·yah cha — मेरो छालाको समस्या छ

I have high/low blood pressure.
me·ro *rak*·ta·cahp *bha*·de·ko/ *gha*·ṭe·ko cha — मेरो रक्तचाप बढेको/ घटेको छ

I have a weak heart.
me·ro *mu*·ṭu *kam*·jor cha — मेरो मुटु कमजोर छ

I've had my vaccinations.
me·ro khop *li*·sak·yo — मेरो खोप लिइसक्यो

I have my own syringe.
ma·sã·ga *ahph*·no *si*·rinj cha — मसँग आफ्नो सिरिन्ज छ

Is that a new syringe you're using?
tyo *su*·i ra *si*·rinj *na*·yãh ho? — त्यो सूई र सिरिन्ज नयाँ हो ?

I don't want a blood transfusion.
ma·lai *ra*·gat *li*·na man *par*·dai·na — मलाई रगत लिन मन पर्दैन

I'm on medication for ...
ma ...·ko *au*·sa·dhi *lin*·dai·chu — म ...को औषधि लिदैछु

I'm on a special diet.
ma *khah*·nah *bãh*·dhe·ko chu — म खाना बारेको छु

I need a new pair of glasses.
ma·lai *na*·yãh *cash*·mah *cah*·hi·yo — मलाई नयाँ चश्मा चाहियो

alternative treatments

अर्को उपचारहरू

Traditional Ayurvedic medicines from plants are prepared in Nepal, while Tibetan medicines are another alternative. Massage therapists are everywhere and chiropractors can also be found.

Ayurvedic medicine	ah·yur·*be*·dah	आयुर्वेद
Ayurvedic tonic	ra·*sah*·di	रसादि
faith healer	*dhah*·mi/*jhãh*·kri	धामी/ झाक्री
herbal treatment	ja·ḍi·*bu*·ṭi	जडीबूटी
massage	*mah*·lis	मालिस
meditation	dhyahn	ध्यान
midwife	dhai	धाई
shaman/witchdoctor	*jahn*·ne	जान्ने
Tibetan medicine	ti·*be*·tan *ḍahk*·ṭa·ri	तिबेतन डाक्टरी
traditional doctor	*bai*·dha	बैध्य
witch (m/f)	*bok*·si	बोक्सी
yoga	*yo*·gah	योगा

parts of the body

अङ्गप्रत्यङ्ग

My ... hurts.
me·ro ... *dukh*·yo — मेरो ... दुख्यो

I have a pain in my ...
me·ro ...·mah du·*khai* cha — मेरो ...मा दुखाई छ

I've burned my ...
me·ro ...·mah *pol*·yo — मेरो ...मा पोल्यो

I can't move my ...
me·ro ... ca·*lau*·na *sak*·di·na — मेरो ... चलाउन सक्दिन

He/She broke his/her ...
wa·*hãh*·ko ... *bhãhc*·yo — वहाँको ... भाच्यो

ankle	go·li·*gãh*·ṭho	गोलीगाँठो
anus	*mal*·dwahr	मलद्धार
appendix	*a*·peṇ·ḍiks	अपेण्डीक्स
arm	*pah*·khu·rah	पाखुरा
back	*pi*·ṭhũ	पिठ्युँ
backbone	ḍhahḍ	ढाड
bladder	*mu*·trah·sha·ya	मूत्राशय
blood	*ra*·gat	रगत
body	ji·*u*	जीउ
bone	hahḍ	हाड
brain	*gi*·di	गिदी
breast	stan	स्तन
buttock	cahk	चाख
calf	pĩ·*ḍu*·lah	पिंडुला
cheek	*gah*·lah	गाला
chest	*chah*·ti	छाती
ear	kahn	कान
elbow	ku·*hi*·no	कुहिनो
eye	*ãh*·khah	आँखा
face	*a*·nu·hahr	अनुहार
finger	*aũ*·lah	औंला
foot	*khuṭ*·ṭah	खुट्टा
hair	ka·*pahl*	कपाल
hand	haht	हात
head	*ṭau*·ko	टाउको
heart	*mu*·ṭu	मुटु
hip	cahk	चाक
jaw	bang·*gah*·rah	बङ्गारा
joint	*jor*·ni	जोर्नी
kidney	mir·*gau*·lah	मृगौला
knee	*ghũ*·ḍah	घुँडा
leg	*go*·ḍah	गोडा
lips	oṭh	ओठ

SAFE TRAVEL

liver	*ka*·le·jo	कलेजो
lung	*phok*·so	फोक्सो
mouth	mukh	मुख
muscle	*mãh*·sha·pe·shi	मांशपेशी
nails	nang	नङ
neck	*ghãh*·ṭi	घाँटी
nose	nahk	नाक
penis	*ling*·ga	लिङ्ग
rib	*ka*·rang	करङ
shoulder	kãhdh	काँध
skin	*chah*·lah	छाला
stomach	peṭ	पेट
teeth/tooth	dãhṭ	दाँत
testicles	*aṇ*·ḍa	अण्ड
throat (inside)	*ga*·lah	गला
throat (outside)	*ghãh*·ṭi	घाँटी
tongue	*ji*·bro	जिब्रो
vagina	*yo*·ni	योनि
vein	*na*·sah	नसा
womb/uterus	*pah*·ṭhe·ghar	पाठेघर
wrist	*nah*·ḍi	नाडी

at the chemist

औषधि पसलमा

Nepalese pharmacies stock a wide range of Western medicines, available without prescription. They can be good places to go for medical advice.

I need something for ...
...·ko *lah*·gi, *au*·sa·dhi *di*·nu·hos — ...को लागि, औषधि दिनुहोस

Please give me ...	*ma*·lai ... *di*·nu·hos	मलाई ... दिनुहोस
aspirin	*ais*·pi·rin	आईसपिरिन
bandages	*paṭ*·ṭi	पट्टी
iodine	*ai*·ḍin	आयोडिन
medicine	*au*·sa·dhi	औषधि

Do I need a prescription for ...?
...·ko *lah*·gi *au*·sa·dhi·vi·dhi *li*·nu·par·cha? — ...को लागि औषधि विधि लिनुपर्छ ?

I have a prescription.
me·ro *au*·sa·dhi·vi·dhi cha — मेरो औषधि विधि छ

How many times a day?
din·ko *ka*·ti *pa*·ṭak? — दिनको कति पटक ?

(Twice) a day.
din·ko (*du*·i·pa·ṭak) — दिनको (दुइपटक)

With food.
khah·nah·sã·ga — खानासँग

Can I drive on this medication?
yo *au*·sa·dhi *li*·e·ra, *gah*·ḍi ca·*lau*·nu·hun·cha? — यो औषधि लिएर, गाडी चलाउनुहुन्छ ?

SUSTAINABLE TRAVEL

WIth climate change now an ongoing concern, the matter of sustainability becomes an important part of the travel vernacular. In practical terms, this means assessing our impact on the environment and local cultures and economies – and acting to make that impact as positive as possible. Here are some basic phrases to get you on your way …

communication & cultural differences

I'd like to learn some of your local dialects.

ma·*lah*·i sthah·*ni*·ya *bo*·li ra *bhah*·shah *sik*·na man·*lah*·gyo	मलाई स्थानीय बोली र भाषा सिक्न मनलाग्यो

Would you like me to teach you some English?

ma ta·pah·ĩ·*lah*·i a·li·*ka*·ti ang·*gre*·ji *bhah*·shah si·kah·*i*·di·ũ?	म तपाईलाई अलिकति अङ्ग्रेजी भाषा सिकाईदिउँ?

Is this a local or national custom?

yo sthah·*ni*·ya ki desh·bha·*ri*·ko ca·*lan* ho?	यो स्थानीय कि देशभरिको चलन हो ?

I respect your customs.

ma ta·pah·ĩ·ha·*ru*·ko ca·*lan*·ko *ij*·jat *gar*·chu	म तपाईहरुको चलनको इज्जत गर्छु

community benefit & involvement

I'd like to volunteer my skills.

ma·*lah*·i ah·*phu*·le jah·*ne*·ko ku·rah·*ha*·ru si·kah·*u*·na man·*par*·cha	मलाई आफुले जानेको कुराहरु सिकाउन मनपर्छ

Are there any volunteer programs available in the area?
tyas ṭhah·*ũ*·mah ku·*nai*
swa·yam·*se*·bak
kahr·ya·kram·*ha*·ru chan?
त्यस ठाउँमा कुनै
स्वयंसेवक
कार्यक्रमहरु छन् ?

What sorts of issues is this community facing?
ya·*hãh*·kah mahn·che·ha·*ru*·le
kas·to ki·*sim*·ko
du·kha·*kash*·ṭa *bhog*·nu
pa·ri·ra·*he*·ko cha?
यहाँका मान्छेहरुले
कस्तो किसिमको
दुख–कष्ट भोग्नु
परिरहेको छ ?

agriculture problem	kri·*shi*·ko sa·*mas*·yah	कृषिको समस्या
deforestation	ban bi·*nahsh*	वन विनाश
drinking water problem	*khah*·ne pah·*ni*·ko sa·*mas*·yah	खाने पानीको समस्या
electricity	bi·*ju*·li	बिजुली
flood/landslide problem	bah·*ḍhi* pa·hi·*ro*·ko sa·*mas*·yah	बाढी पहिरोको समस्या
lack of education	shi·*chyah*·ko ka·*mi*	शिक्षाको कमी
migration problem	ba·*sah*·i·sa·*rah*·i·ko sa·*mas*·yah	बसाई–सरा इको समस्या

environment

Where can I recycle this?
ma yo *ka*·hãh ri·sah·*i*·kal
gar·na sak·*chu*?
म यो कहाँ रिसाइकल
गर्न सक्छु ?

transport

Can we get there by public transport?
hah·*mi tya*·hãh bas·*bah*·ṭa
jah·*na* sak·*chaũ*?
हामी त्यहाँ बसबाट
जान सक्छौं ?

Can we get there by bike?
hah·*mi tya*·hãh
sah·i·*kal*·mah jah·*na*
sak·*chaũ*?
हामी त्यहाँ
साइकलमा जान
सक्छौं ?

I'd prefer to walk there.

ma·*lah*·i *tya*·hãh hĩ·*ḍe*·ra *jah*·na man·*lahg*·cha	मलाई त्यहाँ हिडेर जान मनलाग्छ

accommodation

I'd like to stay at a locally run hotel.

ma·*lah*·i ya·*hĩ*·ko mahn·*che*·le ca·lah·*e*·ko ho·*ṭel*·mah *bas*·na man·*par*·cha	मलाई यहाँको मान्छेले चलाएको होटेलमा बस्न मनपर्छ

Can I turn the air conditioning off and open the window?

ma e·*si* ban·*da* ga·*re*·ra jhyahl kho·*lũ*?	म ए.सी. बन्द गरेर झ्याल खोलुँ ?

There's no need to change my sheets.

me·*ro* o·*chyahn*·ko *tan*·nah *pher*·nu par·*dai*·na	मेरो ओछ्यानको तन्ना फेर्नु पर्दैन

shopping

Where can I buy locally produced goods/souvenirs?

sthah·*ni*·ya mah·nis·ha·*ru*·le ta·*yahr* ga·*re*·kah sah·mahn·*ha*·ru ka·*hãh* *kin*·na pah·*in*·cha?	स्थानीय मानिसहरुले तयार गरेका सामानहरु कहाँ किन्न पाइन्छ ?

food

Do you sell locally produced food?

ta·*pah*·ĩ sthah·*ni*·ya ma·*nis*·le ba·nah·*e*·ko *khah*·nah *bec*·nu·*hun*·cha?	तपाई स्थानीय मानिसले बनाएको खाना बेच्नुहुन्छ ?

Do you sell organic produce?

ta·*pah*·ĩ de·*shi*·mal ra ki·*rah* *mahr*·ne au·*sha*·dhi na·*rah*·khi ut·*pah*·dan ga·*re*·ko *khah*·nah *bec*·nu·*hun*·cha?	तपाई देशीमल र किरा मानेर औषधि नराखी उत्पादन गरेको खाना बेच्नुहुन्छ ?

Which Nepali food should I try?

ma kun ne·*pah*·li *khah*·nah *khah*·ũ?	म कुन नेपाली खाना खाउँ ?

sightseeing

Does your company hire local guides?

ta·pah·*ĩ*·ko kam·pa·*ni*·le sthah·*ni*·ya ga·hi·ḍha·ru·*lah*·i bhah·*ḍah*·mah lin·*cha*?	तपा इरूको कम्पनीले स्थानीय गाईडहरुलाई भाडामा लिन्छ ?

Does your company donate money to charity?

ta·pah·*ĩ*·ko kam·pa·*ni*·le dahn·*dhar*·ma gar·*ne* sãs·thah·*lah*·i *can*·dah din·*cha*?	तपाईको कम्पनीले दान–धर्म गनेर् संस्थालाई चन्दा दिन्छ ?

Does your company visit local businesses?

ta·pah·*ĩ*·ko kam·*pa*·ni sthah·*ni*·ya byah·*pahr* bya·ba·sah·ya·*ha*·ru *her*·na jahn·*cha*?	तपाईको कम्पनी स्थानीय व्यापार व्यवसायहरु हेर्न जान्छ ?

Are cultural tours available?

sãhs·*kri*·tik bhra·maṇ·*ha*·ru *gar*·na pah·*in*·cha?	साँस्कृतिक भ्रमणहरु गर्न पाईन्छ ?

Does the guide speak local dialects?

gah·*iḍ*·le sthah·*ni*·ya *bo*·li ra *bhah*·sha bol·*cha*?	गाइडले स्थानीय बोली र भाषा बोल्छ ?

In this dictionary, the following notation applies in regard to parts of speech:

Nouns are not indicated unless they can be mistaken for adjectives, in which case they're followed by (n). Likewise, adjectives are only followed by (adj) when their use can be mistaken for a noun. Verbs are preceded by 'to'. This serves to distinguish a verb from its noun counterpart, eg, 'to book' versus 'book'.

A

to be able (can)	*sak*·nu	सक्नु
abortion	*gar*·bha·paht	गर्भपात
about	-*bah*·re	-बारे
above	-*mah*·thi	-माथि
abroad	bi·*desh*	बिदेश
to accept (agree to)	*mahn*·nu	मान्नु

Do you accept/agree?
ta·*paĩ mahn*·nu·hun·cha? तपाई मान्नुहुन्छ ?

I accept/agree.
ma *mahn*·chu म मान्छु

accident	dur·*gha*·ṭa·nah	दुर्घटना
accommodation (rented)	*ḍe*·rah	डेरा
to ache	*dukh*·nu	दुख्नु
across	-*pah*·ri	-पारि
activist	*kahr*·ya·kahr	कार्यकार
actor	a·bhi·*ne*·tah/ a·bhi·*ne*·tri **(m/f)**	अभिनेता/ अभिनेत्री
addict	lat *bha*·ya·ko *mahn*·che	लत भएको मान्छे
addiction	lat	लत
address	ṭhe·*gah*·nah	ठेगाना
administration	pra·*shah*·san	प्रशासन
to admire	*tah*·riph *gar*·nu	तारिफ गर्नु
admission (to enter)	*bhar*·nah	भर्ना
to admit	swi·*kahr gar*·nu	स्वीकार गर्नु
adult (n)	*ba*·yask	बयस्क
advice	sal·*lah*·ha	सल्लाह
to advise	sal·*lah*·ha *di*·nu	सल्लाह दिनु

aerogram	*ha*·wai·pa·tra	हवाईपत्र
aeroplane	*ha*·wai·ja·hahj	हवाईजहाज
to be afraid	ḍa·*rau*·nu	डराउनु
after	-*pa*·chi	-पछि
(in the) afternoon	*diũ*·so	दिउँसो
again	*phe*·ri	फेरि
against	bi·*rodh*	बिरोध
age	*u*·mer	उमेर
aggressive	*nir*·da·yi	निर्दयी
ago	*a*·ghi	अघि
to agree to	*mahn*·nu	मान्नु

I don't agree.
ma *mahn*·di·na — म मान्दिन

Agreed!
man·jur *bha*·yo! — मन्जुर भयो !

agriculture	*khe*·ti·pah·ti	खेतीपाती
ahead	*a*·ghi	अघि
aid	sa·*ha*·yog	सहयोग
air	*hah*·wah	हावा
air-conditioned	bah·tah·nu·*ku*·lit	बातानुकुलीत
airmail	*ha*·wai·ḍahk	हवाईडाक
airport	*bi*·mahn·stal	बिमानस्थल
airport tax	*bi*·mahn·stal·ko kar	बिमानस्थलको कर
alarm clock	*ghaṇ*·ṭi *gha*·ḍi	घण्टी घडी
alcohol	*rak*·si	रक्सी
all	*sa*·bai	सबै
all day	*din*·bha·ri	दिनभरि
allergy	*a*·lahr·ji	एलर्जी
to allow	*a*·nu·ma·ti *di*·nu	अनुमति दिनु

It's allowed.
a·nu·ma·ti cha — अनुमति छ

It's not allowed.
a·nu·ma·ti *chai*·na — अनुमति छैन

almost	*jhan*·ḍai	झण्डै
alone	*ek*·lai	एक्लै
along	-*bha*·ri • -*hun*·dai	-भिर • -हुँदै
already	*a*·ghi	अघि
also	*pa*·ni	पनि
altitude	*uc*·cai	उचाई
always	*sa*·dhaĩ	सधैं
amateur	*la*·ha·ḍi	लहडी
ambassador	*rahj*·dut	राजदूत

among	*ma*·dhye	मध्ये
anaesthetic	nish·*ce*·tak	निश्चयतक
ancient	*prah*·cin	प्राचीन
and	ra	र
and then/so	*a*·ni	अनि
anger	ris	रिस
to get angry	ri·*sau*·nu	रिसाउनु
animal	ja·*nah*·war	जनावर
ankle	go·li·*gāh*·ṭho	गोलीगाँठो
annoyed	*dik*·ka	दिक्क
annual	*bahr*·sik	वार्षिक
to answer	*ut*·tar *di*·nu	उत्तर दिनु
ant	ka·*mi*·lah	कमिला
antibiotics	ahṇ·ṭi·bi·*yo*·ṭik	आण्टीबीयोटीक
antique (n)	pu·*rah*·no *bas*·tu	पुरानो बस्तु
any	*ke*·hi	केही
anyone	*ko*·hi	कोही
anything	*ke*·hi	केही
anywhere	*ja*·hāh	जहाँ
apartment	*ḍe*·rah	डेरा
appendix	*a*·peṇ·ḍiks	अपेण्डीक्स
apple	syau	स्याउ
appointment	bheṭ *gar*·ne sa·*ma*·ya	भेट गर्ने समय
approximately	*lag*·bhag	लगभग
archaeological	pu·rah·*tat*·wi·ya	पुरातत्वीय
architecture	*vahs*·tu·ka·lah	वास्तुकला
to argue	*ba*·has *gar*·nu	बहस गर्नु
argument	*ba*·has	बहस
arm	*pah*·khu·rah	पाखुरा
to arrive	*pug*·nu	पुग्नु
art	ka·*lah*	कला
art gallery	ka·*lah*·ko ghar	कलाको घर
arthritis	bahth	बाथ
artist	*ka*·lah·kahr	कलाकार
artwork	ka·*lah* kahm	कला काम
ashtray	*ahsh*·ṭre	आस्ट्रे
to ask	*sodh*·nu	सोध्नु
to ask for	*mahg*·nu	माग्नु
aspirin	*ais*·pi·rin	आईसपिरिन
asthma	*dam*·ko *bya*·thah	दमको ब्यथा
asthmatic	*dam bya*·thah·ko *ro*·gi	दम ब्यथाको रोगी
at	-mah	-मा
atmosphere	bah·yu·*maṇ*·ḍal	बायुमण्डल
autorickshaw	*ṭyahm*·pu	टयाम्पु
available	*pain*·cha	पाइन्छ
awful	bi·*rak*·ta·lahg·do	बिरक्तलाग्दो

B

baby	*bac*·cah	बच्चा
baby bottle	dudh khu·*wau*·ne *si*·si	दूध खुवाउने सिसी
baby food	*bac*·cah·ko *khah*·nah	बच्चाको खाना
babysitter	*bac*·cah *her*·ne *mahn*·che	बच्चा हेर्ने मान्छे
back	*pi*·ṭhũ	पिठ्युँ
backbone	ḍhahḍ	ढाड
backpack	*jho*·lah	झोला
at the back (behind)	pa·*chah*·ḍi	पछाडि
bad	kha·*rahb*	खराब
bag	*jho*·lah	झोला
baggage	*mahl*·sah·mahn	मालसामान
baggage claim	*mahl*·sah·mahn *li*·ne ṭhaũ	मालसामान लिने ठाउँ
balcony	*bahr*·da·li	बार्दली
ball	*bha*·kun·ḍo	भकुन्डो
band	bahṇḍ	बाण्ड
bandage	*paṭ*·ṭi	पट्टी
bank	baĩk	बैंक
banknote	*baĩk*·noṭ	बैंकनोट
bar	bahr	बार
barber	ha·*jahm*	हजाम
to bargain	*mol*·tol *gar*·nu	मोलतोल गर्नु
barley	jau	जौ
basil	*tul*·si	तुलसी
basket	*ṭo*·ka·ri	टोकरी
bat	*ca*·me·ro	चमेरो
to bathe	nu·*hau*·nu	नुहाउनु
bathroom	snahn *kak*·sha • *bahṭh*·rum	स्नान कक्श • बाथरुम
battery	*ma*·sa·lah	मसला
to be	*hu*·nu	हुनु
beach	ba·*lau*·ṭe ki·*nahr*	बलौटे किनार
bean	*si*·mi	सिमी
bear	*bhah*·lu	भालु
beard	*dah*·hri	दाह्री
beautiful	*sun*·dar	सुन्दर
because	*ki*·na·bha·ne	किनभने
bed	khahṭ	खाट
bedbug	u·*ḍus*	उडुस
bedding	bi·*chyau*·nah	बिछ्यौना
bedroom	*khahṭ*·ko *ko*·ṭhah	खाटको कोठा
bee	*mau*·ri	मौरी
beef	*gai*·ko *mah*·su	गाईको मासु

beer	*bi*·yar	बियर
beer (rice)	chyahng	छ्यांङ
beer (millet)	*tum*·bah	तूम्बा
before	*a*·ghi	अघि
beggar	*mahg*·ne	माग्ने
to begin	*su*·ru *gar*·nu	सुरु गर्नु
behind	pa·*chah*·ḍi	पछाडि
belief	bi·*shwahs*	विश्वास
to believe	bi·*shwahs gar*·nu	विश्वास गर्नु
below	*ta*·la	तल
belt	*pe*·ṭi	पेटी
beside	*cheu*·mah	छेउमा
best	sab·*bhan*·dah *rahm*·ro	सबभन्दा राम्रो
bet	*bah*·ji	बाजी
better	jhan *rahm*·ro	झन् राम्रो
between	*bic*·mah	बीचमा
bicycle	*sai*·kal	साइकल
big	*ṭhu*·lo	ठूलो
bill	bil	बिल
binoculars	*dur*·bin	दूरबीन
biography	*ji*·va·ni	जीवनी
bird	*ca*·rah	चरा
birth certificate	*jan*·ma pra·*mahṇ*·pa·tra	जन्म प्रमाणपत्र
birthday (official)	*ja*·yan·ti	जयन्ती
birthday (personal)	*jan*·ma·din	जन्मदिन
biscuit	*bis*·kuṭ	बिस्कुट
to bite	*ṭok*·nu	टोक्नु
to bite (snake only)	*ḍas*·nu	डस्नु
bitter	*ti*·to	तीतो
black	*kah*·lo	कालो
B&W (film)	*kah*·lo *se*·to (ril)	कालो सेतो (रील)
blanket	*kam*·mal	कम्बल
to bleed	*ra*·gat *au*·nu	रगत आउनु
to bless	*ah*·shir·bahd *di*·nu	आशीबार्द दिनु
blessing	*ah*·shir·bahd	आशीबार्द
blind (adj)	*an*·dho	अन्धो
blizzard	*hiũ*·ko *ãh*·dhi	हिउँको आँधी
blood	*ra*·gat	रगत
blood group	*ra*·gat sa·*mu*·ha	रगत समूह
blood pressure	*rak*·ta·cahp	रक्तचाप
low/high blood pressure	*gha*·ṭe·ko/*bha*·de·ko *rak*·ta·cahp	घटेको/बढेको रक्तचाप
blood test	*ra*·gat·ko jãhc	रगतको जाँच
blouse	*co*·lo	चोलो
blue	*ni*·lo	निलो

to board	*caḍh*·nu	चढ्नु
boat	*ḍung*·gah	डुङ्गा
body	ji·*u*	जीउ
boiled water	u·*mah*·le·ko *pah*·ni	उमालेको पानी
bomb	*go*·lah	गोला
bone	hahḍ	हाड
book	ki·*tahb*	किताब
to book	*sany*·cit *gar*·nu	संचित गर्नु
bookshop	ki·*tahb pa*·sal	किताब पसल
boots	buṭ	बुट
border	si·*mah*·nah	सिमाना
boring	*wahk*·ka *hu*·ne	वाक्क हुने
to borrow	*sah*·paṭ *li*·nu	सापट लिनु
boss	*mah*·lik	मालिक
both	*du*·bai	दुबै
bottle	*si*·si	सिसी
bottle opener	*si*·si *khol*·ne	सिसी खोल्ने
(at the) bottom	*pīd*(·mah)	पींद(मा)
box	*bah*·kas	बाकस
boy	*ke*·ṭah	केटा
boyfriend	*pre*·mi	प्रेमि
brain	*gi*·di	गिदी
branch	*hãh*·gah	हाँगा
brassware	*pi*·tal·ko *sah*·mahn	पितलको सामान
brave	ba·*hah*·dur	बहादुर
bread	*ro*·ṭi	रोटी
bread (flat)	ca·*pah*·ti	चपाती
bread (deep fried)	*pu*·ri	पुरी
bread (loaf of)	*pau*·ro·ṭi	पाउरोटी
to break	*phuṭ*·nu • *bhãhc*·nu	फुट्नु • भाच्नु फेर्नु
breakfast	bi·*hah*·na·ko *khah*·nah	बिहानको खाना
breast	stan	स्तन
to breathe	sahs *pher*·nu	सास फेर्नु
bribe	ghus	घूस
to bribe	ghus *di*·nu	घूस दिनु
bridge	pul	पुल
bright	u·*jyah*·lo	उज्यालो
to bring	*lyau*·nu	ल्याउनु
broken	*phuṭ*·yo	फुट्यो
brother (elder)	dai	दाई
brother (younger)	bhai	भाइ
brothers	dah·ju·*bhai*	दाजुभाई
brown	*khai*·ro	खैरो
bruise	coṭ	चोट
brush	*bu*·rus	बुरुस

DICTIONARY

to brush (hair)	ka·*pahl kor*·nu	कपाल कोर्नु
to brush (teeth)	dãht *mahjh*·nu	दाँत माझ्नु
bucket	*bahl*·ṭin	बाल्टिन
Buddhism	*bud*·dha *dhar*·ma	बुद्ध धर्म
bug (insect)	*ki*·rah	कीरा
buff meat	*rãh*·gah·ko *mah*·su	राँगाको मासु
buffalo	*rãh*·gah/*bhaĩ*·si **(m/f)**	राँगा/भैंसी
to build	u·*bhyau*·nu	उभ्याउनु
building	*bha*·wan	भवन
to burn	*pol*·nu	पोल्नु
bus	bas	बस
bush (shrub)	boṭ	बोट
business	*be*·pahr	व्यापार
businessperson	*be*·pah·ri	व्यापारी
busy	*bes*·ta	बेस्त
but	*ta*·ra	तर
butter	*ma*·khan	मखन
butterfly	*pu*·ta·li	पुतली
button	ṭãhk	टाँख
to buy	*kin*·nu	किन्नु

I'd like to buy ...
ma·lai ... *kin*·na man *lahg*·yo — मलाई ... किन्न मन लाग्यो

Where can I buy a ticket?
ṭi·kaṭ *ka*·hãh *kin*·na *sa*·kin·cha? — टिकट कहाँ किन्न सकिन्छ ?

by	-le	-ले

C

cabbage	ban·dah·*ko*·bi	बन्दाकोबी
cafe	*kyah*·phe	क्याफे
calendar	*sam*·bat	सम्बत
to call	bo·*lau*·nu	बोलाउनु
camera	*kyah*·me·rah	क्यामेरा
camera shop	*kyah*·me·rah *pa*·sal	क्यामेरा पसल
to camp	*shi*·bir *gar*·nu	शिविर गर्नु

Can we camp here?
hah·mi *ya*·hãh *shi*·bir *gar*·nu·hun·cha? — हामी यहाँ शिविर गर्नुहुन्छ ?

camping	*shi*·bir	शिविर
camp site	*shi*·bir *gar*·ne ṭhaũ	शिविर गर्ने ठाउँ
can (to be able)	*sak*·nu	सक्नु

We can do it.
hah·mi *gar*·na *sak*·chaũ — हामी गर्न सक्छौं

I can't do it.
ma *gar*·na *sak*·di·na — म गर्न सक्दिन

can	ṭin	टिन
can opener	ṭin *khol*·ne	टिन खोल्ने
to cancel	*rad*·da *gar*·nu	रद्द गर्नु
candle	*main*·bat·ti	मैनबत्ती
cap	*ṭo*·pi	टोपी
capital city	*rahj*·dhah·ni	राजधानी
capitalism	*pũ*·ji·bahd	पूजीबाद
car	*mo*·ṭar	मोटर
cardamom (black)	a·*laĩ*·ci	अलैंची
cardamom (green)	*su*·ku·mel	सुकुमेल
cards	tahs	तास
to care (about)	*pyah*·ro *gar*·nu	प्यारो गर्नु
to be careful	hos *gar*·nu	होस गर्नु

Be careful!
hos *gar*·nu·hos! — होस गर्नुहोस !

to take care of	*ja*·tan *gar*·nu	जतन गर्नु
carpet	ga·*laĩ*·cah	गलैंचा
carrot	*gah*·jar	गाजर
to carry	*bok*·nu	बोक्नु
carry basket	*ḍo*·ko	डोको
cashew	*kah*·ju	काजु
cashier	kha·*jahny*·ci	खजाञ्ची
cassette	ṭep	टेप
castle	*ma*·hal	महल
cat	bi·*rah*·lo	बिरालो
cauliflower	*kau*·li	काउली
cave	*gu*·phah	गुफा
to celebrate	ma·*nau*·nu	मनाउनु
cemetery	ci·*hahn*	चिहान
centre	bic	बीच
century	sha·*tahb*·di	शताब्दि
ceramics	*mah*·ṭah·kah	माटाका
	bhãh·ḍah·*kũ*·ḍah	भाँडाकुडा
cereal	*an*·na	अन्न
certain	*pak*·kah • *nish*·cit	पक्का • निश्चित

Are you certain?
ta·*paĩ*·lai *nish*·cit cha? — तपाईलाई निश्चित छ ?

I'm certain.
ma·lai *nish*·cit cha — मलाई निश्चित छ

certificate	pra·*mahṇ*·pa·tra	प्रमाणपत्र
chain	*si*·kri	सिक्री
chair	mec	मेच
championship	sar·ba·bi·*je*·tah	सर्बविजेता
chance	dau	दाउ
to change (money)	*sahṭ*·nu	साट्नु
small change	*khu*·drah *pai*·sah	खुद्रा पैसा
charming	ra·*mai*·lo	रमाइलो
cheap	*sas*·to	सस्तो

Cheat!
ṭhag! ठग !

to check	jāh·*cau*·nu	जचाउँन
cheek	*gah*·lah	गाला
cheese	cij	चीज
chemist	*au*·sa·dhi *pa*·sal	औषधि पसल
chess	*bud*·dhi·cahl	बुद्धिचाल
chest	*chah*·ti	छाती
chicken	*ku*·khu·rah	कुखुरा
chicken meat	*ku*·khu·rah·ko *mah*·su	कुखुराको मासु
child	*bac*·cah	बच्चा
childminding	*bac*·cah *her*·ne	बच्चा हेर्ने
children (own)	cho·rah·*cho*·ri	छोराछोरी
children (general)	ke·ṭah·*ke*·ṭi	केटाकेटी
chilli pepper	khur·*sah*·ni	खुर्सानी
chocolate	*cak*·leṭ	चक्लेट
choko squash	is·*kus*	ईस्कुस
cholera	*hai*·jah	हैजा
to choose	*chahn*·nu	छान्नु
Christian	*i*·sai	ईसाई
Christianity	*i*·sai *dhar*·ma	ईसाई धर्म
church	*gir*·jah·ghar	गीर्जाघर
cigarette	*cu*·roṭ	चुरोट
cigarette paper	*cu*·roṭ *kah*·gaj	चुरोट कागज
cinema	*si*·ne·mah	सिनेमा
cinnamon	*dahl*·ci·ni	दाल्चिनी
circus	ta·*mah*·sah	तमासा
citizen	*nah*·ga·rik	नागरिक
city	*sha*·har	शहर
city centre	*sha*·har·ko bic	शहरको बीच
city wall	*sha*·har·ko par·*khahl*	शहरको पर्खाल
class (social)	*bar*·ga	बर्ग
class system	*bar*·ga·ko *thi*·ti	बर्गको थिति
to clean	sa·*phah gar*·nu	सफा गर्नु

clerk	*ba*·hi·dahr	बहिदार
clever	ca·*lahkh*	चलाख
cliff	bhir	भीर
to climb	*caḍh*·nu	चढ्नु
clinic	ci·kit·*sah*·la·ya	चिकित्सालय
clock	*bhit*·te *gha*·ḍi	भि त्ते घडी
to close	*ban*·da *gar*·nu	बन्द गर्नु
closed	*ban*·da	बन्द
cloth	*ka*·pa·ḍah	कपडा
clothing	*lu*·gah	लुगा
clothing store	*lu*·gah *pa*·sal	लुगा पसल
cloud	*bah*·dal	बादल
cloudy	*bad*·li	बदली
cloves	lwahng	ल्वाङ्ग
coast	ki·*nahr*	किनार
coat	koṭ	कोट
cobbler	*sahr*·ki	सार्की
cockroach	*sãhng*·glo	साङ्ला
coconut	*na*·ri·wal	नरिवल
coffee	*ka*·phi	कफी
coin	*mu*·drah	मुद्रा
cold (weather)	*jah*·ḍo	जाडो
cold (to the touch)	*ci*·so	चिसो

It's cold.
jah·ḍo/*ci*·so cha — जाडो/चिसो छ

cold water	*ci*·so *pah*·ni	चिसो पानी
cold (viral infection)	*ru*·ghah	रुघा
to have a cold	*ru*·ghah *lahg*·nu	रुघा लाग्नु
colleague	*sã*·gi	संगी
to collect	ja·*mau*·nu	जमाउनु
college	ma·hah·bi·*dyah*·la·ya	महाबिद्यालय
colour	rang	रङ्ग
comb	*kãi*·yo	काईंयो
to come	*au*·nu	आउनु
comedy	*hah*·sya·pur·ṇa *ra*·ca·nah	हास्यपुर्ण रचना
comfortable	*ah*·rahm	आराम
communism	*sahm*·ya·bahd	साम्यबाद
communist	*sahm*·ya·bah·di	साम्यबादी
companion	*sah*·thi	साथी
company	*kam*·pa·ni	कम्पनी
compass	di·shah·*su*·cak *yan*·tra	दिशासूचक यन्त्र
compassion	ka·*ru*·ṇah	करुणा
concert	*kan*·sarṭ	कन्सर्ट

condom	ḍhahl	ढाल
to confirm	*pak*·kah *gar*·nu	पक्का गर्नु
Congratulations!		
ba·dhai!	बधाइ !	
conservative	pu·rah·tan·*bah*·di	पुरातनबादी
to be constipated	*di*·sah *kas*·nu	दिसा कस्नु
constipation	*di*·sah *ka*·se·ko	दिसा कसेको
consulate	*rahj*·du·tah·vahs	राजदूतावास
contaminated	*ju*·ṭho	जुठो
contraception	*gar*·bha·ni·rodh	गर्बनिरोधक
contraceptive device	*pa*·ri·bahr ni·*yo*·jan·ko *sah*·dhan	परिवार नियोजनको साधन
contract	*ṭhek*·kah	ठेक्का
convent	*ahsh*·ram	आश्रम
conversation	ku·rah·*kah*·ni	कुराकानी
cook	*bhahn*·se	भान्से
to cook	pa·*kau*·nu	पकाउनु
cool (adj)	*shi*·tal	शीतल
Cool!		
kha·ta·rah !	खतरा !	
cooperative (n)	*sah*·jhah	साझा
coriander (dried)	*dha*·ni·yāh	धनिया
coriander (fresh)	*ha*·ri·yo *dha*·ni·yāh	हरियो धनिया
corn	*ma*·kai	मकै
corner	*ku*·nah	कुना
corrupt	*bhras*·ṭa	भ्रष्ट
corruption	*bhras*·ṭah·cahr	भ्रष्टाचार
to cost	*lahg*·nu	लाग्नु
How much does it cost to go to ...?		
... *jah*·na·lai *ka*·ti *pai*·sah *lahg*·cha?	... जानलाई कति पैसा लाग्छ ?	
cotton	*su*·ti	सुती
cough	*kho*·ki	खोकी
to count	*gan*·nu	गन्नु
country	desh	देश
countryside	*sha*·har *bah*·hi·ra·ko bheg	शहर बाहिरको भेग
coupon	*ku*·pan	कुपन
court (legal)	*a*·dah·lat	अदालत
courtyard	cok	चोक
cow	gai	गाई
cowshed	goṭh	गोठ

craft	ka·*lah*	कला
cramp	*baū*·dyai	दुखाई
crazy	*bau*·lah·hah	बौलाहा
cream	tar	तर
credit	u·*dhah*·ro	उधारो
credit card	*kre*·diṭ kahrḍ	क्रेडिट कार्ड

Can I pay by credit card?
kre·diṭ kahrḍ·le *tir*·nu·hun·cha? क्रेडिट कार्डले तिर्नुहुन्छ ?

creek	*kho*·lah	खोला
cremation	dah·ha·*sā*·skahr	दाह संस्कार
crocodile	*go*·hi	गोही
crop	*bah*·li	बाली
cross-country trail	*go*·re·ṭo *bah*·ṭo	गोरेटो बाटो
crow	kahg	काग
crowd	hul	हूल
cucumber	*kāh*·kro	काँक्रो
to cuddle	*kahkh*·mah *cyahp*·nu	काखमा च्याप्नु
to cultivate	*khan*·jot *gar*·nu	खनजोत गर्नु
cultural show	sāh·*skri*·tik pra·*dar*·shan	साँस्कृतिक प्रदर्शन
culture	sā·*skri*·ti	सँस्कृति
cumin	*ji*·rah	जीरा
cup	kap	कप
cupboard	da·*rahj*	दराज
curd (yogurt)	*da*·hi	दही
current affairs	*tah*·jah *kah*·ro·bahr	ताजा कारोबार
curtain	*par*·dah	पर्दा
customs	*bhan*·sahr	भन्सार
cut (n)	ghau	घाउ
to cut	*kahṭ*·nu	काट्नु
CV (resume)	*bai*·yo·ḍah·ṭah	बाइयोडाटा
to cycle	*sai*·kal ca·*lau*·nu	साइकल चलाउनु
cycling	*sai*·kal ca·*lau*·ne	साइकल चलाउने
cyclist	*sai*·kal ca·*lau*·ne *mahn*·che	साइकल चलाउने मान्छे

D

dad	bah	बा
daily	*din*·hū	दिनहुँ
dairy	dug·dha·*shah*·lah	दूग्धशाला
dairy products	*dudh*·ko *khah*·nah	दूधको खाना
damp	*o*·si·lo	ओसिलो
to dance	*nahc*·nu	नाच्नु
dancer	*nar*·ta·ki	नर्तकी

dangerous	*kha*·ta·rah	खतरा
dark	ã·*dhyah*·ro	अध्याँरो
date (appointment)	bheṭ *gar*·ne sa·*ma*·ya	भेट गर्ने समय
date (*Bikram* calendar)	*ga*·te	गते
date (Gregorian calendar)	*tah*·rikh	तारिख
dates (fruit)	cho·*ha*·rah	छोहरा
daughter	*cho*·ri	छोरी
dawn	bi·*hahn*	विहान
day	din	दिन
in (six) days	(cha) din *pa*·chi	(छ) दिन पछि
day after tomorrow	*par*·si	पर्सी
day before yesterday	*as*·ti	अस्ती
dead	*ma*·re·ko	मरेको
deaf	*ba*·hi·ro	बहिरो
death	*mri*·tyu	मृत्यु
to decide	*nir*·ṇa·ya *gar*·nu	निर्णय गर्नु
deck of cards	tahs	तास
deep	*ga*·hi·ro	गहिरो
deer	*mri*·ga • *ha*·riṇ	मृग • हरिण
to defecate	*di*·sah *gar*·nu	दिसा गर्नु
deforestation	ban·bi·*nahs*	वन विनाश
degree (extent)	u·*pah*·dhi	उपाधि
delayed (late)	a·*be*·lah	अबेला
delicious	*mi*·ṭho	मीठो
delirium	*mur*·chah	मुर्छा
democracy	pra·*jah*·tan·tra	प्रजातन्त्र
demonstration	ju·*lus*	जुलूस
dentist	*dãht*·ko *ḍahk*·ṭar	दाँतको डाक्टर
to deny	na·*mahn*·nu	नमान्नु
to depart	pras·*thahn gar*·nu	प्रस्थान गर्नु
departure	pras·*thahn*	प्रस्थान
descendant	san·*tahn*	सन्तान
design	*na*·mu·nah	नमुना
destination	*la*·cha • u·*de*·shya	लक्ष्य • उदेश्य
to destroy	nahsh *gar*·nu	नाश गर्नु
development	bi·*kahs*	बिकास
diabetes	ma·dhu·*me*·ha	मधुमेह
diabetic	ma·dhu·*me*·ha *ro*·gi	मधुमेह रोगी
diaper	*bac*·cah·ko *ṭah*·lo	बच्चाको टालो
diarrhoea	*jhah*·ḍah • *pa*·khah·lah	झाडा • पखाला
diary	din·*car*·yah	दिनचर्या
dice/die	*go*·ṭi	गोटी

dictatorship	tah·nah·*shah*·hi	तानाशाही
dictionary	*shab*·da·kosh	शब्दकोश
to die	*mar*·nu	मर्नु
different	*pha*·rak	फरक
difficult	*gah*·hro	गाह्रो
dinner	bhaht	भात
direct (from a to b)	*si*·dhah	सिधा
direct (manner)	*si*·dhah	सिधा
direction	*di*·shah	दिशा
director	ḍai·*rek*·ṭar	डाईरेक्टर
dirty	*pho*·hor	फोहोर
disabled	a·*pahng*·ga	अपाङ्ग
disadvantage	be·*phai*·dah	बेफाइदा
discount	chuṭ	छुट
to discount	gha·*ṭau*·nu	घटाउनु
to discover	*pat*·tah *lau*·nu	पत्ता लाउनु
discrimination	*pa*·cha·paht	पक्षपात
disease	rog	रोग
dish (container)	*bhā̃h*·ḍah	भाँडा
dish (food)	*pa*·ri·kahr	परिकार
disinfectant	ji·vah·ṇu·*ra*·hit	जिवाणुरहित
distance (eg, 3 km)	kos	कोस
dizzy	ring·*ga*·ṭah	रिङ्गटा
to do	*gar*·nu	गर्नु

What are you doing?
ta·*paĩ* ke *gar*·nu·hun·cha? — तपाई के गर्नुहुन्छ ?

I didn't do it.
mai·le *ga*·ri·nã — मैले गरिन

doctor	*ḍahk*·ṭar	डाक्टर
dog	*ku*·kur	कुकुर
doll	*pu*·ta·li	पुतली
dome	*stu*·pah	स्तुपा
donkey	*ga*·dhah	गधा
door	*ḍho*·kah	ढोका
double	*do*·bar	दोबर
double bed	*du*·i·ja·nah·ko khahṭ	दुईजनाको खाट
double room	*du*·i·ja·nah·ko *ko*·ṭhah	दुईजनाको कोठा
down	*ta*·la	तल
downhill	o·*rah*·lo	ओरालो
downward	*ta*·la·ti·ra	तलतिर
dozen	*dar*·jan	दर्जन
drama (play)	*nah*·ṭak	नाटक
dramatic	*nah*·ṭa·ki·ya	नाटकीय

dream	*sa*·pa·nah	सपना
to dream	*sa*·pa·nah *dekh*·nu	सपना देख्नु
dress	*jah*·mah	जामा
to dress	*lu*·gah la·*gau*·nu	लुगा लगाउनु
drink	pahn	पिउने पदार्थ
to drink	pi·*u*·nu	पिउनु
drinking water	*khah*·ne *pah*·ni	खाने पानी
to drive	*hãhk*·nu	हाक्नु
drowsy	ung	लठ्ठीएको
drug (illegal)	na·*sah*·lu *au*·sa·dhi	नसालु औषधि
drug (legal)	*o*·kha·ti	ओखती
drug addiction	*o*·kha·ti·ko lat	ओखतीको लत
drums	da·*mah*·hah • ḍhol	दमाहा • ढोल
to be drunk	*rak*·si *lahg*·nu	रक्सी लाग्नु
dry	*suk*·khah	सुख्खा
to dry (clothes)	*(lu*·gah) su·*kau*·nu	(लुगा) सुकाउनु
duck	hãhs	ह्रास
during	a·*ba*·dhi	अवधि
dusk	*san*·dhyah·kahl	सन्ध्याकाल
dust	*dhu*·lo	धूलो
dysentery	ra·gat·*mah*·si	रगतमासी

E

each	*ha*·rek	हरेक
eagle	cil	चील
ear	kahn	कान
early	*sa*·be·rai	सबेरै

It's early.
sa·be·rai ho सबेरै हो

to earn	ka·*mau*·nu	कमाउनु
earring	ṭap	टप
Earth	*pri*·thi·bi	पृथ्वी
earth (soil)	*mah*·ṭo	माटो
earthquake	bhuĩ·*cah*·lo	भूईंचालो
east	*pur*·ba	पुर्व
easy	*sa*·ji·lo	सजिलो
to eat	*khah*·nu	खानु
economical	kam·*khar*·chi·lo	कम खर्चिलो
economy	*ar*·tha bya·*bas*·thah	अर्थ ब्यबस्था
education	*shi*·chah	शिक्षा
eel	bahm	बाम
egg	phul • *aṇ*·ḍah	फुल • अण्डा
eggplant	*bhahṇ*·ṭah	भाण्टा

elbow	ku·*hi*·no	कुहिनो
election	cu·*nahb*	चुनाब
electricity	*bi*·ju·li	बिजुली
elephant	*haht*·ti	हात्ती
else	*a*·ru	अरु
email	*i*·mel	इमेल
embarrassed	*laj*·jit	लज्जित
embarrassment	lahj	लाज
embassy	*rahj*·du·tah·vahs	राजदूतावास
embroidery	buṭ·ṭah	बुट्टा
emergency	*ah*·pat	आपत्
employee	*jah*·gi·re	जागिरे
employer	*mah*·lik/*mah*·lik·ni **(m/f)**	मालिक/मालिकनी
empty	*khah*·li	खाली
end	*an*·ta	अन्त
to end	*an*·ta *hu*·nu	अन्त हुनु
endangered species	*kha*·ta·rah·mah *par*·ne *bar*·ga	खतरामा पर्ने वर्ग
energy	*shak*·ti	शक्ति
engagement	*vahg*·dahn	वाग्दान
engine	*in*·jin	इन्जिन
engineer	in·ji·*ni*·yar	इन्जिनियर
English	ang·*gre*·ji	अङ्ग्रेजी
to enjoy	*maj*·jah *lahg*·nu	मज्जा लाग्नु
enough	pra·*shas*·ta	प्रशस्त
to be enough	*pug*·nu	पु ग्नु

Enough!
bha·yo ! भयो !

to enter	*pas*·nu	पस्नु

Do not enter.
pra·besh ni·*sedh* प्रबेश निषेध

entertaining	*maj*·jah *lahg*·ne	मज्जा लाग्ने
envelope	khahm	खाम
environment	bah·tah·*ba*·raṇ	वातावरण
epilepsy	*chah*·re rog	छारे रोग
equal	ba·*rah*·bar	बराबर
equality	sa·*mahn*·tah • ba·*rah*·ba·ri	समानता • बराबरी
equipment	*sah*·mahn	सामान
evening	*be*·lu·kah	बेलुका
event	*gha*·ṭa·nah	घटना
Everest (Mount)	sa·gar·mah·*thah*	सगरमाथा
every	*ha*·rek	हरेक

every day	*ha*·rek din	हरेक दिन
exact(ly)	ṭhik	ठीक
example	u·*dah*·ha·raṇ	उदाहरण
excellent	*ut*·tam	उत्तम
exchange	*sah*·ṭo	साटो
to exchange	*sahṭ*·nu	साट्नु
exchange rate	*sahṭ*·ne reṭ	साट्ने रेट
excluded	*bah*·hek	बाहेक

Excuse me.
ma·lai mahph *gar*·nu·hos — मलाई माफ गर्नुहोस

exercise book	*kah*·pi	कापि
exhibition	pra·*dar*·sha·ni	प्रदर्शनी
exile	desh ni·*kah*·lah	देश निकाला
exit	ni·*kahs*	निकास
exotic	bi·*ci*·tra	विचित्र
to expect	a·*pe*·chah *gar*·nu	अपेक्षा गर्नु
expensive	ma·*hā*·go	महंगो
experience	*a*·nu·bhab	अनुभब
to experience	*a*·nu·bhab *gar*·nu	अनुभब गर्नु
exploitation	*sho*·saṇ	शोषण
export	*nir*·yaht	निर्यात
to export	*nir*·yaht *gar*·nu	निर्यात गर्नु
to extend	*thap*·nu	थप्नु
eye	*āh*·khah	आँखा

F

face	*a*·nu·hahr	अनुहार
factory	kahr·*khah*·nah	कारखाना
factory worker	kahr·*khah*·nah·ko *maj*·dur	कारखानाका मजदूर
faeces	*di*·sah	दिसा
fair (festival)	*me*·lah	मेला
faith	bi·*shwahs*	विश्वास
falcon	bahj	बाज
fall (autumn)	*sha*·rad *ri*·tu	शरद ऋतु
to fall	*khas*·nu	खस्नु
false	*jhu*·ṭo	झूटो
family	*pa*·ri·bahr	परिवार
famous	pra·*sid*·dha	प्रसिद्ध
fan (cooling)	*pā*·khah	पंखा
far	*ṭah*·ḍhah	टाढा
farm	*khet*·bah·ri	खेतबारी
farmer	ki·*sahn*	किसान
fast (adj)	*chi*·ṭo	छिटो

fast (n)	*bar*·ta	वार्ता
fat	*mo*·ṭo	मोटो
father	*bu*·wah	बुवा
father-in-law	*sa*·su·rah	ससुरा
fault	*ka*·sur	कसुर
faulty	kahm na·*gar*·ne	काम नगर्ने
fear	ḍar	डर
to fear	*ḍar*·nu	डराउनु
feast	bhoj	भोज
fee	*shul*·ka	शुल्क
to feed	khu·*wau*·nu	खुवाउनु
to feel	*lahg*·nu	लाग्नु
to feel like	man *lahg*·nu	मन लाग्नु
feelings	*cit*·ta	चित्त
female (animal)	*po*·thi	पोथी
female (person)	stri	स्त्री
fence	bahr	बार
fennel	soph	सोफ
fenugreek	*me*·ṭhi	मेठी
festival	*cahḍ*·bahḍ • *jah*·trah	चाडबाड • जात्रा
fever	*ja*·ro	जरो
(a) few	*tho*·rai	थोरै
fiction	*kal*·pit *ka*·thah	कल्पित कथा
field	khet	खेत
fig	*an*·jir	अन्जीर
fight	*jha*·ga·ḍah	झागडा
to fight	*laḍ*·nu	लड्नु
to fill	*bhar*·nu	भर्नु
film (cinema)	philm • cal·*ci*·tra	फिल्म • चलिचत्र
film (photographic)		
colour film	*rang*·gin ril	रंगीन रील
B&W film	*kah*·lo *se*·to ril	कालो सेतो रील
filter	*cahl*·ni	चाल्नी
filtered	*chah*·ne·ko	छानेको
filtered water	*phil*·ṭar *pah*·ni	फिल्टर पानी
to find	*pau*·nu	पाउनु
fine (n)	ja·ri·*mah*·nah	जरिवाना
finger	*aũ*·lah	औंला
fingernail	nang	नङ
fire	*ah*·go	आगो
firewood	*dau*·rah	दाउरा
first	*pa*·hi·lah	पहिला
fish	*mah*·chah	माछा
fish shop	*mah*·chah *pa*·sal	माछा पसल
flag	*jhaṇ*·ḍah	झण्डा

flashlight (torch)	ṭarc	टर्च
flat (adj)	*cyahp*·ṭo	च्याप्टो
flea	u·*pi*·yãh	उपियाँ
flight	u·*ḍahn*	उडान
floor (of house)	bhu·*ĩ*	भूईं
floor (storey)	*ghar*·ko *ta*·lah	घरको तला
flour	*pi*·ṭho	पीठो
flower	phul	फूल
flu	ru·ghah·*kho*·ki·ko *ja*·ro	रुघाखोकीको जरो
fly	*jhĩ*·gah	झिंगा
fog	ku·*i*·ro	कुइरो
to follow	pa·*chyau*·nu	पछ्याउनु
food	*khah*·nah	खाना
food poisoning	*khah*·nah kha·*rahb*	खाना खराब
foot	*khuṭ*·ṭah	खुट्टा
on foot	hĩ·*ḍe*·ra	हिंडेर
football (soccer)	*laht*·te *bha*·kun·ḍo	लात्ते भकुन्डो
footpath	*go*·re·ṭo	गोरेटो
for	-ko *lah*·gi	-को लागि
foreign(er)	bi·*de*·shi	बिदेशी
forest	ban	बन
forever	*sa*·dhaĩ	सधैं
to forget	*bir*·sa·nu	बिर्सनु

I forget.
ma *bir*·san·chu — म बिर्सन्छु

Forget it! (Don't worry!)
bhai·go ! — भैगो !

to forgive	maph *gar*·nu	माफ गर्नु
fork	*kãh*·ṭah	काँटा
fortnight	*pan*·dhra din	पन्ध्र दिन
fox	*phyau*·ro	प्याउरो
free (at liberty)	swa·*tan*·tra	स्वतन्त्र
free (of charge)	*sit*·taĩ	सित्तैं
freedom	swa·*tan*·tra·tah	स्वतन्त्रता
to freeze	*jam*·nu	जम्नु
fresh	*tah*·jah	ताजा
fried	*bhu*·ṭe·ko	भुटेको
friend	*sah*·thi	साथी
friendly	*mi*·lan·sahr	मिलनसार
to frighten	ḍa·*rau*·nu	डराउनु
frog	*bhyah*·gu·to	भ्यागुतो
from (place)	-*bah*·ṭa	-बाट
from (time)	-*de*·khi	-देखि

in front of	-a·*gah*·ḍi	-अगाडि
frost	tu·*sah*·ro	तुसारो
frostbite	tu·*sah*·ro·le *khah*·ya·ko	तुसारोले खायको
fruit	*phal*·phul	फलफूल
fruit picking	*phal*·phul *ṭip*·ne	फलफूल टिप्ने
full	*bha*·ri	भारी
fun	*maj*·jah	मज्जा
to have fun	*maj*·jah *lahg*·nu	मज्जा लाग्नु
to make fun of	*hãh*·so u·*ḍau*·nu	हाँसो उडाउनु
funeral	ma·*lahm*	मलाम
future (n)	bha·*bi*·sya	भविष्य

G

game (sport)	khel	खेल
garage	*gyah*·rej	ग्यारेज
garbage	*mai*·lah	मैला
garden	ba·*gaĩ*·cah	बगैंचा
gardening	*mah*·li·ko kahm	मालीको काम
garlic	*la*·sun	लसुन
gas	gyãhs	ग्याँस
gas cylinder	gyãhs *si*·lin·ḍar	ग्याँस सिलीन्डर
gate	*ḍho*·kah	ढोका
gay man	*sa*·ma·ling·ga	समिलङ्ग
	sam·bho·gi *pu*·rus	सम्भोगी पुरुष
gem	ju·*hah*·raht	जुहारात

Get lost!
bhahg ! — भाग !

to get off (bus)	*or*·la·nu	ओर्लनु
to get up	*uṭh*·nu	उठ्नु
ghat	ghahṭ	घाट
ghee	ghi·*u*	घिउ
gift	*u*·pa·hahr	उपहार
ginger	*a*·du·wah	अदुवा
girl	*ke*·ṭi	केटी
girlfriend	*pre*·mi·kah	प्रेमिका
to give	*di*·nu	दिनु

Please give me ...
ma·lai ... *di*·nu·hos — मलाई ... दिनुहोस

glass	gi·*lahs*	गिलास
to go	*jah*·nu	जानु

Let's go.
jaũ — जाऔं

DICTIONARY

We'd like to go to ...
hah·mi·lai ...·mah *jah*·na man *lahg*·yo हामीलाई ...मा जान मन लाग्यो

Go straight ahead.
si·dhah *jah*·nu·hos सिधा जानुहोस

to go on foot	hĩ·*ḍe*·ra *jah*·nu	हिंडेर जानु
goal	gol	गोल्
goalkeeper	*gol*·ki	गोल्की
goat	*bahkh*·ro	बाख्रो
goatmeat	*kha*·si·ko *mah*·su	खसीको मासु
god	*de*·va·tah	देवता
God	*bha*·ga·bahn	भगबान
goddess	*de*·va·tah	देवता
gold (n)	sun	सुन
gold (adj)	*sun*·ko	सुनको
good	*rahm*·ro	राम्रो
goodbye	na·ma·*ste*	नमस्ते
goodnight	shu·bha·*rah*·tri	शुभरात्री
goods	*sah*·mahn	सामान
government	sar·*kahr*	सरकार
gram	grahm	ग्राम
grandchildren	nah·ti·*nah*·ti·ni	नातिनातिनी
grandfather	*bah*·je	बाजे
grandmother	*ba*·jyai	बज्यै
grape	*ã*·gur	अंगुर
grapefruit	*bho*·ga·ṭe	भोगटे
grass	ghãhs	घाँस
grateful	gun *mahn*·ne	घुम्ने
great (powerful)	bi·*shahl*	बिशाल

Great!
kha·ta·rah! खतरा !

greedy	*lo*·bhi	लोभी
green	*ha*·ri·yo	हरियो
Gregorian calendar	*is*·vi *sam*·bat	इस्वी सम्बत्
grey	*khai*·ro	खैरो
to grow (crop)	ub·*jau*·nu	उब्जाउनु
to grow (in size)	*baḍh*·nu	बढ्नु
guava	*am*·bah	अम्बा
to guess	*an*·dahj *gar*·nu	अन्दाज गर्नु
guest	*pah*·hu·nah	पाहुना
guesthouse	*pah*·hu·nah ghar	पाहुना घर
guide	*bah*·ṭo de·*khau*·ne *mahn*·che	बाटो देखाउने मान्छे
guidebook	nir·*de*·shan·ko ki·*tahb*	निर्देशनको किताब

english–nepali

guilty	a·pa·*rah*·dhi	अपराधी
not guilty	a·pa·*rah*·dhi *hoi*·na	अपराधी होइन
guitar	gi·*tahr*	गितार
gym	*byah*·yahm·shah·lah	ब्यायामशाला
gymnastics	*byah*·yahm	ब्यायाम

H

hair	ka·*pahl*	कपाल
hairbrush	ka·*pahl kor*·ne bu·*rus*	कपाल कोर्ने बुरुस
hairpin	*kãh*·ṭah	काँटा
half	*ah*·dhah	आधा
half a litre	*ah*·dhah *li*·ṭar	आधा लिटर
hallucination	bhram	भ्रम
hammer	ghan	घन
hand	haht	हात
handbag	byahg	ब्याग
handicraft	*has*·ta·ka·lah	हस्तकला
handkerchief	ru·*mahl*	रुमाल
handmade	*haht*·le *ba*·ne·ko	हातले बनेको
handsome	*sun*·dar	सुन्दर
happy	*khu*·si	खुसी

Happy Birthday!
jan·ma·din·ko shu·bha·*kah*·ma·nah! जन्मदिनको शुभकामना !

hard (difficult)	*gah*·hro	गाह्रो
hard (not soft)	*ka*·ḍah	कडा
harness	sahj	काठी कस्नु
hashish	*ca*·res	चरेस
hat	ṭop	टोपी
to have	cha	छ

Do you have ...?
ta·*paĩ* ... cha? तपाई ... छ ?

I have ...
ma ... cha म ... छ

he (pol)	*wa*·hãh	वहाँ
he (inf)	*u*·ni • tyo • yo	ऊनी • त्यो • यो
head	*ṭau*·ko	टाउको
headache	*ṭau*·ko *dukh*·yo	टाउको दुख्यो
headstrap	*nahm*·lo	नाम्लो
health	*swahs*·thya	स्वास्थ्य
health post	ci·kit·*sah*·la·ya	चिकित्सालय
to hear	*sun*·nu	सुन्नु

heart	*mu*·ṭu	मुटु
heat	rahp	राप
heater (electric)	*hi*·ṭar	हिटर
heaven	*swar*·ga	स्वर्ग
heavy	*ga*·hraũ	गह्रौं
hell	*na*·rak	नरक
hello	na·ma·*ste*	नमस्ते

Hello? (answering a call)
ha·*jur?* हजुर ?

helmet	pha·*lah*·me *ṭo*·pi	फलामे टोपी
to help	*mad*·dat *gar*·nu	मद्दत गर्नु

Help!
gu·*hahr*! गुहार !

hemp	*pa*·ṭu·wah	पटुवा
hemp powder	bhahng	भाङ्ग
hen	*ku*·khu·ri	कुखुरी
herb	ja·ḍi·*bu*·ṭi	जडीबूटी
here	*ya*·hãh	यहाँ
high	*u*·co	उचो
to hike	*pai*·dal *gar*·nu	पैदल गर्नु
hiking	*pai*·dal *yah*·trah	पैदल यात्रा
hiking route	*pai*·dal·ko *bah*·ṭo	पैदल बाटो
hill	*ḍãh*·ḍah	डाँडा
hillperson	pa·*hah*·ḍi	पहाडी
Hindu	*hin*·du	हिन्दू
Hindu calendar	*bik*·ram *sam*·bat	बिक्रम सम्बत्
Hinduism	*hin*·du *dhar*·ma	हिन्दू धर्म
hip (n)	cahk	चाक
to hire	*bhah*·ḍah·mah *li*·nu	भाडामा लिनु

I want to hire ...
ma ... *bhah*·ḍah·mah *li*·nu *par*·yo म ... भाडामा लिनु पर्यो

hobby	cahkh	चाख
hole	pwahl	प्वाल
holiday	*bi*·dah	बिदा
holy	pa·*bi*·tra	पवित्र
home	ghar	घर
homeless	su·kum·*bah*·si	सुकुम्वासी
honest	i·*mahn*·dahr	इमान्दार
honey	*ma*·ha	मह
honeymoon	pra·*mod*·kahl	प्रमोदकाल

hookah	*huk*·kah	हुक्का
horrible	*ghin*·lahg·do	घिनलाग्दो
horse	*gho*·ḍah	घोडा
horseriding	*gho*·ḍah *caḍh*·na	घोडा चढ्न
hospital	*as*·pa·tahl	अस्पताल
hospitality	*bya*·ba·hahr	ब्यबहार
hot (to the touch)	*tah*·to	तातो
hot (weather)	*gar*·mi	गर्मी

It's hot.
gar·mi cha — गर्मी छ

hot water	*tah*·to *pah*·ni	तातो पानी
to be hot	*gar*·mi/*tah*·to *lahg*·nu	गर्मी/तातो लाग्नु
hotel	*ho*·ṭel	होटेल
hour	*ghaṇ*·ṭah	घण्टा
house	ghar	घर
housework	ba·ḍhahr·*kũ*·ḍhahr	घरायसी काम
how (quality)	*kas*·to	कस्तो
how (means)	*ka*·sa·ri	कसरी

How do I get to ...?
...·mah *ka*·sa·ri *jah*·ne? — ...मा कसरी जाने ?

How do you say ...?
...·lai ke *bhan*·cha? — ...लाई के भान्छ ?

how much/many	*ka*·ti	कति
hug	ã·*gah*·lo	अंगालो
human (n)	*mah*·nis	मानिस
human rights	mah·nab·*a*·dhi·kahr	मानवअधिकार
humid	*bahs*·pi·ya	बाष्पीय
(one) hundred	(ek) say	(एक) सय
hungry	bhok	भोक

Are you hungry?
ta·*paĩ*·lai bhok *lahg*·yo? — तपाईलाई भोक लाग्यो ?

I'm hungry.
ma·lai bhok *lahg*·yo — मलाई भोक लाग्यो

to hurry	ha·*tahr gar*·nu	हतार गर्नु
(in a) hurry	ha·*tahr*	हतार
hurt	coṭ	चोट
to hurt (ache)	*dukh*·nu	दुख्नु
to hurt (cause someone pain)	du·*khau*·nu	दुखाउनु
husband (own)	*log*·ne	लोग्ने

husband (someone else's)	*sri*·mahn	श्रीमान
hut	*jhu*·pro	झुप्रो

I

I	ma	म
ice	*ba*·raph	बरफ
ice axe	*gaĩ*·ti	गैंती
ice cream	*khu*·wah *ba*·raph	खुवा बरफ
ice peak	hi·*mahl*	हिमाल
idea	bi·*cahr*	बिचार
identity card	*pa*·ri·ca·ya *pa*·tra	पिरचय पत्र
idol	*mur*·ti	मुर्ति
if	*ya*·di • *bha*·ne	यदि • भने
ill	bi·*rah*·mi	बिरामी
illegal	*ni*·yam·bi·rodh	नियम विरोध
illness	rog	रोग
imagination	*kal*·pa·nah	कल्पना
imitation (fake)	*nak*·kal	नक्कल
immediately	tu·*run*·tai • *a*·hil·yai	तुरून्तै • अहिल्यै
immigration	a·*dhyah*·ga·man	अध्यागमन
import	*ah*·yaht	आयात
to import	*ah*·yaht *gar*·nu	आयात गर्नु
important	ma·*hat*·twa·pur·ṇa	महत्वपुर्ण

It's important.
ma·*hat*·twa·pur·ṇa cha — महत्वपुर्ण छ

It's not important.
ma·*hat*·twa·pur·ṇa *chai*·na — महत्वपुर्ण छैन

impossible	a·*sam*·bhab	असम्भब
imprisonment	kah·rah·*bahs*	काराबास
in	-mah	-मा
in front of	-a·*gah*·ḍi	-अगाडि
incense burner	dhup *dah*·ni	धुप दानि
including	*sa*·met	समेत
incomprehensible	na·*bu*·jhi·ne	नबुझिने
inconvenient	a·*su*·bi·dhah	असुबिधा
India	*bhah*·rat	भारत
indigestion	*a*·pac	अपच
industry	*u*·dyog	उद्योग
inflammation	*sun*·ni·ye·ko *a*·bas·thah	सुन्निएको अबस्था
influenza	ru·ghah·*kho*·ki·ko *ja*·ro	रुघाखोकीको जरो
informal	a·nau·pa·*cah*·rik	अनौपचारिक
information	jahn·*kah*·ri	जानकारी

to inject	*bhi*·tra pa·*sau*·nu	भित्र पसाउनु
injection	*su*·i	सूई
injury	coṭ	चोट
ink	*ma*·si	मसी
insect	*ki*·rah	कीरा
inside	*bhi*·tra	भित्र
instructor	*shi*·chak • a·*dhyah*·pak	शिक्षक • अध्यापक
insurance	*bi*·mah	बिमा
interesting	cahkh *lahg*·do	चाख लाग्दो
intermission	*bish*·rahm	बिश्राम
international	an·tar·*rah*·sṭri·ya	अन्तर्राष्ट्रिय
interview	an·tar·*bahr*·tah	अन्तवार्ता
to invite	*nim*·tah *gar*·nu	निम्ता गर्नु
iodine	*ai*·ḍin	आयोडिन
Islam	is·*lahm dhar*·ma	इस्लाम धर्म
island	*ṭah*·pu • dwip	टापु • द्वीप
it	tyo • yo	त्यो • यो
to itch	ci·*lau*·nu	चिलाउनु

J

jackal	syahl	स्याल
jail	*jhyahl*·khah·nah	झ्यालखाना
jar	su·*rah*·hi	सुराही
jealous	*ḍah*·hah	डाहा
jeans	*jin*·painṭ	जीनपाइन्ट
Jew/Jewish	ya·*hu*·di	यहुदी
jewel	ju·*hah*·raht	जुहारात
jewellery	*ga*·ha·nah	गहना
job	kahm	काम
job advertisement	*kahm*·ko pra·*cahr*	कामको प्रचार
joke	khyahl • *ṭhaṭ*·ṭah	ख्याल • ठट्टा

I'm joking.
mai·le khyahl *ga*·re·ko — मैले ख्याल गरेको

journalist	*pa*·tra·kahr	पत्रकार
journey	*yah*·trah	यात्रा
Judaism	ya·*hu*·di *dhar*·ma	यहुदी धर्म
judge	nyah·*yah*·dhish	न्यायाधीश
jug	su·*rah*·hi	सुराही
juice	ras	रस
to jump	u·*phra*·nu	उफ्रनु
jumper (sweater)	*swi*·ṭar	स्विटर
jungle	ban	बन
justice	*nyah*·ya	न्याय

K

keen (to ...)	... *gar*·ne *ut*·suk	... गनेर् उत्सुक
kerosene	ma·ṭi·*tel*	मिटतेल
key	*sãh*·co	साँचो
to kick	*laht*·ta·le hir·*kau*·nu	लात्ताले हिकार्उनु
kidney	mir·*gau*·lah	मृगौला
to kill	*mahr*·nu	मार्नु
kilogram	*ki*·lo	किलो
kilometre	*ki*·lo	किलो
kind (type)	*ki*·sim	किसिम
kindergarten	*nar*·sa·ri	स्कुल
kindness	*da*·yah	दया
king	*rah*·jah	राजा
kiss	mwaĩ	म्वाई
to kiss	mwaĩ *khah*·nu	म्वाई खानु
kitchen	*bhahn*·chah	भान्छा
kitten	bi·*rah*·lah·ko *chau*·ro	बिरालाको छाउरो
knee	*ghũ*·ḍah	घुँडा
knife	*cak*·ku • *khu*·ku·ri	चक्कु • खुकुरी
to know (person)	*cin*·nu	चिन्नु
to know (something)	*thah*·ha *hu*·nu	थाहा हुनु

I don't know.
ma·lai *thah*·ha *chai*·na — मलाई थाहा छैन

knowledge	*thah*·ha	थाहा

L

lace (shoe)	*phit*·tah	फित्ता
lake	tahl	ताल
lamp	*bat*·ti	बत्ती
lamp (ceremonial)	*ci*·rahg	चीराग
lamp (made of sacred butter)	dip	दिप
land	*jag*·gah	जग्गा
landslide	*pa*·hi·ro	पहिरो
language	*bhah*·sah	भाषा
large	*ṭhu*·lo	ठूलो
last	*an*·tim • *ga*·ya·ko	अन्तिम • गएको
last month	*ga*·ya·ko *ma*·hi·nah	गयको महीना
last night	*hi*·jo *rah*·ti	हिजो राति
last week	*ga*·ya·ko *hap*·tah	गएको हप्ता
last year	*ga*·ya·ko *bar*·sa	गएको वर्ष
late	*ḍhi*·lo	ढिलो

It's late.
ḍhi·lo cha — ढिलो छ

to laugh	*hãhs*·nu	हाँस्नु
to launder	*dhu*·nu	धुनु
laundry	*lu*·gah·dhu·ne ṭhaũ	लुगाधुने ठाउँ
law	*kah*·nun	कानुन
lawyer	*wa*·kil	वकील
laxative	ju·*lahph*	जुलाफ
lazy	*al*·chi	अल्छी
leader	*ne*·tah	नेता
leaf	paht	पात
to learn	*sik*·nu	सिक्नु
leather	*chah*·lah	छाला
leathergoods	*chah*·lah·ko *sah*·mahn	छालाको सामान
to leave	*choḍ*·nu	छोड्नु
ledge	cheu	छेउ
leech	*ju*·kah	जुका
left	*bah*·yãh	बायाँ
leg	*go*·ḍah	गोडा
legal	*kah*·nu·ni	कानुनी
to legalise	*kah*·nu·ni *ah*·dhahr *di*·nu	कानुनी आधार दिनु
lemon	*kah*·ga·ti	कागती
lens	*ai*·nah	ऐना
lentils	dahl	दाल
black lentils	*kah*·lo dahl	कालो दाल
brown lentils	*khai*·ro dahl	खैरो दाल
red lentils	*mu*·sur dahl	मुसुर दाल
leopard	*ci*·tu·wah	चितुवा
leper	*kus*·ṭhi	कुष्ठी
leprosy	*kus*·ṭa·rog	कुष्टरोग
lesbian	stri *sam*·bho·gi *ai*·mai	स्त्री सम्भोगी आईमाई
less	kam	कम
letter	*ci*·ṭhi	चिठी
liar	ḍhãhṭ	झुठो बोल्ने मानिस
library	pus·ta·*kah*·la·ya	पुस्तकालय
lice/louse	*jum*·rah	जुम्रा
to lie (down)	*laḍ*·nu	लड्नु
to lie (dishonest)	*ḍhãhṭ*·nu	ढाट्नु
life	*ji*·van • *jin*·da·gi	जीवन • जिन्दगी
light (n)	*bat*·ti	बत्ती
light (colour)	*phi*·kah	फिक्का
lightbulb	cim	चिम
lightning	*bi*·ju·li *cam*·kai	बिजुली चम्काई

lightweight	ha·*lu*·kah	हलुका
like	*jas*·to	जस्तो
to like	man *par*·nu	मन पर्नु
line	*re*·khah	रेखा
lion	*sĩ*·ha	सिंह
lips	oṭh	ओठ
to listen	*sun*·nu	सुन्नु
little (small)	*sah*·no	सानो
a little (bit)	*a*·li *a*·li • a·li·*ka*·ti	अलिअलि • अलिकति
to live (life)	*bāhc*·nu	बाँच्नु
to live (somewhere)	*bas*·nu	बस्नु

Long live ...!
ja·ya ...! जय ...!

liver	*ka*·le·jo	कलेजो
lizard	che·*pah*·ro	छेपारो
load	*bhah*·ri	भारी
local	*sthah*·ni·ya	स्थानीय
location	ṭhaũ	ठाउँ
lock	*tahl*·cah	ताल्चा
to lock	*tahl*·cah *gar*·nu	ताल्चा गर्नु
lodge	laj	लज
long	*lah*·mo	लामो
to look	*her*·nu	हेर्नु
to look after	*her*·bi·cahr *gar*·nu	हेरविचार गर्नु
to look for	*khoj*·nu	खोज्नु
loose	*khu*·ku·lo	खुकुलो
to lose	ha·*rau*·nu	हराउनु
loss	*nok*·sahn	नोक्सान
lost	ha·*rau*·na	हराउनु
a lot	*dhe*·rai	धेरै
loud	*uc*·ca	उच्च
love (general)	*mah*·yah	माया
love (romantic)	prem	प्रेम

I love you.
ma ta·*paĩ*·lai *mah*·yah *gar*·chu म तपाईलाई माया गर्छु

low	*ho*·co	होचो
to lower	gha·*ṭau*·nu	घटाउनु
luck	*bhah*·gya	भाग्य
lucky	bhah·gya·*mah*·ni	भाग्यमानी
luggage	*mahl*·sah·mahn	मालसामान
lump	*ḍal*·lo	डल्लो

lunch	*ca*·me·nah	चमेना
lunchtime	*ca*·me·nah·ko *be*·lah	चमेनाको बेला
lung	*phok*·so	फोक्सो
luxury	bi·*lahs*	बिलास

M

machine	kal	कल
made of	-ले *ba*·ne·ko	-ले बनेको
magazine	*pa*·tri·kah	पत्रिका
magician	*jah*·du·gar	जादुगर
mail	ḍãhk	डाँक
mailbox	pa·tra·*many*·ju·sah	पत्र मञ्जुषा
main road	pra·*mukh bah*·ṭo	प्रमुख बाटो
main square	pra·*mukh* cok	प्रमुख चोक
majority	dhe·rai·*ja*·so	धेरैजसो
to make	ba·*nau*·nu	बनाउनु
malaria	*au*·lo	औलो
male (animal)	*bhah*·le	भाले
male (person)	nar	नर
male & female (adj)	nar·*nah*·ri	नरनारी
man & woman (n)	nar·*nah*·ri	नरनारी
man (formal)	pu·*rus*	पुरुष
man (husband)	*log*·ne·mahn·che	लोग्नेमान्छे
man (old)	*bu*·ḍho	बूढो
man (young)	*ke*·ṭah	केटा
mankind	*mah*·nab	मानब
manager	*hah*·kim	हाकिम
mandarin	*sun*·ta·lah	सुन्तला
mango	ãhp	आँप
many	*dhe*·rai	धेरै
map	*nak*·sah	नक्सा

Please show me on the map.
nak·sah·mah *ma*·lai de·*khau*·nu·hos — नक्सा मलाई देखाउनुहोस

marijuana	*gãh*·jah	गाँजा
market	ba·*jahr*	बजार
weekly market	haht ba·*jahr*	हात बजार
marriage	bi·*hah*	विवाह
to marry	bi·*hah gar*·nu	विवाह गर्नु
mask	ma·*kuṇ*·ḍo	मकुण्डो
massage	*mah*·lis	मालिस
mat	*gun*·dri	गुन्द्री
matches	*sa*·lai	सलाइ
mattress	*ḍa*·sa·nah	डसना
maybe	*shah*·yad	शायद

me	*ma*·lai	मलाई
meal	khah·nah	खाना
to measure	*nahp*·nu	नाप्नु
measurement	nahp	नाप
meat	*mah*·su	मासु
mechanic	*mi*·stri	मिस्त्री
medal	*tak*·mah	तक्मा
medicine	*au*·sa·dhi	औषधि
meditation	dhyahn	ध्यान
to meet	*bheṭ*·nu	भेट्नु

I'll meet you.
ma ta·*paī*·lai *bheṭ*·chu — म तपाईलाई भेट्छु

melon	*tar*·bu·jah	तरबुजा
to melt	pa·*gahl*·nu	पगाल्नु
member	sa·*das*·ya	सदस्य
meningitis	me·nī·*jai*·ṭis	मेनिन्जाईटीस
menstruation	*ma*·hi·nah·bah·ri	महीनाबारी
menu	*men*·yu	मेन्यु
message	*kha*·bar	खबर
metal	*dhah*·tu	धातु
middle	bic	बीच
midnight	ma·*dhya*·raht	मध्यरात
military service	*sai*·nik *se*·bah	सैनिक सेबा
milk	dudh	दूध
millet	*ko*·do	कोदो
million	das lahkh	दस लाख
mind	man	मन
mine	*me*·ro	मेरो
minute	*mi*·naṭ	मिनट

Just a minute.
ek·chin — एकछिन

mirror	*ai*·nah	ऐना
miscarriage	*rak*·ta·paht	रक्तपात
to miss (bus)	*chal*·nu	छल्नु
mistake	*gal*·ti	गल्ती
to mix	mi·*sau*·nu	मिसाउनु
modern	ah·*dhu*·nik	आधुनिक
moisturiser	*mukh*·mah la·*gau*·ne krim	मुखमा लगाउने क्रीम
moment	*ek*·chin	एकछिन
monastery	*gum*·bah • bi·*hahr* • ba·*hahl*	गुम्बा • बिहार • बहाल

money	*pai*·sah	पैसा
mongoose	*nyau*·ri *mu*·sah	न्याउरी मूसा
monk (Buddhist)	*bhi*·chu • *lah*·mah	भिक्षु • लामा
monkey	*bãh*·dar	बाँदर
monsoon	*bar*·khah	बाख्रा
month	*ma*·hi·nah	महीना
this month	yo *ma*·hi·nah	यो महीना
monument	*smah*·rak	स्मारक
moon	*can*·dra·mah	चन्द्रमा
moon (dark)	*aũ*·si	औंसी
moon (full)	*pur*·ṇi·mah	पुर्णिमा
more	*a*·ru	अरू
morning	bi·*hah*·na	बिहान
mosque	*mas*·jid	मस्जिद
mosquito	lahm·*khuṭ*·ṭe	लामखुट्टे
mosquito net	jhul	झुल
mother	*ah*·mah	आमा
mother-in-law	*sah*·su	सासू
motorcycle	*mo*·ṭar *sai*·kal	मोटर साइकल
mountain	pa·*hahḍ*	पहाड
mountain bike	*maun*·ṭen baik	माउन्टेन बाइक
mountain climbing	*pa*·hahḍ *caḍh*·nu	पहाड चढ्ने
mountain hut	pa·*hah*·ḍi *jhu*·pro	पहाडी झुप्रो
mountain path	pa·*hah*·ḍi *bah*·ṭo	पहाडी बाटो
high mountain path	hi·*mahl*·ko *bah*·ṭo	हिमालको बाटो
mountain range	*shre*·ṇi	श्रेणी
mountaineer	par·ba·*tah*·ro·hi	पर्वतारोही
mouse	*mu*·sah	मूसा
moustache	*jũ*·gah	जुङ्गा
mouth	mukh	मुख
to move	ca·*lau*·nu	चलाउनु
movie	philm	फिल्म
much	*dhe*·rai	धेरै
mucus	kaph	कफ
mud	*hi*·lo	हिलो
multicoloured	*rang*·gin	रंगीन
mum	*ah*·mai	आमै
muscle	*mãh*·sha·pe·shi	मांशपेशी
museum	sã·gra·*hah*·la·ya	संग्रहालय
mushroom	cyau	च्याउ
music	*sang*·git	सङ्गीत
musician	*sang*·git·kahr	सङ्गीतकार
Muslim	*mu*·sal·mahn	मुसलमान
mute	*lah*·ṭo	लाटो
mutton	*bhẽ*·ḍah·ko *mah*·su	भेंडाको मासु
my	*me*·ro	मेरो

N

name	nahm	नाम
napkin	ru·*mahl*	रुमाल
narcotic	*lah*·gu *au*·sa·dhi	लागु औषधि
narrow	*sãh*·ghu·ro	साँघुरो
nationality	*rah*·sṭri·ya·tah	राष्ट्रियता
nature	*pra*·kri·ti	प्रकृति
nausea	*wahk*·wah·ki	वाकवाकि
near	*na*·jik	नजीक
nearby	*na*·ji·kai	नजिकै
necessary	*ah*·ba·shyak	आबश्यक
neck	*ghãh*·ṭi	घाँटी
necklace	*mah*·lah	माला
needle (sewing)	*si*·yo	सियो
needle (syringe)	*si*·rinj	सिरिन्ज
Nepalese knife	*khu*·ku·ri	खुकुरी
net	jahl	जाल
never	*ka*·hi·le *hoi*·na	कहिले होइन
new	*na*·yãh	नयाँ
news	*sa*·mah·cahr	समाचार
newspaper	*a*·kha·bahr	अखबार
next	*ar*·ko • *au*·ne	अर्को • आउने
next month	*ar*·ko *ma*·hi·nah	अर्को महीना
next week	*ar*·ko *hap*·tah	अर्को हप्ता
next year	*ar*·ko *bar*·sa	अर्को बर्ष
next to	*na*·jik	नजीक
nice	*rahm*·ro	राम्रो
nickname	*u*·pa·nahm	उपनाम
night	raht	रात
no (definition)	*hoi*·na	होइन
no (location)	*chai*·na	छैन
no (permission)	*hun*·dai·na	हुन्दैन
noise	*ah*·wahj	आवाज
noisy	*hal*·lah	हल्ला
none	*ke*·hi *pa*·ni	केही पनि
noon	ma·*dhyahn*·ha	मध्यान्ह
no one	*ko*·hi (*pa*·ni)	कोही (पनि)
north	*ut*·tar	उत्तर
nose	nahk	नाक
notebook	*kah*·pi	कापी
nothing	*ke*·hi (*pa*·ni)	केही (पनि)
novel	*u*·pan·yahs	उपन्यास
now	*a*·hi·le	अहिले
nowadays	hi·jo·*ah*·ja	हिजोआज

number	*sang*·khyah	संख्या
nurse	nars	नर्स

O

oats	jai	जइ
obvious	*spas*·ṭa	स्पष्ट
ocean	*ma*·hah·sah·gar	महासागर
o'clock	*ba*·jyo	बज्यो
occupation	*pe*·shah	पेशा
of	-ko	-को
offence	dos	दोष
to offend	*a*·pa·mahn *gar*·nu	अपमान गर्नु
to offer	*di*·nu	दिनु
office	kahr·*yah*·la·ya	कार्यालय
office worker	kar·ma·*cah*·ri	कर्मचारी
often	*ak*·sar	अक्सर

Oh!
oho! • e! ओहो ! • ऐ !

oil	tel	तेल
ointment	*ma*·la·ham	मलहम
OK	*ṭhik* cha • *hun*·cha • has	ठीक छ • हुन्छ • हस
old (man/woman)	*bu*·ḍho/*bu*·ḍhi	बुढा/बूढी
old (thing)	pu·*rah*·no	पुरानो
old city	pu·*rah*·no *sha*·har	पुरानो शहर
on	-mah	-मा
on foot	hĩ·*ḍe*·ra	हिंडेर
on time	ṭhik sa·*ma*·ya·ko	ठीक समयको
once	*ek*·co·ṭi	एकचोटी
onion	pyahj	प्याज
only	*mah*·trai	मात्रै
open	*kho*·le·ko	खोलेको
to open	*khol*·nu	खोल्नु
opening	ud·*ghah*·ṭan	उद्घाटन
opera	*sang*·git·ma·ya *nah*·ṭak	सङ्गीतमय नाटक
opinion	*rah*·ya	राय
opportunity	*mau*·kah	मौका
opposite (point of view)	*bi*·pa·rit	बिपरीत
opposite (side)	*ul*·ṭo	उल्टो
or	ki	कि
oral	*mau*·khik	मौखिक
orange (adj)	*sun*·ta·lah rang	सुन्तला रङ्ग
orange (n)	*sun*·ta·lah	सुन्तला

order	*ah*·desh	आदेश
to order	*ah*·desh *di*·nu	आदेश दिनु
ordinary	sah·*dhah*·raṇ	साधारण
organisation	*sang*·gha	संघ
to organise	*ban*·do·bas·ta mi·*lau*·nu	बन्दोबस्त मिलाउनु
original	*mau*·lik	मौलिक
ornament	*ga*·ha·nah	गहना
other	*ar*·ko • *a*·ru	अर्को • अरु
otherwise	*na*·tra	नत्र
out(side)	*bah*·hi·ra	बाहिर
over	-*mah*·thi	-माथि
overnight	*raht*·bha·ri	रातभरि
overseas	bi·*desh*(·mah)	बिदेश(मा)
to owe	riṇ *lahg*·nu	ऋण लाग्नु

I owe you.
mai·le ta·*paĩ*·lai riṇ *lahg*·yo — मैले तपाईलाई ऋण लाग्यो

You owe me.
ta·*paĩ*·le *ma*·lai riṇ *lahg*·yo — तपाईले मलाई ऋण लाग्यो

owl	*ul*·lu	उल्लु
own	*ahph*·no	आफ्नो
to own	*ahph*·no ba·*nau*·nu	आफ्नो बनाउनु
owner	*sah*·hu·ji/*sah*·hu·ni **(m/f)**	साहुजी/साहुनी
ox	*go*·ru	गोरु
oxygen	*prahṇ*·bah·yu	प्राणवायु

P

package	*po*·ko • *baṭ*·ṭah	पोको • बट्टा
packet	*po*·ko • *baṭ*·ṭah	पोको • बट्टा
padlock	*tahl*·cah	ताल्चा
page	*pan*·nah	पन्ना
pagoda	*ga*·jur	गजुर
pain	du·*khai*	दुखाई
painful	*du*·khad	दु :खद
to paint	*ci*·tra ba·*nau*·nu	चित्र बनाउनु
painter	*ci*·tra·kahr	चित्रकार
painting	*ci*·tra • *thahng*·kah	चित्र • थाङ्का
painting (art)	*ci*·tra·ka·lah	चित्रकला
pair (n)	jor	जोर
palace	*dar*·bahr	दरबार
pale	*phi*·kah	फिका
pan (cooking)	*bah*·ṭah	बाटा
pan (frying)	*tahp*·ke	ताप्के
pan (wok)	ka·*rah*·hi	कराही

paper	*kah*·gaj	कागज
parcel	pu·*lin*·dah	पुलिन्दा
parents	*ah*·mah *bu*·wah	आमा बुवा

Pardon?
ha·*jur?* हजुर ?

park	u·*dyahn*	उद्यान
to park	*gah*·ḍi *rok*·nu	गाडि रोक्नु
parliament (building)	*sã*·sad (*bha*·wan)	संसद (भवन)
parrot	*su*·gah	सुगा
part	*khaṇ*·ḍa	खण्ड
to participate	bhahg *li*·nu	भाग लिनु
particular	bi·*shes*	विशेष
party (feast)	bhoj	भोज
party (political)	dal	दल
pass (n)	*bhan*·jyahng	भन्ज्याङ
passive	*nis*·kri·ya	निष्कृय
passenger	*yah*·tri	यात्री
passport	rah·ha·*dah*·ni	राहदानी
passport number	rah·ha·*dah*·ni·ko *sang*·khyah	राहदानीको सङ्ख्या
past (time)	*bhut*·kahl	भूतकाल
pasture	*khar*·ka	खर्क
path	*bah*·ṭo	बाटो
patient (adj)	*sa*·ha·ne • dhai·*rya*·shil	सहने • धैर्यशील
to pay	*tir*·nu	तिर्नु
payment	bhuk·*tah*·ni	भुक्तानी
peace	*shahn*·ti	शान्ति
peach	*ah*·ru	आरु
peacock	ma·*yur*	मयुर
peak	cu·*cu*·ro	चुचुरो
peanut	*ba*·dahm	बदाम
pear	*nahs*·pah·ti	नास्पाती
peas	*ke*·rau	केराउ
pedestrian	*pai*·dal *yah*·tri	पैदल यात्री
pen	*ka*·lam	कलम
pencil	*si*·sah·ka·lam	सिसाकलम
penis	*ling*·ga	लिङ्ग
penknife	*cak*·ku	चक्कु
people	*mahn*·che·ha·ru • *ja*·na·tah	मान्छेहरू • जनता
pepper	*ma*·ric	मरिच
green pepper	*bhẽ*·ḍah khur·*sah*·ni	भेंडा खुर्सानी
per cent	*pra*·ti·shat	प्रतिशत

DICTIONARY

perfect	a·*tyut*·tam	अति उत्तम
performance	*nah*·ṭak	नाटक
period pain	*ma*·hi·nah·bah·ri·ko du·*khai*	मिहनाबारीको दुखाई
permanent	*sthah*·yi	स्थायी
permanent collection	*sthah*·yi *sang*·gra·ha	स्थायी सङ्ग्रह
permission	*a*·nu·ma·ti	अनुमति
permit	*a*·nu·ma·ti·pa·tra	अनुमतिपत्र
to permit	*a*·nu·ma·ti *di*·nu	अनुमति दिनु
persecution	*a*·tyah·cahr	अत्याचार
person	*mahn*·che	मान्छे
personal	*byak*·ti·gat	व्यक्तिगत
personality	*byak*·ti·twa	व्यक्तित्व
to perspire	pa·*si*·nah *au*·nu	पसिना आउनु
pet	*pahl*·tu ja·*nah*·war	पाल्तु जनावर
petition	*bin*·ti·pa·tra	बिन्तीपत्र
petroleum	*kha*·nij tel	खनिज तेल
pharmacy	*au*·sa·dhi *pa*·sal	औषधि पसल
pheasant	*kah*·lij	कालिज
to phone	phon *gar*·nu	फोन गर्नु
phone book	*phon*·ko ki·*tahb*	फोनको किताब
photo	*tas*·bir	तस्वीर

Can I take a photo?
tas·bir *khic*·nu·hun·cha? तस्वीर खिच्नुहुन्छ ?

photographer	*tas*·bir *khic*·ne *ka*·lah·kahr	तस्वीर खिच्ने कलाकार
photography	*tas*·bir *khic*·ne ka·*lah*	तस्वीर खिच्ने कला
pick(axe)	*gaĩ*·ti	गैंती
to pick up	*li*·na *au*·nu	लिन आउनु
pickle (relish)	a·*cahr*	अचार
piece	*ṭuk*·rah	टुक्रा
pig	*sũ*·gur	संगुर
pigeon	*pa*·re·wah	परेवा
pill	*go*·li	गोली
the Pill	*pa*·ri·bahr ni·*yo*·jan·ko *au*·sa·dhi	परिवार नियोजनको औषधि
pillow	si·*rah*·ni	सिरानी
pillowcase	si·*rah*·ni·ko khol	सिरानीको खोल
pine tree	*sal*·lah·ko rukh	सल्लाको रूख
pineapple	*bhuĩ*·ka·ṭa·har	भुँईकटहर
pink	gu·*lah*·phi	गुलाफी
pipe	*cu*·roṭ paip	चुरोट पाईप
place	ṭhaũ	ठाउँ

plains	*ma*·desh • ta·*rai*	मदेश • तराई
plains dweller	*ma*·de·si	मदेसी
plane	*ha*·wai·ja·hahj	हवाईजहाज
planet	*sã*·sahr • *gra*·ha	संसार • ग्रह
plant	*bi*·ru·wah	बिरूवा
to plant	*rop*·nu	रोप्नु
plate	thahl	थाल
plateau	*sa*·ma·tal *ṭah*·ku·ro	समतल टाकुरो
platform (cremation)	ghahṭ	घाट
platform (stage)	u·*ṭhah*·ya·ko ṭhaũ	उठाएको ठाउँ
play (theatre)	*li*·lah	लीला
to play cards	tash *khel*·nu	तास खेल्नु
to play (game)	*khel*·nu	खेल्नु
to play (music)	ba·*jau*·nu	बजाउनु
to play sport	*khel*·kud *khel*·nu	खेलकुद खेल्नु
player	khe·*lah*·ḍi	खेलाडि
playing cards	tash	तास
to plug	*bu*·jo *lau*·nu	बुजो लाउनु
plum	ah·ru·*ba*·kha·ḍah	आरुबखडा
pocket	*khal*·ti	खल्ती
poetry	*ka*·bi·tah	किताब
to point (out)	de·*khau*·nu	देखाउनु
poker (fire)	su·*i*·ro	सुइरो
police	pra·*ha*·ri	प्रहरी
politician	rahj·*ni*·ti·gyã	राजनीतिज्ञ
politics	*rahj*·ni·ti	राजनीति
pollen	pa·*rahg*	पराग
pollution	*du*·sit	दुषित
pomegranate	a·*nahr*	अनार
pond	*po*·kha·ri	पोखरी
poor	*ga*·rib	गरिव
popular	*lok*·pri·ya	लोकप्रिय
pork	*sũ*·gur·ko *mah*·su	सुंगुरको मासु
porter	*bha*·ri·yah	भरिया
portrait	*ah*·kri·ti·ci·tra	आकृति चित्र
possible	*sam*·bhab	सम्भव

It's (not) possible.
sam·bhab cha (*chai*·na) सम्भव छ (छैन)

postage	*ḍãhk*·khar·ca	डाँक खबर
postcard	*posṭ*·kahrḍ	पोष्टकार्ड
postcode	*posṭ*·koḍ	पोस्टकोड
poster	*par*·cah	पर्चा
post office	*hu*·lahk *aḍ*·ḍah	हुलाक अड्डा

DICTIONARY

potato	*ah*·lu	आलु
pot (ceramic)	*bhāh*·ḍo	भाँडो
pottery	*mah*·ṭah·kah *bhāh*·ḍah	माटाका भाँडा
poverty	da·*ri*·dra·tah	दिरद्रता
power	*shak*·ti	शक्ति
prayer	*man*·tra • *prahr*·tha·nah	मन्त्र • प्रार्थना
to prefer	bes *lahg*·nu	बेस लाग्नु
pregnant	*gar*·bha·va·ti	गर्भवती
present (gift)	*u*·pa·hahr	उपहार
present (time)	*bar*·ta·mahn	वर्तमान
president	*rah*·sṭra·pa·ti	राष्ट्रपित
pressure	*thi*·cai	भाँडा
pretty	*rahm*·ro	राम्रो
to prevent	*rok*·nu	रोक्नु
price	mol	मोल
pride	*gar*·ba	गर्व
priest	pu·*jah*·ri	पूजारी
prime minister	pra·*dhahn man*·tri	प्रधानमन्त्री
print (artwork)	*cha*·pai	छपाइ
prison	*jhyahl*·khah·nah	झ्यालखाना
prisoner	*kai*·di	कैदी
private	*ni*·ji	निजी
problem	sa·*mas*·yah	समस्या
process	*kahm*·ko *bi*·dhi	कामको विधि
to process	*pra*·kri·yah ca·*lau*·nu	प्रक्रिया चलाउनु
procession (march)	ju·*lus*	जुलूस
procession (wedding)	*jan*·ti	जन्ती
produce	ut·*pah*·dan	उत्पादन
to produce	ut·*pah*·dan *gar*·nu	उत्पादन गर्नु
producer	ut·*pah*·dak	उत्पादक
profession	*pe*·shah	पेशा
professional	khahs *pe*·shah bi·*gyã*	खास पेशा बिज्ञ
profit	*nah*·phah	नाफा
programme	*kah*·rya·kram	कार्यक्रम
projector	*pra*·che·pak	प्रक्षेपक
promise	*ba*·can	बचन
to promise	*ba*·can *di*·nu	बचन दिनु
proposal	*pras*·tahb	प्रस्ताब
proprietor	*sah*·hu·ji/*sah*·hu·ni **(m/f)**	साहुनी/साहुजी
prostitute	*be*·shyah	बेश्या
to protect	ba·*cau*·nu	बचाउनु
protected forest	ba·*cah*·ye·ko ban	बचायेको बन
protected species	ba·*cah*·ye·ko *bar*·ga	बचायेको वर्ग
protest	bi·*rodh*	बिरोध
to protest	bi·*rodh gar*·nu	बिरोध गर्नु

protest march	ju·*lus*	जुलूस
public (adj)	*sahr*·ba·ja·nik	सार्वजनिक
public (n)	*ja*·na·tah	जनता
public toilet	shau·*cah*·la·ya	शौचालय
to pull	*tahn*·nu	तान्नु
pump	pamp	पम्प
puncture	pwahl	प्वाल
to punish	*dan*·ḍa *di*·nu	दन्ड दिनु
puppy	*ku*·kur·ko *chau*·ro	कुकुरको छाउरो
pure	*co*·kho	चोखो
purple	*pyah*·ji	प्याजी
to push	gha·*ceḍ*·nu	घचेड्नु
to put (down)	*rahkh*·nu	राख्नु
to put in	*hahl*·nu	हाल्नु

Q

qualifications	*yog*·ya·tah	योग्यता
quality	gun	गुन
queen	*rah*·ni	रानी
question	*prash*·na	प्रश्न
quick(ly)	*chi*·ṭo	छिटो
quiet	*shahn*·ta	शान्त
quietly	bi·*stah*·rai	बिस्तारै
quilt	*si*·rak	सिरक

R

rabbit	kha·*rah*·yo	खरायो
race (culture)	*jah*·ti	जाति
race (sport)	dauḍ	दौड
racing bike	*re*·sing baik	रेसिङ्ग बाइक
racism	*jah*·ti·bahd	जातिबाद
radio	*re*·ḍi·yo	रेडियो
radish	*mu*·lah	मुला
to rain	*pah*·ni *par*·nu	पानी पर्नु

It's raining.
pah·ni *par*·cha — पानी पर्छ

rainy season	*bar*·saht	वर्षात
raisin	dahkh	दाख
rally	ja·*maht*	जमात
to rape	ba·*laht*·kahr *gar*·nu	बलात्कार गर्नु
rare	*dur*·labh	दुर्लभ
rash	sujh	सुज
rat	*mu*·sah	मूसा
raw	*kãh*·co	काँचो

razorblade	*pat*·ti	पत्ती
to read	*paḍh*·nu	पढ्नु
ready	*ta*·yahr	तयार
to realise	bodh *gar*·na *sak*·nu	बोध गर्न सक्नु
reason	*kah*·raṇ	कारण
receipt	bil	बिल
to receive	*prahp*·ta *gar*·nu	प्राप्त गर्नु
recent	*hahl*·sahl·ko	हालसालको
recently	*hahl*·sah·lai	हालसालै
to recognise	*cin*·nu	चिन्नु
to recommend	si·*phah*·ris *gar*·nu	सिफारिस गर्नु
to recover	*ni*·ko·hu·nu	निकोहुनु
recyclable	ri·*sai*·kal *gar*·na *sa*·ki·ne	रीसाइकल गर्न सिकने
recycling	ri·*sai*·kal	रीसाइकल
red	*rah*·to	रातो
referee	ma·*dhyas*·tha	मध्यस्थ
reference	pra·*mahṇ*·pa·tra	प्रमाणपत्र
refugee	sha·ra·*ṇahr*·thi	शरणार्थी
to refund	phar·*kau*·nu	फर्काउनु
to refuse	*a*·swi·kahr *gar*·nu	अस्वीकार गर्नु
region	*che*·tra	क्षेत्र
regional	prah·*de*·shik	प्रादेशिक
regulation	*ni*·yam	नियम
relationship	*mi*·lahp	मिलाप
to relax	*ah*·rahm *gar*·nu	आराम गर्नु
religion	*dhar*·ma	धर्म
religious	*dhahr*·mik	धार्मिक
remaining	*bãh*·ki	बाँकी
to remember	sam·*jha*·nu	सम्झनु
remote	*dur*·gam	दुर्गम
rent	*bhah*·ḍah	भाडा
to rent	*bhah*·ḍah·mah *li*·nu	भाडा लिनु
to repair	*mar*·mat *gar*·nu	मर्मत गर्नु
to repeat	do·ha·*rau*·nu	दोहराउनु
republic	gaṇ·*rah*·jya	गणराज्य
request	*a*·nu·rodh	अनुरोध
reservation	*sany*·cit	सञ्चित
to reserve	*sany*·cit *gar*·nu	सञ्चित गर्नु
resignation	rah·ji·*nah*·mah	राजीनामा
to respect	*mahn*·nu	मान्नु
responsibility	jim·me·*dah*·ri	जिम्मेवारी
to rest	*ah*·rahm *li*·nu	आराम लिनु
restaurant	bho·ja·*nah*·la·ya	भोजनालय
resting place (tree)	cau·*tah*·rah	चौतारा

resume (CV)	*bai*·yo·ḍah·ṭah	बायोडाटा
retired	a·wa·*kahsh li*·ya·ko	अवकाश लियको
to return	*phar*·ka·nu	फर्कनु
return ticket	*jah*·ne·au·ne *ṭi*·kaṭ	जानेआउने टिकट
review	sa·*mah*·lo·ca·nah	समालोचना
revolution (people's)	*krahn*·ti	क्रान्ती
rhinoceros	*gaĩ*·ḍah	गैंडा
rhododendron	lah·li·*gu*·rāhs	लालीगुँरास
rhythm	*la*·ya • tahl	लय • ताल
rib	*ka*·rang	करङ
rice (beaten)	*cyu*·rah	च्यूरा
rice (cooked)	bhaht	भात
rice (uncooked)	*cah*·mal	चामल
rice (unhusked)	dhahn	धान
rich	*dha*·ni	धनी
rickshaw	*rik*·shah	रीक्सा
to ride (a horse)	*caḍh*·nu	चढ्नु
right (correct)	ṭhik	ठीक
right (not left)	*dah*·yāh	दायाँ
to be right (correct)	*mil*·nu	मिल्नु

You're right.
ta·*paĩ*·le ṭhik *bhan*·nu *bha*·yo — तपाईले ठीक भन्नु भयो

right now	*a*·hil·yai	अहिल्यै
rights	*a*·dhi·kahr	अधिकार
human rights	mah·nab·*a*·dhi·kahr	मानव अधिकार
ring (of phone)	*ghaṇ*·ṭi	घण्टी
ring (on finger)	*aũ*·ṭhi	औंठी
to ring (bell)	*baj*·nu	बज्नु

I'll give you a ring.
ma ta·*paĩ*·lai phon *gar*·chu — म तपाईलाई फोन गर्छु

to rip off	*ṭhag*·nu	ठग्नु
ripe	*pah*·ke·ko	पाकेको
risk	*kha*·ta·rah	खतरा
river	*na*·di	नदी
road (route)	*bah*·ṭo	बाटो
road (paved)	*sa*·ḍak	सडक
road map	*bah*·ṭo·ko *nak*·sah	बाटोको नक्सा
to rob	*cor*·nu	चोर्नु
rock	*pa*·ha·ro	पहरो
to roll (up)	*ber*·nu	बेर्नु
to roll (move)	*guḍ*·nu	गुड्नु
romance	*mi*·ṭho·pan • *pre*·mah·lahp	मीठोपन • प्रेमालाप

room	*ko*·ṭhah	कोठा
room number	*ko*·ṭhah·ko *nam*·bar	कोठाको नम्बर
rooster	*bhah*·le *ku*·khu·rah	भाले कुखुरा
rope	*ḍo*·ri	डोरी
rough	*khas*·ro	खस्रो
round	*go*·lo	गोलो
to row (a boat)	(*ḍung*·gah) ca·*lau*·nu	(डुङ्गा) चलाउनु
to rub	*dal*·nu	दल्नु
rubbish	*pho*·hor	फोहोर
rug	*sah*·no ga·*laĩ*·cah	सानो गलैंचा
ruins	bhag·*nah*·ba·shes	भग्नावशेष
rule (regulation)	*ni*·yam	नियम
to run (away)	da·*gur*·nu	दगुर्न
rupees	ru·*pi*·yãh	रुपियाँ

S

sad	*du*·khi	दु :खी
safe (adj)	su·*ra*·chit	सुरक्षित
safe (n)	su·*ra*·chit ṭhaũ	सुरक्षित ठाउँ
safety pin	huk	हुक
saffron	*ke*·shar	केशर
saint (Hindu)	ma·*haht*·mah	महात्मा
saint (Muslim)	pir	पीर
salary	*ta*·lab	तलब
sale	*bi*·kri	बिक्रि
salt	nun	नुन
salty	nu·*ni*·lo	नुनिलो
same	u·*hi*	उही
sand	*bah*·lu·wah	बालुवा
sandal	*cap*·pal	चप्पल
sari	*sah*·ḍi	साडी
to save	ba·*cau*·nu	बचाउनु
to say	*bhan*·nu	भन्नु
to scale	*caḍh*·nu	चढ्नु
scared	*ḍar*·lahg·do	डरलाग्दो
scarf	do·*paṭ*·ṭah	दोपट्टा
scenery	*dri*·shya	दृश्य
school	bi·*dyah*·la·ya	बिद्यालय
science	bi·*gyahn*	बिज्ञान
scientist	bai·*gyah*·nik	बैज्ञानिक
scissors	*kaĩ*·ci	कैंची
to score	*prahp*·ta *gar*·nu	प्राप्त गर्नु
sculpture	*mur*·ti·ka·lah	मुर्तिकला
sea	sa·*mu*·dra	समुद्र
seaside	sa·*mu*·dra·ko ki·*nahr*	समुद्रको किनार

seat	ṭhaũ	ठाउँ
to be seated	*ba*·si *rahkh*·nu	बसी राख्नु
second (adj)	*dos*·rah	दोस्रा
second (n)	*se*·keṇḍ	सेकेण्ड
secret (adj)	*gop*·ya	गोप्य
secretary	*sa*·cib	सचिव
to see (look at)	*her*·nu	हेर्नु
to see (observe)	*dekh*·nu	देख्नु

We'll see!
he·*raũ!* हेरौं !

I see. (understand)
bujh·yo बुझ्यो

See you later.
phe·ri *bhe*·ṭaũ·lah! फेरी भेटौंला !

See you tomorrow.
bho·li *bhe*·ṭaũ·lah! भोलि भेटौंला !

seed	bi·*u*	बीउ
selfish	*swahr*·thi	स्वार्थी
to sell	*bec*·nu	बेच्नु
to send	pa·*ṭhau*·nu	पठाउनु
sensible	bi·*be*·ki	बिबेकी
sentence (prison)	*nir*·ṇa·ya	निर्णय
sentence (words)	*bah*·kya	बाक्य
to separate	chu·*ṭyau*·nu	छुटयाउनु
serious	*gam*·bhir	गम्भीर
servant	*no*·kar	नोकर
to serve	*se*·bah *gar*·nu	सेबा गर्नु
service	*se*·bah	सेबा
sesame seed	*til*·ko bi·*u*	तिलको बिउ
several	*a*·nek	अनेक
to sew	si·*u*·nu	सिउनु
sex (gender)	*ling*·ga	लिङ्ग
sex (intercourse)	*sam*·bhog	संभोग
to have sex	*sam*·bhog *gar*·nu	संभोग गर्नु
sexism	ai·mai·*pra*·ti·ko *ghri*·ṇah	आईमाईप्रतिको घृणा
sexy	*sam*·bho·gi	सम्भोगी
shade	*shi*·tal	शीतल
shadow	*chah*·yāh	छायाँ
shampoo	*dhu*·lai	धुलाइ
shape	*ah*·kahr	आकार
to share	*bāhḍ*·nu	बाड्नु
to shave	*khau*·ra·nu	खौरनु

shawl	*oḍh*·ne	ओढ्ने
she (inf)	*u*·ni • tyo • yo	ऊनी • त्यो • यो
she (pol)	*wa*·hãh	वहाँ
sheep	*bhẽ*·ḍah	भेंडा
sheet (bed)	*tan*·nah	तन्ना
sheet (paper)	tau	ताउ
shelter	bahs	बास
shelves	da·*rahj*	दराज
ship	*pah*·ni·ja·hahj	पानीजहाज
shirt	ka·*mij*	कमिज
to shiver	*kahm*·nu	काम्नु
shoe(s)	*jut*·tah	जुत्ता
shoe shop	*jut*·tah *pa*·sal	जुत्ता पसल
to shoot	*hahn*·nu	हान्नु
shop	*pa*·sal	पसल
shopkeeper	*pa*·sa·le • *sah*·hu	पसले • साहु
to go shopping	*kin*·mel *jah*·nu	किनमेल जानु
short (height)	*puḍh*·ko	पुढ्को
short (length)	*cho*·ṭo	छोटो
shortage	*ka*·mi	कमी
shorts	*kaṭ*·ṭu	कट्टू
shoulder	kãhdh	काँध
to shout	ka·*rau*·nu	कराउनु
show	*khel*·bahḍ	खेलबाड
to show	de·*khau*·nu	देखाउनु
shower	snahn	स्नान
to shower	nu·*hau*·nu	नुहाउनु
shrine	*de*·wal	देवल
to shut	*ban*·da *gar*·nu	बन्द गर्नु
shyness	lahj	लाज
sick	bi·*rah*·mi	बिरामी
sickness	rog	रोग
side	cheu	छेउ
this side	*wah*·ri	वारी
that side	*pah*·ri	पारी
to sign	*sa*·hi *gar*·nu	सही गर्नु
signature	*sa*·hi	सही
signpost	sang·ket·*cin*·ha	सांकेतिक चिन्ह
silence	*maun*·tah	मौनता
silk	*re*·sham	रेशम
silver (adj)	*cãh*·di·ko	चाँदीको
silver (n)	*cãh*·di	चाँदी
similar	*us*·tai	उस्तै
simple	*sa*·ral	सरल
sin	pahp	पाप

since (May)	*(mai)*·de·khi	(मे)देखि
to sing	*gau*·nu	गाउनु
singer	*gah*·yak/*gah*·yi·kah **(m/f)**	गायक/गायिका
single (unique)	*ek*·lo	एक्लो
single (unmarried)	*ek*·lai	एक्लै
single man	ku·*mahr*	कुमार
single room	*ek*·ja·nah·ko *ko*·ṭhah	एकजनाको कोठा
single woman	ku·*mah*·ri	कुमारी
singlet	*gan*·ji	गन्जी
sister (elder)	*di*·di	दिदी
sister (younger)	*ba*·hi·ni	बहिनी
sisters	di·di·*ba*·hi·ni	दिदीबहिनी
sitting posture	*ah*·san	आसन
situation	a·*bas*·thah	अबस्था
size	saij	साइज
to ski	is·*ki khel*·nu	इस्की खेल्नु
skiing	is·*ki khel*·na	इस्की खेल्न
skin	*chah*·lah	छाला
sky	*ah*·kahsh	आकाश
to sleep	*sut*·nu	सुत्नु
sleeping bag	*sut*·ne *jho*·lah	सुत्ने झोला
sleeping pills	su·*tau*·ne *au*·sa·dhi	सुताउने औषधि
sleepy	*ni*·drah	निद्रा
slow	*ḍhi*·lo	ढिलो
slowly	bi·*stah*·rai	बिस्तारै
small	*sah*·no	सानो
smell	bahs	बास
to smell (create a scent)	ga·*nhau*·nu	गन्हाउनु
to smell (with nose)	*sũgh*·nu	सुँघ्नु
to smile	*hãhs*·nu	हाँस्नु
to smoke (cigarettes)	*dhum*·ra·pahn *gar*·nu	धूम्रपान गनरु
smoking	*dhum*·ra·pahn	धूम्रपान
snack	*khah*·jah	खाजा
snake	*sar*·pa	सर्प
snow	hiũ	हिउँ
snow peak	hi·*mahl*	हिमाले
soap	*sah*·bun	साबुन
socialist	sa·*mahj*·bah·di	समाजबादी
sock	*mo*·jah	मोजा
soil	*mah*·ṭo	माटो
soldier	si·*pah*·hi	सिपाही
solid	ṭhos	ठोस
some	*ke*·hi • *ku*·nai	केही • कुनै
someone	*ko*·hi	कोही

something	*ke*·hi	केही
sometimes	ka·hi·le·*kah*·hĩ	कहिलेकाँही
son	*cho*·rah	छोरा
song	git	गीत
soon	*cãh*·ḍai	चाँदै
sore	*du*·khe·ko	दुखेको
sorry (condolence)	*da*·yah	दया
sorry (regret)	*duh*·khit	दु :खित
I'm sorry. (apology) mahph *gar*·nu·hos		माफ गनुर्होस
soul (spirit)	*aht*·mah	आत्मा
sound	*ah*·wahj	आवाज
soup	*su*·ru·wah	सुरुवा
sour	*a*·mi·lo	अमीलो
south	*da*·chiṇ	दक्षिण
souvenir	*ci*·no	चिनो
souvenir shop	*ci*·no *pa*·sal	चिनो पसल
to sow	*rop*·nu	रोप्नु
soybeans	*bhaṭ*·mahs	भटमास
space (outer space)	an·ta·*ri*·cha	अन्तरिक्ष
space (room to move)	ṭhaũ	ठाउँ
to speak	*bol*·nu	बोल्नु
special	bi·*shes*	विशेष
specialist	bi·she·*sa*·gyã	विशेषज्ञ
speed	*ga*·ti • beg	गित • बेग
to spend	*khar*·ca *gar*·nu	खर्च गर्नु
spice	*ma*·sa·lah	मसला
spicy	*pi*·ro	पिरो
spider	*mah*·ku·rah	माकुरा
spinach	pah·*lung*·go	पालुङ्गो
spirit (soul)	*aht*·mah	आत्मा
spoon	*cam*·cah	चम्चा
sport	*khel*·kud	खेलकुद
sprain	*mar*·kai	मर्काइ
spring (coil)	spring	स्प्रिङ
spring (season)	*ba*·san·ta *ri*·tu	बसन्त ऋतु
square (shape)	bar·ga·*che*·tra	वर्ग क्षेत्र
square (town centre)	cok	चोक
squirrel	*lo*·khar·ke	लोखर्के
stage (n)	*rang*·ga·manyc	रङ्गमञ्च
stairs	bha·*ryahng*	भर्याङ्ग
stale	*bah*·si	बासी
stamp (postage)	*ṭi*·kaṭ	टिकट

to stand	u·*bhi*·nu	उभिनु
standard	star	स्तर
star(s)	*tah*·rah	तारा
to start	*su*·ru *gar*·nu	सुरु गर्नु
stationer	ci·ṭhi·*pa*·tra *pa*·sal	चिठीपत्र पसल
statue	*mur*·ti	मुर्ति
to stay (remain)	*ra*·ha·nu	रहनु
to stay (sit)	*bas*·nu	बस्नु
to steal	*cor*·nu	चोर्नु
steam	bahph	बाफ
steep downhill	bhi·*rah*·lo	भिरालो
steep uphill	*ṭhah*·ḍo	ठाडो
step	*khuḍ*·ki·lo	खुडिकलो
stick	*laṭh*·ṭhi	लठ्ठी
stomach	peṭ	पेट
stomachache	peṭ *du*·khe·ko	पेट दुखेको
stone	*ḍhung*·gah	ढुङ्गा
stop (bus)	bas bi·*sau*·ni	बस बिसौनी
to stop	*rok*·nu	रोक्नु

Stop! (pol)
rok·nu·hos! रोक्नुहोस !

Stop! (inf)
rok! रोक !

stork	*dha*·nesh • *nil*·ca·rah	धनेश • नीलचरा
storm	*hu*·ri	हुरी
story	*ka*·thah	कथा
stove (electric)	*hi*·ṭar	हिटर
stove (kerosene/gas)	sṭobh	स्टोभ
stove (wood)	*cu*·lo	चूलो
straight	*si*·dhah	सिधा
strange	a·*nau*·ṭho	अनौठो
stranger	a·pa·*ri*·cit *byak*·ti	अपरिचित व्यक्ति
stream	*kho*·lah	खोला
street	*sa*·ḍak	सडक
strength	bal	बल
strike	*haḍ*·tahl	हडताल
string	*ḍo*·ri	डोरी
to stroll	*ghum*·nu	घुम्नु
strong	*ba*·li·yo	बलियो
stubborn	*a*·ṭer	अटेर
student	bi·*dyahr*·thi	विद्यार्थी
studio	ci·tra·*shah*·lah	चित्रशाला
stupid	*mur*·kha	मुर्ख

style	*dhãh*·cah • *shai*·li	ढाँचा • शैली
suburb	kãhṭh	काँठ
suburbs of ...	...·ko kãhṭh	...को काँठ
success	*sa*·phal·tah	सफलता
suddenly	a·*cah*·nak	अचानक
to suffer	*du*·kha *pau*·nu	दु :ख पाउनु
sugar	*ci*·ni	चिनी
sugar cane	*u*·khu	उखु
suitcase	*bah*·kas	बाकस
summer	*gar*·mi *mau*·sam	गर्मी मौसम
sun	*sur*·ya	सुर्य
sunny	gha·*mai*·lo	घमाईलो
sunrise	*sur*·yo·da·ya	सुर्योदय
sunset	sur·*yahs*·ta	सुर्यास्त

Sure.
pak·kah पक्का

surface mail	*gah*·ḍi·bah·ṭa posṭ	गाडीबाट पोस्ट
surname	thar	थर
surprise	a·*cam*·ma	अचम्म
to survive	*bãhc*·nu	बाँच्नु
sweater (jumper)	*swi*·ṭar	स्विटर
sweet	*gu*·li·yo	गुलियो
to swim	*pau*·ḍi *khel*·nu	पौडी खेल्नु
swimming	*pau*·ḍi	पौडी
sword	*tar*·bahr	तरबार
sympathy	sa·*hah*·nu·bhu·ti	सहानुभूति
synthetic	*kri*·trim *bas*·tu·bah·ṭa ba·*nah*·ya·kah *ku*·rah	कृत्रिम बस्तुबाट बनायका कुरा
syringe	*si*·rinj	सिरिन्ज

T

table	*ṭe*·bul	टेबुल
tail	*puc*·char	पुच्छर
tailor	*su*·ci·kahr	सूचिकार
to take	*li*·nu	लिनु
to take away	*lag*·nu	लग्नु
to take a photo	*tas*·bir *khic*·nu	तस्वीर खिच्नु
to talk	*ku*·rah *gar*·nu	कुरा गर्नु
tall	*a*·glo	अग्लो
tasty	*mi*·ṭho	मीठो
tax	kar	कर
taxi	*ṭyahk*·si	ट्याक्सी
tea	*ci*·yah	चिया

teacher	*shi*·chak	शिक्षक
teaching	*shi*·chaṇ	शिक्षण
team	*ṭo*·li	टोली
technique	*ta*·ri·kah	तरिका
telegram	tahr	तार
telephone	phon	फोन
telephone centre	phon *aḍ*·ḍah	फोन अड्डा
to telephone	phon *gar*·nu	फोन गर्नु
telescope	*dur*·bin	दूरबीन
television	*ṭe*·li·bhi·jan	टेलिभिजन
to tell	*bhan*·nu	भन्नु
temperature (fever)	*ja*·ro	जरो
temperature (weather)	*tahp*·kram	तापक्रम
temple (Buddhist)	*stu*·pah	स्तुपा
temple (Hindu)	*man*·dir	मन्दिर
temporary	a·*sthah*·yi	अस्थायी
tent	pahl	पाल
tenth	*da*·saũ	दसौं
terrible	*ḍar*·lahg·do	डरलाग्दो
test	jãhc	जाँच
tetanus	*dha*·nu·rog	धनुरोग
than	-*bhan*·dah	-भन्दा
to thank	*dhan*·ya·bahd *di*·nu	धन्यबाद दिनु

Thank you.
dhan·ya·bahd धन्यबाद

that	tyo	त्यो
theatre	*a*·bhi·na·ya	अभिनय
there	*tya*·hãh	त्यहाँ
these	yi	यी
they (informal)	*u*·ni·ha·ru	उनीहरू
they (formal)	*wa*·hãh·ha·ru	वहाँहरु
thick	*bahk*·lo	बाक्लो
thief	cor	चोर
thin (animal/person)	*du*·blo	दुब्लो
thin (thing)	*pah*·ta·lo	पातलो
thing (abstract)	*ku*·rah	कुरा
thing (material)	cij • *bas*·tu	चीज • बस्तु
things	*cij*·bij	चीजबीज
to think	bi·*cahr gar*·nu	बिचार गर्नु
third (3rd)	*tes*·rah	तेस्रा
thirst	*tir*·khah	तीर्खा
this	yo	यो
those	ti	ती
thought	bi·*cahr*	बिचार

thread	*dhah*·go	धागो
throat (inside)	*ga*·lah	गला
throat (outside)	*ghãh*·ṭi	घाँटी
thunder	*gar*·jan	गर्जन
thunderstorm	megh·*gar*·jan *ta*·thah *bar*·sah	मेघ गर्जन तथा वर्षा
Tibetan dress	*cu*·bah	चुबा
tick	*kir*·no	किर्नो
ticket	*ṭi*·kaṭ	टिकट
ticket office	*ṭi*·kaṭ *aḍ*·ḍah	टिकट अड्डा
tiger	bahgh	बाघ
to be tight	*ka*·si·nu	कसिनु
to tighten	*kas*·nu	कस्नु
time	sa·*ma*·ya	समय
time (instance)	*pa*·ṭak	पटक
timetable	sa·*ma*·ya *tah*·li·kah	समय तालिका
tin (can)	ṭin	टिन
tin opener	ṭin *khol*·ne	टिन खोल्ने
tip (money)	*ba*·kas	बाकस
to be tired	*thahk*·nu	थाक्नु
tired	*tha*·kai	थकाइ
to	-mah • -lai	-मा • -लाई
tobacco	*sur*·ti	सुर्ती
today	*ah*·ja	आज
together	sahth·*sah*·thai	साथसाथै
toilet (flushing)	*bahṭh*·rum	बाथरुम
toilet (pit)	*car*·pi	चर्पी
toilet (public)	shau·*cah*·la·ya	शौचालय
toilet paper	*ṭwai*·leṭ *pe*·par	ट्वाईलेट पेपर
tomato	gol·*bhẽ*·ḍah	गोलभेंडा
tomorrow	*bho*·li	भोलि
tomorrow afternoon	*bho*·li *diũ*·so	भोलि दिउँसो
tomorrow evening	*bho*·li *be*·lu·kah	भोलि बेलुका
tomorrow morning	*bho*·li bi·*hah*·na	भोलि बिहान
tongue	*ji*·bro	जिब्रो
tonight	*ah*·ja *rah*·ti	आज राति
too (also)	*pa*·ni	पनि
too (much)	*dhe*·rai • *sah*·hrai	धेरै • साह्रै
too expensive	*dhe*·rai ma·*hã*·go	धेरै महंगो
tooth	dãht	दाँत
toothache	dãht *du*·khe·ko	दाँत दुखेको
toothbrush	dãht *mahjh*·ne *bu*·rus	दाँत माझ्ने बुरुस
toothpaste	*many*·jan	मञ्जन
torch (flashlight)	ṭarc	टर्च
to touch	*chu*·nu	छुनु

tour (journey)	*bhra*·maṇ	भ्रमण
to tour	*ghum*·nu	घुम्नु
tourism	par·*ya*·ṭan	पर्यटन
tourist	par·*ya*·ṭak	पर्यटक
tourist information office	par·*ya*·ṭan kahr·*yah*·la·ya	पर्यटन कार्यालय
towards	-*ti*·ra	-तिर
towel	ru·*mahl*	रुमाल
tower	*a*·glo *bha*·wan	अग्लो भवन
town	*na*·gar	नगर
track (footprints)	*hī*·ḍe·ko chahp	हिंडेको छाप
track (path)	*go*·re·ṭo	गोरेटो
trade union	*kahm*·ko sa·*mi*·ti	कामको सिमित
trader	*sah*·hu	साहु
traffic	ah·wat·*jah*·wat *gar*·ne *bas*·tu	आवतजावत गर्ने बस्तु
trail	*go*·re·ṭo • *sah*·no *bah*·ṭo	गोरेटो • सानो बाटो
train	*rel*·gah·ḍi	रेलगाडी
to translate	*ul*·thah *gar*·nu	उल्था गर्नु
to travel	*yah*·trah *gar*·nu	यात्रा गर्नु
travel office	*yah*·trah·ko *ṭi*·kaṭ *aḍ*·ḍah	यात्राको टिकट अड्डा
travel sickness	*gah*·di·mah *lahg*·ne *wahk*·wahk	गाडीमा लाग्ने वाकवाक
traveller	*yah*·tri	यात्री
travellers cheque	*ṭrah*·bhlar cek	ट्राभलर चेक
tree	rukh	रूख
trekking	*pai*·dal *yah*·trah	पैदल यात्रा
trip	*yah*·trah	यात्रा
trousers	*su*·ru·wahl	सुरुवाल
truck	ṭrak • *la*·ri	ट्रक • लरी
true	*sa*·hi	सही

It's true.
sa·tya ho — सत्य हो

trust	bi·*shwahs*	विश्वास
to trust	bi·*shwahs gar*·nu	विश्वास गर्नु
truth	*sa*·tya	सत्य
to try	*ko*·sis *gar*·nu	कोसिस गर्नु
to try on	*la*·gai *her*·nu	लगाई हेर्नु
T-shirt	*gan*·ji	गन्जी
tuberculosis	*cha*·ya·rog	क्षयरोग
tune	tahn	तान
tunic	*dau*·rah	दौरा
turmeric	*be*·sahr	बेसार

to turn	*moḍ*·nu	मोड्नु

Turn left/right.
bah·yāh/*dah*·yāh *moḍ*·nu·hos बायाँ/दायाँ मोड्नुहोस

twice	*du*·i *pa*·ṭak	दुइ पटक
twins	jam·*lyah*·hah	जुम्ल्याहा
type	*ki*·sim	किसिम
to type	ṭaip *gar*·nu	टाइप गर्नु
typhoid	*ṭai*·phaiḍ	टाइफाइड
typical	*na*·mu·nah *hu*·ne	नमूना हुने
tyre	*ṭah*·yar·cak·kah	टायरचक्का

U

umbrella	*chah*·tah	छाता
uncomfortable	*a*·sa·ji·lo	असिजलो
under	-*mu*·ni	-मुनि
underpants	*kaṭ*·ṭu	कट्ट
to understand	*bujh*·nu	बुझ्नु
to undress	phu·*kahl*·nu	फुकाल्नु
unemployed	be·*kahr*	बेकार
unemployment	be·*kah*·ri	बेकारी
union	sa·*mi*·ti	सिमित
universe	*bi*·shwa	विश्व
university	bi·shwa·bi·*dyah*·la·ya	विश्वविद्यालय
unripe	*kāh*·co	काँचो
unsafe	a·*su*·ra·chit	असुरक्षित
until (June)	*(jun)*·sam·ma	(जुन)सम्म
unusual	a·*nau*·ṭho	अनौठो
up	*mah*·thi	माथि
up there	u *mah*·thi	उ माथि
uphill	u·*kah*·lo	उकालो
upward	*mahs*·ti·ra	मास्तिर
urgent	ja·*ru*·ri	जरुरी
to urinate	*pi*·sahb *gar*·nu	पिसाब गर्नु
urine	*pi*·sahb	पिसाब
useful	*kahm*·lahg·ne • *gu*·ni	कामलाग्ने • गुनी
useless	*bi*·nah·kahm·ko • *rad*·di	बिनाकामको • रद्दी
usually	*ak*·sar	अक्सर
utensil	*bhā*·ḍah	भाँडा

V

vacant	*khah*·li	खाली
vacation (holiday)	*bi*·dah	बिदा
vaccination	khop	खोप

valley	u·*pa*·tya·kah	उपत्यका
valuable	*dah*·mi • a·*mul*·ya	दामी • अमूल्य
value	bhau • mol • *mul*·ya	भाउ • मोल • मूल्य
van	*mahl*·gah·ḍi	मालगाडी
vegetables	tar·*kah*·ri	तरकारी
vegetarian	sah·kah·*hah*·ri	साकाहारी

I'm vegetarian.
ma sah·kah·*hah*·ri hũ — म साकाहारी हुँ

vegetation	*ba*·nas·pa·ti	वनस्पति
vehicle	*gah*·ḍi	गाडी
vein	*na*·sah	नसा
venereal disease	*bhi*·rĩ·gi	भिरङ्गी
venue	sthahn	स्थान
very	*dhe*·rai • *ek*·dam	धेरै • एकदम
vest	*is*·ṭa·koṭ	इस्टकोट
view	*dri*·shya	दृश्य
village	gaũ	गाउँ
vine	*la*·ha·rah	लहरा
vineyard	*ang*·gur·ko ba·*gaĩ*·cah	अङ्गुरको बगैंचा
visa	*bhi*·sah	भिसा
to visit	*bheṭ*·na *jah*·nu	भेट्न जानु
vitamin	*bhi*·ṭah·min	भिटामिन
voice	swar	स्वर
to vomit	*bahn*·tah *gar*·nu	बान्ता गर्नु
to vote	mat kha·*sahl*·nu	मत खसा ल्नु
vulture	*gid*·dha	गिद्ध

W

to wait	*par*·kha·nu	पर्खनु

Wait!
par·kha·nu·hos! — पर्खनुहोस !

waiter	*be*·rah	बेरा
to walk	*hĩḍ*·nu	हिंड्नु
wall (boundary)	*par*·khahl	पर्खाल
wall (inner)	*bhit*·tah	भित्ता
wall (outer)	*gah*·ro • sãhdh	गारो • साँध
to want	*cah*·ha·nu	चाहनु

I want ...
ma·lai ... *cah*·hi·yo — मलाई ... चाहियो

Do you want ...?
ta·*paĩ*·lai ... *cah*·hi·yo? — तपाईलाई ... चाहियो ?

war	*la*·ḍaī	लडाई
wardrobe	da·*rahj*	दराज
warm	*nyah*·no	न्यानो
to warn	ce·*tah*·wa·ni *di*·nu	चेतावनी दिनु
to wash (dishes)	*mahjh*·nu	माझ्नु
to wash (people)	nu·*hau*·nu	नुहाउनु
to wash (things/ face/hands/feet)	*dhu*·nu	धुनु
watch	*gha*·ḍi	घडी
to watch	*her*·nu	हेर्नु
water	*pah*·ni	पानी
water (boiled)	u·*mah*·le·ko *pah*·ni	उमालेको पानी
water (drinking)	*khah*·ne *pah*·ni	खाने पानी
water (mineral)	*mi*·na·ral *wah*·ṭar	मिनरल वाटर
water bottle	*pah*·ni·ko *bo*·tal	पानीको बोतल
waterfall	*jhar*·nah	झरना
wave	chahl	छाल
way	*bah*·ṭo	बाटो

Please tell me the way to ...
... *jah*·ne kun *bah*·ṭo ho? ... जाने कुन बाटो हो ?

Which way?
kun *bah*·ṭo? कुन बाटो ?

Way Out
ni·*kahs* निकास

we	*hah*·mi(·ha·ru)	हामी (हरू)
weak	*kam*·jor	कमजोर
wealthy	*dha*·ni	धनी
to wear	la·*gau*·nu	लगाउनु
weather	*mau*·sam	मौसम
wedding	bi·*hah*	विवाह
wedding cake	bi·*hah*·ko kek	विवाहको केक
wedding present	bi·*hah*·ko *u*·pa·hahr	विवाहको उपहार
week	*hap*·tah	हप्ता
this week	yo *hap*·tah	यो हप्ता
to weigh	*jokh*·nu	जोख्नु
weight	*jo*·khai	जोखा इ
welcome (n)	*swah*·ga·tam	स्वागतम
to welcome	*swah*·gat *gar*·nu	स्वागत गर्नु
welfare	*bha*·lai	भलाइ
well (adj)	*san*·cai	सन्चै
west	*pash*·cim	पश्चिम
wet	*bhi*·je·ko	भिजेको
what	ke	के

What's he/she saying?
wa·hāh ke *bhan*·nu·hun·cha? वहाँ के भन्नुहुन्छ ?

What time is it?
ka·ti *ba*·jyo? कति बज्यो ?

wheat	*ga*·hū	गहुँ
wheel	*cak*·kah	चक्का
wheelchair	*pahng*·grah	पाङ्ग्रा
	bha·ya·ko mec	भएको मेच
when	*ka*·hi·le	कहिले

When does it leave?
ka·ti *ba*·je *choḍ*·cha? कति बजे छोड्छ ?

where	*ka*·hāh	कहाँ

Where's the bank?
baĩk *ka*·hāh cha? बैंक कहाँ छ ?

which	kun	कुन
white	*se*·to	सेतो
who	ko	को

Who is it?
ko ho? को हो ?

Who are they?
wa·hāh·ha·ru ko ho? वहाँहरु को हो ?

whole	*sing*·gai	सिङ्गै
whose	*kas*·ko	कस्को
why	*ki*·na	किन

Why is the museum closed?
sā·gra·*hah*·la·ya *ki*·na *ban*·da ho? संग्रहालय किन बन्द हो ?

wide	*pha*·rah·ki·lo	फराकिलो
wife (own)	*swahs*·ni	स्वास्नी
wife (someone else's)	sri·*ma*·ti	श्रीमती
wild animal	*jang*·ga·li ja·*nah*·war	जङ्गली जनावर
to win	*jit*·nu	जित्नु
wind	*hah*·wah	हावा
window	jhyahl	झ्याल
windblown	*hah*·wah	हावा
windy	*hah*·wah *lahg*·ne	हावा लाग्ने
wing(s)	*pa*·khe·ṭah	पखेटा
winner	bi·*je*·tah	बिजेता
winter	*jah*·ḍo *ma*·hi·nah	जाडो महिना

wire	tahr	तार
wise	*bud*·dhi·mahn	बुद्धिमान्
to wish	*ic*·chah *gar*·nu	ईच्छा गर्नु
with	-*sã*·ga • -*si*·ta • -le	-सँग • -सित • -ले
within	-*bhi*·tra	-भित्र
within an hour	ek *ghaṇ*·ṭah·bhi·tra	एक घण्टाभित्र
without	-*bi*·nah	-बिना
without filter	*cahl*·ni·bi·nah	चाल्नीबिना
wok (pan)	ka·*rah*·hi	कराही
woman (inf)	*ai*·mai	आईमाई
woman (pol)	*ma*·hi·lah	महिला
woman (old)	*bu*·ḍhi	बूढी
woman (wife)	*swahs*·ni·mahn·che	स्वास्नीमान्छे
woman (young)	*ke*·ṭi	केटी
wonderful	a·*cam*·ma *rahm*·ro	अचम्म राम्रो
wood	kahṭh	काठ
wooden article	*kahṭh*·bah·ṭa *ba*·ne·ko *bas*·tu	काठबाट बनेको बस्तु
wool	un	ऊन
word	*shab*·da	शब्द
work	kahm	काम
to work	kahm *gar*·nu	काम गर्नु
work permit	*kahm*·ko *a*·nu·ma·ti *pa*·tra	कामको अनुमतिपत्र
worker	*maj*·dur • *kahm*·dahr	मजदुर • कामदार
worker (office)	kar·ma·*cah*·ri	कर्मचारी
workplace	kahr·*yah*·la·ya	कार्यालय
workshop	*kahr*·ya·shah·lah	कार्यशाला
world	sã·*sahr*	संसार
World Cup	warlḍ kap	वर्ल्ड कप
worm (animal)	*ki*·rah	कीरा
worms (intestinal)	*ju*·kah	जुका
worried	pir	पीर
to worry	pir *gar*·nu	पीर गर्नु
worse	jhan *na*·rahm·ro	झन नराम्रो
worship	*pu*·jah	पूजा
worth	bhau • mol • *mul*·ya	भाउ • मोल • मूल्य
wound	ghau	घाउ
to write	*lekh*·nu	लेख्नु
writer	*le*·khak	लेखक
writing paper	*lekh*·ne *kah*·pi	लेख्ने कापी
wrong (amiss)	*be*·ṭhik	बेठीक
wrong (incorrect)	*ga*·lat	गलत
wrong (injustice)	an·*yah*·ya	अन्याय

I'm wrong. (not right)
ma *ga*·lat chũ — म गलत छुँ

I'm wrong. (my fault)
ma *ga*·lat hũ — म गलत हुँ

Y

yak	*caũ*·ri·gai	चौरीगाई
yak meat	*caũ*·ri·gai·ko *mah*·su	चौरीगाईको मासु
yam	*ta*·rul	तरुल
year	*bar*·sa • sahl	वर्ष • साल
this year	yo *bar*·sa	यो वर्ष
yellow	pa·*hẽ*·lo	पहेंलो
yes	ha·*jur*	हजुर
yesterday	*hi*·jo	हिजो
yesterday afternoon	*hi*·jo *diũ*·so	हिजो दिउँसो
yesterday evening	*hi*·jo *be*·lu·kah	हिजो बेलुका
yesterday morning	*hi*·jo bi·*hah*·na	हिजो बिहान
yet	*a*·jha·sam·ma	आजसम्म
yeti	*ye*·ti	यती
yoga	*yo*·gah	योगा
yogurt	*da*·hi	दही
you (sg)	*ti*·mi/ta·*paĩ* **(inf/pol)**	तिमी/तपाई
you (pl)	*ti*·mi·ha·ru/ ta·*paĩ*·ha·ru **(inf/pol)**	तिमीहरू/ तपाईहरु
young	ja·*wahn*	जवान
youth	*yu*·bak	युबक

Yuck!
chi! — छि !

Z

zodiac	*rah*·shi·ca·kra	राशिचक्र
zone	*any*·cal	अञ्चल
zoo	*ci*·ḍi·yah·khah·nah	चिडियाखाना

D

E

F

G

H

I

J

K

L

M

T

V

W

NUMBERS

0	शुन्य	*sun*·ya	11	एघार	e·*ghah*·ra
1	एक	*ek*	12	बाह्र	*bah*·hra
2	दुइ	*du*·i	13	तेह्र	*te*·hra
3	तीन	tin	14	चौध	*cau*·dha
4	चार	cahr	15	पन्ध्र	*pan*·dhra
5	पाँच	pāhc	16	सोह्र	*so*·hra
6	छ	cha	17	सत्र	*sa*·tra
7	सात	saht	18	अठार	a·*ṭhah*·ra
8	आठ	ahṭh	19	उन्नाईस	un·*nais*
9	नौ	nau	20	बीस	bis
10	दस	das	100	एक सय	ek say

SIGNS

बन्द	**Closed**
खतरा	**Danger**
प्रबेश	**Entrance**
निकास	**Exit**
प्रबेश निषेध	**No Entry**
खुला	**Open**
रोक्नुहोस	**Stop**
शौचालय	**Toilets**